Seashell Virgin

Seashell Virgin

A Nacho Mama's Patio Café Novel

Steve Schatz

Any Summer Sunday Books ∆∆∆ Bloomington, IN

Any Summer Sunday Books
520 S Walnut #3306
Bloomington, IN 47402

www.AnySummerSunday.com

ISBN: 978-1-953029-07-2

Cover Design by James @ GoOnwrite.com/
Editor - Jill French

Ordering Information:
Quantity sales. Special discounts are available on quantity
purchases. Contact Sales@AnySummerSunday.com 765.346.9227
Distributed through Ingram. Audio by FindawayVoices.com

Other Books by Steve Schatz

From Absolute Love Publishing
Adima Rising
Adima Returning

From Any Summer Sunday Books
Any Summer Sunday at Nacho Mama's Patio
Café
Who Plugged the Dyke?
Ghost Girl | A Mystery

It's Fiction

Acknowledgments

Thanks to those brave few who attacked beta versions of the book — Theresa Atkinson, Carol Campbell, Erica Berent, and Pat Vint. Jeff Doshier for essential aid kicking over my brain box. Deb Walsh and Wednesday for ultimate fabulousity. Rox for the bosom of the sisterhood. Erica Berent for the Any Summer Sunday logo and many years of friendship. Carp Combs for an essential insight into Brown County. Sharon and JO for the krewe which started the madness.

Dedication

As always — to my beloved ... who endures this weird old man with remarkable grace.

Chapter 1 - Some Days Suck

Gone! A fourteen-foot truck packed to the tits with geegaws, gowns, and glamour—spirited away. I had parked it right here, less than thirty minutes before, obvious as a zit on a first date, across the street from Hoosier Daddy, the town's only gay bar. Close, so when I got stuck carrying everything TiaRa del Fuego chose into the dressing rooms backstage, I'd have less of a struggle. I had already been far too butch for a day off. I had planned for a day full of napping, occasional attempts at cleaning, some light reading, and more napping. Then Beau showed up far too early and ever since, I had been far too active for someone of my tender years and with my lack of motivation.

All that splendor had not just walked itself into the van. No, these arms, these legs, and this back had been repeatedly besmirched by physical effort and all were letting their displeasure be known. When I'd pulled up to the bar a few minutes earlier, I wanted, needed, and deserved a drink, possibly two—while I described the glories that awaited in the truck to TiaRa and Suave. Timmy had laid the groundwork and my ebullience had sealed the deal. TiaRa had said she positively hungered for the gowns and baubles. Suave KitTan had declared she already had a plan to sneak a quantity of the lovely things into her store, Suave Delights, while evading the watchful eye of her devoted husband Foxy, who had once again decreed no new stock was allowed until there were sales to match. Suave was always much more interested in acquisition than disposition. All that remained between me and a lovely lie down was the actual hand over. So, we went out to complete the exchange. Simple. But there the truck wasn't.

"Are you sure you parked it here?" asked TiaRa in much the same tone a mother uses when asking, "Where did you see it last?"

Swallowing my frustration, I managed to contain my impulse to point out that my age and mental abilities had not declined to such an extent that I would have forgotten where I had parked the truck in such a short time. TiaRa, a delicate being, did not deserve snippy replies, despite my rising alarm.

The truck had been either towed or stolen. One possibility was expensive, and the other horrifying. I had just promised the contents to TiaRa and Suave and I hated to disappoint them. Far worse, the truck was actually the property of my latest job. I had only recently been given keys to the shop and knew where the keys to the truck were kept. No one had been at work when Beau's moving emergency arose. The truck wasn't scheduled to be used, so I had borrowed it without asking. I just left a note for Brian, the owner. I knew this was generally acceptable. Others had done it, but I was new and hadn't taken the liberty before. If the truck was in any way damaged, I would be looking for a new job. If it had been stolen, I might be looking for a lawyer. I do not handle stress well. My mouth tends to make talking motions without actually forming words. Tia and Suave looked at me with growing concern.

Maybe the churchies, I thought.

Several adherents of the storefront charismatic church down the block from Hoosier Daddy were always out proving their intolerance by shouting at anyone approaching the bar. Reverend Harry Felcher had moved his congregation of hate mongers from a bankrupt auto-parts store in nearby Martinsville a couple of months ago, to be closer to the sin and cameras of a larger, more tolerant city. Never one to turn down an opportunity to get his picture in the paper or on the news, he and his sycophants had taken to marching a picket line in front of their church, protesting the immoral decadancing and other horrors they were sure went on inside the bar. On Sundays, when the old hobby store that lay between the church and the bar was closed, they tried to extend their picket all the way to Daddy's front door, but the owners quickly got an injunction.

A red line, painted on the sidewalk clearly announced how far Felcher and his followers could come without being charged with trespass. They were always an irritant, but perhaps they had branched out into car theft. I looked across the street at the odd collection of Southern Indiana inbreds who had nothing better to do on a Thursday afternoon than parade their prejudices, while they worshiped a young man who had spent his short time on the earth mixing it up with twelve other men out in the hot, sweaty sands. They were shuffling in a circle like zombies waiting for the brain buffet to open. None looked devious enough to be hiding a recent felonious act. While a good thief should be able to act innocent, I just could not stretch my view of any one of them to have the ingenuity to break into a truck in broad daylight, hot-wire said truck, and finally drive off with a pile of gowns and homo couture, hide the booty, and hurry back to resume their march to nowhere.

"Perhaps we should return to Daddy's," suggested Suave. "Nacho is cooking on the patio and will know what to do."

Nacho Mama was the proprietor of the café, located inside Hoosier Daddy. A gruff restaurateur of uncertain gender with a penchant for muumuus and cigars, Nacho had mysterious interests, talents, and associations that extended far beyond making the best nachos this side of heaven. Nacho was one of those people you turn to in a crisis.

My mind had overextended itself. Too much had happened too quickly and I could only nod. Suave performed an elegant swivel and headed back to the bar. TiaRa glided after her. I stumbled in their wake.

Passing through the dark bar, past the ever-present line of stool-beperched antique queens, each sucking on a never-empty drink, we turned right, through the curtains, onto the patio and into Nacho's domain. TiaRa went directly to the kitchen door and knocked. I held my breath. No one disturbed Nacho when the kitchen or office doors were closed. I was fond of TiaRa and did not wish to see her hurt.

Nothing happened.

Tia knocked again, louder.

"Go away! If I wanted to see anyone, I'd tell 'em," shouted Nacho.

I took a step back.

Tia was untroubled and knocked again. Not one of our group would dare do this, but TiaRa raised her voice to be heard through the door. "It is TiaRa del Fuego, Nacho dear. You are needed."

Almost immediately the door was flung open and there stood Nacho, with ever-present cigar belching foul-smelling smoke. Nacho's glare softened. TiaRa was the only person who Nacho treated with anything approaching sweetness. "Oh, Miss Tia. I wasn't expecting ..."

TiaRa waved away the words. I had never heard Nacho come close to apologizing for anything. If I hadn't been so upset about the box truck and its precious cargo, this would have floored me.

"Nacho, dear," Tia said. "We seem to have a bit of a problem."

4

"I'm busy. Spill it quick."

Tia explained.

Nacho glared at me. "How much did you have to drink, BB?"

Nacho's gaze was, at the best of times intimidating. However, I knew I was on solid ground. "Only one and it wasn't strong. I specifically asked for more juice than usual, because I was so parched. You see I have been ..."

Nacho held up a hand. "I asked a question that required a one-word answer, not your life story. Are you sure where you parked it?"

Before I could explain, Nacho waved the cigar in my face. "One-word answer BB. Like I said, I'm busy."

I sighed. "Yes. I'm sure."

Nacho shrugged. "Call the cops. See if they towed it. I'm guessing you don't know the license plate number."

I began to explain that I had borrowed the truck from work, but again a cloud of choking smoke cut me off.

"Call your work. Get the number of the plate. Then call the cops. If it ain't towed, it can't be that hard to find a box truck in town. Good thing it's not the beginning of the semester. There'd be too many to count, with the students moving in." Nacho turned back to the kitchen. "And don't feel you have to tell me how it turns out. I don't care."

I dithered. "I really hate to call Brian. Technically I didn't ask him. It's just that Beau said we had to move fast because Opal's house had been broken into and he was afraid the crooks would return."

Nacho stopped and turned. "Opal? You talkin' about Opal Milbank? The old broad who boinked half the rich guys in the state in her time?"

That surprised me. I hadn't heard of Opal Hungerford

Milbank before that morning, when Beau turned up on my doorstep in the midst of a major meltdown, crying she had been found dead by the police responding to a burglar alarm. That Nacho knew of her opened new avenues of inquiry into both Nacho and the lady in question. I opened my mouth to begin to delve, but Nacho shook the cigar in my face.

"Nuh uh. Stuff those questions back up your butt, BB. I can see them bubblin' out and in case you forgot, I said I'm busy. You ain't getting more outta me now. But if the stuff that got stolen belonged to the Milbank broad, there may be more going on than just swiping a truck. Is Roger still out front messing with the churchies?"

I shook my head. "His latest trick showed up a bit before me. They were putting on a show for the churchies. Roger had him bent over the chair and was spanking him and they both were moaning very theatrically. The churchies were heading for the safety of the church before their eyes or souls melted. When I went out to get the stuff from the truck, Roger and his friend were gone and the churchies were back."

Nacho nodded. "Give him a call first. You'll screw up his plans for the afternoon, but he'll only yell for a little while. Then call the police. Give Roger a fifteen-minute lead."

Nacho turned back to the kitchen. "I've still got a place to run and don't have time for this now. Tell Roger to keep me up-to-date."

Nacho went back into the kitchen and slammed the door.

We looked at each other. "We shall wait here, BB," said Suave. "Having us out there will only confuse matters and slow the process. I believe in situations like this, speed is of the essence. Should you need us, we are at the ready."

TiaRa touched my arm. "Be strong BB. We are not abandoning you. We are creating a more efficient picture for investigation. Suave and I have no extra knowledge, but figuring that out will waste valuable time. I shall call Roger now. He will be more compliant in giving up his recreation if the request comes from me. You go out front, wait fifteen minutes, then call the police."

I nodded and headed through the curtains, into the dark bar, past the row of old queens, who hadn't moved except to empty a glass or two, and out to the street where the truck I had borrowed without asking, was no longer waiting for me. I sighed and thought about the ruined promise of a lovely day off and the real possibility of a new job hunt. Some days it just wasn't a good idea to get out of bed and this was turning out to be the mother of all such days. And it was supposed to have been a pleasant, quiet Thursday.

Chapter 2 - Beau In Tears

I had not planned to spend the day packing a truck and then losing it. I had wonderful plans for a day filled with a whole lot of nothing. This was *supposed* to be a day off. I had planned to sleep well into the morning, perhaps even until noon, my own personal best. Despite my plan, many hours before I found myself pacing the street, missing a truck that didn't belong to me, that was filled with splendid little geegaws that didn't belong to me, I had been jolted awake by some beast leaning on my doorbell. I stumbled to the door, anger and alarm jostling for my attention while sleep tugged hopelessly back toward my waiting bed. Mornings do not find me at my sharpest. On my porch stood Beau, tears streaming down his face.

"Miss Opal Hungerford Milbank is dead," he wailed before I was able to say anything. Now Beau is less of a morning person than I am. Seeing him awake and in such a state at this hour (before noon) usually meant he had spent the evening falling in love and had awakened to find he had been abandoned and his new *amour de jour* was gone. This was not an uncommon occurrence.

However, he did not seem to be excruciatingly hungover, which was nearly *de rigor* for falling in love and being dumped in the space of an evening. Every few months, Beau would forget what happened last time, would see a new pair of tight pants, and get drunk enough to swoop on the fella.

Should said fella be similarly looped, a beautiful friendship often resulted which lasted until either all the liquor was consumed or a night of sleep led to a sober appraisal and the young hottie would depart, offering a sliding scale of promises to call or hurtful proclamations hurled at the still love-struck Beau.

I had put these ego-rending activities behind me a few years before, when one young hottie I had bagged, as it were, returned to make amends, having admitted his night with me was his own personal bottom which had driven him into the rooms of AA. That was not the bottom I had been hoping would be explored. Being the publicly acknowledged lowest point of a young man's life had not been on my must-do list. That memory had, so far, been remarkably effective in stiffening my resolve and unstiffening my member, even when I had over indulged. Beau still allowed himself to occasionally wallow in such demoralizing dances. However, I had never heard of these tangos ending in death. In addition, Beau rarely indulged in *femmes* real, imagined, or becoming. And Opal was not a name I had ever heard applied to a male of any variety.

I stepped back, leaving the door open and set about making coffee. It was too early to be receiving visitors, but Beau was one of my best friends. Friends do not require the social niceties extended to a visitor nor can they be denied because of lack of poise or preparation. One simply is with a friend. They have seen you at your worst and often return the favor. This is a bedrock requirement of friendship.

He went straight to his favorite corner of my couch, sniffling all the way. I brought the coffee. He did not drink immediately, but held out his cup like a Victorian street urchin, eyes searching the room. I knew what he wanted. With a sigh I grabbed the coffee liquor and the brandy from the counter and put them on the table in front of him. As he busily applied both to his coffee, I focused my attention on sucking in as much of my own cup as possible without scalding my mouth. This morning, coffee was not a nicety, but a necessity. I knew when he was finished with the ministrations to his coffee, he would return to his wail.

"Someone died?" I asked, knowing it would unplug the dyke. The expected flood of sad emotions poured forth.

"Dear Miss Opal. Such a talent! Such a dream. Such a woman! This world will not see the likes of her again. And now that flaming spirit is quenched." He began to sob. Beau, despite degrees in renaissance poetry and nihilistic philosophy, was at his core a Southern queen and a bit of a dingbat with a flair for the dramatic.

"And who, might one ask, is Miss Opal?"

That stopped him. He stared at me in horror.

"BB! Have you no breeding? No taste? No knowledge of the cultural history of Magawatta?"

I shrugged. Argument was unnecessary. Beau was itching to tell.

"Miss Opal Hungerford Milbank, in addition to being a dear personal friend to both Aunt May and myself was simply the best vocal coach in the Midwest. She had a very exclusive clientele and would only deign to work with people who possessed not only talent, but an advanced sense of style as well as a proper pedigree. She was a doyen of culture. Even more delightful, over the years she has been romantically linked to simply dozens of prominent men in several states. She was vehemently against marriage, feeling it captured the woman while leaving men free to dalliance. She took it upon herself to even the score." A hint of a smile broke through his sadness. "And score she did. Often and enthusiastically."

"And might one ask how you knew her? You are not exactly at the top of the social heap and I've heard you sing. My ears still threaten to bleed."

Beau glared. "I have a lovely voice. Miss Opal said so herself. However, I did not know her professionally. She was compatriot of Miss Mavis Shakleford and I met her while Mavis was still alive."

Mavis Shakleford had been a professor emeritus of ballet and the widow of a bank president. Beau had been her personal assistant. He was initially hired to work around the house, but the two soon discovered a mutual love of strong drink and catty conversation. In her will she stipulated that Beau could live in the grand mansion rent free for as long as he wished. Beau rarely embraced effort or change and the thought of walking away from free rent was anathema, so he was in for the long haul. When his Aunt May had been moved to Magawatta because of her too frequent, far too explicit reminisces of past exploits with now married men, she moved in with him.

"Aunt May and Miss Opal became close friends. They spent hours discussing their love of manly pursuits," he said.

"I don't think that means what you think it does," I interjected.

Beau waved away my objection. "BB, I am simply too disconsolate to be worried about proper implications. Miss Opal shared many a lovely evening with Aunt May and myself. Oh, how we would laugh. Oh, the merriment. And now ..."

I gagged a little bit on my coffee. Beau was sinking into dialog from old bad movies. A little prodding was called for before he put a hand to his forehead and looked, misty eyed into the distance.

"How did she die?"

Beau snapped back to reality and realized his cup was empty. He refilled it, adding a generous helping of spirits.

"Evidently her burglar alarm sounded in the middle of the

night. For a lady of years, she was very technologically savvy and had the absolute finest in security. I believe Roger designed it. The police arrived, but not in time. The culprits had fled. However, when the police went through the house, seeking a way to turn off the alarm, they found her in her bed. Quite dead."

"The burglars killed her?"

"No. The police say she had been dead for a while. Probably scared the life out of those ruffians. They left without taking anything. They just left her lying there ... dead and alone."

This brought on another wave of weeping. When Beau had calmed down again, he continued. "The lawyer just came by to tell May and me. It must have been her heart. She had such a big heart and so vibrant, but she was old ... quite old. She would never divulge her exact age, but she must have been over a hundred. She told stories of lovers she had in the 1920s. While the age of consent was much lower then ... well, you do the math."

"It sounds like she had a good, full, long life," I said. I was thinking of the full day of nothing I had planned and wanted to get on with it. Beau was going to milk his heartbreak for the next few weeks, but the initial emotional explosion had, hopefully, tired him. Having also consumed two well-doctored coffees, I had hopes he might take his melodrama to bed.

"But that is not the least of it," he said, dashing my hopes of escape. "We must go over there. Today! Right away! Before our time is up."

"What do you mean?"

"I told you she was a dear friend," he sounded exasperated, as if I had missed a very obvious point.

"Yes, and?"

"And she has bequeathed to Aunt May all the contents of the house that May might want and can carry away, but that slimy lawyer is only giving her until four this afternoon. After that, he insists everything becomes part of the estate and Aunt May has no claim on it. All that glamour and finery!"

"What?"

Beau nodded. "She has gowns and crystal and jewelry and just scads of things. She has sold off plenty over the years. She hated having old things about. There are entire rooms in the house that are empty. She said she would rather see them empty than packed with dust-covered memories. But there is still a formidable collection. Anything we don't want gets sent to an auction house."

I began to get the picture. My latest job was at Ed's Removal, a company that cleaned out estates, auctioned off anything of value and donated or dumped the rest. Beau was not only here for tea and sympathy. He wanted a freebie clean out. Oh joy. "Which auction house?" I asked.

"Matt Ponce," he said. "You know, he owns that antique mall out near the old depot."

I was quite familiar with MP Downsizers. They had a reputation among those in the business—a bad one. They were known for getting clients by inflating their estimates of what collections would fetch at auction, then they'd make sure any really valuable items were poorly described and photographed so they could snap those up themselves, at bottom dollar. They then sold them through their booths at the antique mall. Plus, Matt, the head of the company, had a reputation for hiring the mean, the drunk, and the dumb, so items were inevitably broken and the places were left a mess. Clients made next to nothing from the auction and had to pay for the clean out.

Matt was a total tool. He was known for heavy drinking and

screwing any woman who would let him. His brother was an Evangelical and a lobbyist for some of the most environmentally irresponsible industry groups in the state. He was widely expected to be the next governor as he had been kissing all the proper butts, had no opinions of his own, and looked good on a poster. The family had money from a string of gas stations that had been closed down by the EPA, sticking the state and the feds with the cost of cleanup. True Indiana royalty.

"We need to meet the lawyer there in less than an hour. The police sealed the house while they investigated and had the soiled things disposed of properly. They have only just unsealed it. We have until four to scavenge. After that, everything belongs to the estate and will be disposed of by this Ponce character. The proceeds are to be donated to Pets Alive and the Humane Society. Ms. Opal did not have animals because of allergies, but she loved them and hated to see them abandoned. We need your eye to help us decide what is worth saving."

More likely he needed my back to help haul things. I could tell there was more.

"We also need a truck to haul away what we want. You would be an absolute angel if you borrowed one from work."

I sighed. I knew I could protest, but Beau was at full wail and I wasn't going to win. I saved my strength for the efforts to come and headed to the bedroom to get dressed. "I'll meet you at your house in thirty minutes with the truck. Be ready. Why don't you try calling Timmy to see if he'll help haul? And put on some work clothes. If you think your whimpering is going to get you out of manual labor, you have another think coming."

Beau looked like he was hoping for another cup of coffee, but I left him in the living room. By the time I dressed and came out, he was gone.

Chapter 3 - At Opal's House

We pulled up in front of ornate metal gates that blocked the circular drive leading to the dearly departed's house. It was more than a house, although a bit less than an estate. Opal's father had been one of the original shopkeepers in town and he had done well and expanded. When his stores spread throughout the Midwest, he sold. With his fortune, he purchased an appointment to the United States Senate and, when not spending the minimum amount of time required in Washington, he lived in splendor in the overblown home he had filled with priceless collectibles from the Continent. He knew the cost of each to the penny and the value of not a one. He knew they were rare and costly and no one in Indiana had one, and that was good enough for him. He acquired a wife using the same measure. She came with a title, a family that had fallen on hard times, and a burning resentment toward the man who purchased and displayed her like another piece in his collection. She gave him a daughter, Opal. She raised the daughter long enough to instill a deep desire for the finer things in life and a deeper disdain for Senator Milbank in particular and gentlemen of leisure in general. Having so schooled the girl, she died, leaving Opal in the care of a string of unremarkable nannies. The senator spent his remaining years slowly disintegrating into alcoholism and gluttony, choking to death while attempting to fit an entire pork tenderloin into his mouth, on a bet during a particularly debauched party, attended by some of the city and state's finest statesmen and whores. The papers reported he died of a broken heart, pining for his lost wife.

Timmy and I were in the truck I had borrowed from work. He had agreed to help in exchange for a shot at some of the booty. Aunt May and Beau were in my car, leading the way. However, there was a bit of a traffic jam blocking access. In front of the gates, two police cars with lights flashing were pulled across the drive, blocking in a newer sporty car of the type favored by overly entitled college males, seeking to impress females of their wealth and prowess. An officer was talking to a prime example of the genre, who was vehemently denying any guilt or knowledge. I believed the second and had doubts about the first. Behind them was a truck poorly painted with pictures of happy elders walking away from their homes with fistfuls of cash, while lettering urged them to call MP Downsizers right away.

Finally, off to the side, parked to ensure no damage came to it, was a very new looking Audi. The owner, obvious because of his very expensive suit and quietly authoritarian demeanor, was talking to another cop who was fast becoming overwhelmed. A short, weaselly looking fellow was doing his best to horn in on the conversation, all the while motioning to the passenger in the MP Downsizers truck, a Southern Indiana inbred hulk, to come represent with some muscle. In the second cop car, a third officer was busy on the radio. We took in this tableau and decided the best course of action was to allow the scene to play out without further direction from any of us. We watched.

Shortly after our arrival, the sergeant who had been talking on the radio hopped out and headed to the cluster at the gate. He ignored the clamor for his attention and focused on the young frat.

"You're Thad Wroks?"

The boy nodded, but said nothing, confident that his family sway had once again come to the rescue.

The sergeant looked at the other cop. "You have his contact information?"

The cop had worked long enough in our little college town so full of overindulged and over privileged young tools of the power elite to know what was coming. He nodded.

The sergeant turned back to the boy. "You're free to go."

"But what about my phone? I've been telling this crap head …"

Both officers' heads snapped back toward the boy and even from this distance, I could feel the menace rise. The boy was smarter than many. He actually noticed his mistake and the consequences that were heading his way and quickly corrected himself.

"I mean this officer. I left my phone here the last time I visited Opal and I need it."

"When were you here, sir? And why?"

"Two or three days ago." Then he smirked. "Miss Opal sometimes asks me to come over to help her … around the house."

He was clearly proud that an old lady found his youthful athleticism attractive and was not trying to hide the implication that he was paid to pleasure her. It didn't occur to him that some might find that a bit icky or at least Freudian and, that he was available for hire, gave a clear indication that his family might still have influence, but they no longer had wealth.

"Two or three days without your phone? I would have thought you would have noticed it was missing a lot sooner."

Thad shook his head. "It's a special phone. Miss Opal got it for me. Only she uses it and I only just noticed I didn't have it." That-I'm-so-studly-and-special smile began to creep across his face again. "I noticed because she usually calls me a few times a week and I hadn't heard from her and ..."

The sergeant cut in. "Fine. If we find the phone, we'll let you know. However, now we need you to leave the scene while we finish our investigation."

"But I need ..."

"Son, you have two choices here. You can leave and if we find the phone, we shall return it to you. Or you can remain and take up our time while we are trying to investigate a death and if you do that, I will have Officer Ridley take you to the station for questioning and of course, your car will be towed. So, I will ask you one more time to leave and let us get on with our job."

The boy wasn't that bright, but he wasn't that dull. With as much attitude as he could muster, he nodded his head and got in his car. Officer Ridley moved his car to allow the boy to back out, which he did and drove off, flipping off the officers, but keeping his hand inside the car, where it expressed his feeling, but did not invite retaliation. A very timid 'fuck you'.

The sergeant now turned to the other group. He focused on the expensive man in the expensive suit. "You Gibson?" he asked.

"That's right. Burton Gibson. I'm the executor of the estate." The man stuck out his hand.

The sergeant ignored it and interrupted. "Got some ID?"

The man drew himself up, insulted. "I don't like your tone. Why should I need to provide ..."

The sergeant interrupted again, obviously not impressed. "If you can prove who you are, I will allow access to the property. That's what my boss just told me to do. There was a break-in here and a death, so we do scheduled drive-bys. That's how we noticed the kid trying to open the gate. Then you pulled up. So, do you have ID or not?"

The cop obviously didn't like the guy. Gibson did not present a lot to like. Self-importance dripped off the lawyer. Of course, maybe the cop just didn't like anyone. Gibson pulled out his wallet and showed the man his ID. The Sargent nodded and turned back to his car, calling out to the other cop, "OK. Let's go." And off they went.

Aunt May walked up to Gibson. "Hello Mr. Gibson. We're here. Our friend BB has borrowed a truck." She nodded in my direction.

At this point, the weaselly man protested. "Hey! I've got the contract for the broad's estate. I don't want Ed's Removal horning in on my business!"

"Mr. Ponce, BB has merely borrowed the truck," said Aunt May. "He is helping us and, as you know, we are to have first choice of any removable items."

"You'll take all the good stuff and leave me the crap," protested Ponce. "I'm gonna watch you and see what you take."

"I am most sure that dear Opal was clear with you when you were hired as to what her wishes were. You have no business here until we are through and I will not have you tromping about trying to rush us while we are trying to do this sad work, while coming to grips with the loss of a dear friend." She turned to the lawyer. "I believe we are to have unimpeded access, is that correct?"

Gibson nodded. "You shouldn't have come, Ponce. I told you not to come until this afternoon. Ms. Claybrook gets first crack at the house."

"But I want ..." began Ponce.

Aunt May broke in. "Then we shall go in, Mr. Gibson. I know the code to open the gate. I am assuming you were not indiscreet enough to give it to this ..." She paused, as if sorting through an assortment of synonyms for slime dweller.

"... gentleman. For if you have, I would suggest you hire a watchman to ensure that after he is finished, the doorknobs and chandeliers are still in place and the copper wiring is still safely located within the walls."

Ponce began to protest, but Gibson cut him off. "I leave you to it, Ms. Claybrook. You have until 4 p.m. Ponce, I'll meet you back here at 4:15 for a walk through." He glared at Ponce until the man, muttering all the way, turned, got in his truck and drove off. Then Gibson, without another word, got back into his Audi and left.

What followed was an orgy of indulgence. So much stuff. So little time. We didn't have the room or strength to take anything large—so we didn't look at the dressers, chifforobes, armoires, or ornate chests that filled the rooms, attic and basement. However, we could and did look *in* them. The collections ranged from the elegant to over-the-top gaudy. I don't have much need for elegance in my life. I like my simple little life and adding something of real value to either décor or wardrobe, instead of elevating, would serve to highlight the depths in which I currently swim. So instead, I aim for the kitschy and bizarre. If the viewer, upon seeing the object, cannot help but wonder, who and more importantly, why this would be conceived and brought forth into creation, then it is for me. Thankfully, Ms. Milbank had not limited her collection to tasteful and refined. There were several pieces of over-the-topistry to be had.

Beau tended to be a tad more snobby in his tastes and sought the small and elegant. Aunt May was not an accumulator. "I have had so much in my life," she said. "Things tend to pass through a time and a place and are really worth only the memory they retrieve. I have now, and have had, more than enough of both objects and memories. My only interest today is in a few things that Opal has mentioned might amuse me because she has related the story behind their acquisition."

So, I was free to indulge my desires for objay darts (the lower-class equivalent of *objet d'art*). I found several wonders of tasteless design, but my life truly became complete when I wandered into the great woman's bedroom. The mattress had been removed by the cleaners (my mind curled away from what it had contained when they found her), but the bed frame remained—a gargantuan carved wood behemoth, replete with angels cavorting on clouds and sunrises. Upon closer inspection I noticed it also had metal posts secured throughout, just perfect for attaching ropes or handcuffs. Upon a bedside table was a tableau of religious icons from many religions and there, amidst the Buddha, Kali and other beings who would make the A list for a party on Olympus, she stood. I stopped and stared. In innocence and glory was a small statue, about eighteen inches tall, of the Blessed Virgin Mary standing on a tiny hilltop decorated with shells while a painted river trickled down into a blue plastic pool. This BVM was sheltered from storms and sin by a large abalone shell, like a bathtub from the sea. It was obviously handcrafted with more love than skill and had been signed on the back by the nuns of an order dedicated to Our Lady of Lourdes, located in a small town in Ohio. To add a special twist, someone had written underneath the name of the sisters' convent, "Oh Sweet Mary. Require my obedience and when I deviate, punish me." They had signed it in a scrawl that looked like "Eppie J". This was tacky times twenty with a pinch of weird thrown in for good measure. Magnificent! I was already imagining a redistribution of the collections in my house to accommodate this new treasure.

As I emerged from the spell cast by my find, I heard Beau and

Timmy ejaculating orgasmic squeals from another room. I was certain they were not indulging in tawdry behavior, so the only conclusion to draw from the explosive rapture was that they had found something or somethings that were tickling their fancies in a particularly good way.

I followed the sounds, clutching the BVM to my chest, unwilling to be separated from her tacky glory.

Down a long hallway, double doors led to a room large enough to be a ballroom. However, it was outfitted more like a shop that handled high-end merchandise for elegant, wealthy, drag queens and prostitutes. Fans, boas, long chiffon gowns, exquisitely beaded—everything from capes to formal wear and shoes enough to make Imelda Marcos hang her head in shame. Beau and Timmy were squealing and dithering from one rack to another, touching and draping splendor over their arms and chests. They clutched garments to themselves like they had discovered long-lost lovers. I am not a clothes person, but I could tell this was an extraordinary collection.

Aunt May came into the room, following the symphony of ecstatic cries and moans. She saw the reason and smiled. "Ah, you've found Opal's costume room."

Beau, looking like he had been dropped in the middle of Santa's workshop had draped furs and boas around his neck, had rings on every finger, and was holding up a very ornate leather outfit resplendent with studs and mesh-covered, strategically placed peek-a-boos. "Why Aunt May," Beau twittered. "I had absolutely no idea Opal was so adventurous. I knew she had gentlemen friends, but I didn't know her tastes were so eclectic."

"Her tastes ran to the mundane, my dear," replied Aunt May. "It was her callers who requested her various adventures. That is one of the reasons we became firm friends. You see, she often needed instruction on how to use a new or unusual accoutrement. I must admit to a certain amount of pride that I was never unable to provide the necessary instruction. Her inquiries often brought back very pleasant or at least interesting memories. For example, that leather piece you are handling reminded me of Marlon Fitzwilliams. He was a most elegant young man. Outstanding in his community. A deacon of his church and a valued employee at the local savings and loan. He looked after his mother who was getting on in years and was unable to do for herself. Yes, he was pleasant to look at and quite well endowed, both in personality and well, endowment. But he was unable to bring any young ladies home, as his mother, while usually quiet and quite proper, occasionally was in the habit of letting fly a resounding volley of curses. No one knew where she had learned such language, but she was versatile and enthusiastic in breadth, length, and volume. It did not trouble him so much, not being able to court, as where his desires lay was in punishment and urination. He loved to put on his very best suit—he had to order a new one each time we had one of our sessions. Then, firmly gagged, he would start bending over my knee and end up ..."

"Aunt May, I must ask you to hold that thought," declared Beau. "I am too enticed by these outfits and if I begin to consider what bodily fluids may have decorated them, I may hesitate to take them with."

"You don't have the closet space to take very many," said Timmy. "Besides they are for a shorter and slimmer ..."

Timmy caught sight of Beau's withering look. "Oh come on, Beau. You aren't a little old lady. And these were tailor-made for a pretty small gal."

Beau had to agree. Then he brightened. "I can take a few drapey things."

"TiaRa might be interested in some," I suggested.

"And Suave could sell some of the more unusual pieces," said Beau. "I'm sure she would split any profits with me and I can always use a few extra dollars. That wouldn't be disrespectful, would it, Aunt May?"

Aunt May shook her head. "I am quite sure it would amuse Opal to no end to have her costumes end up in a drag show or in Suave's shop. But we only have a single truck and a short time, so I suggest we make a plan. I believe I saw a small bar in the library downstairs. Perhaps we should retire there and strategize."

"I'll stay up here and poke around," said Timmy, who didn't drink any more. "I haven't seen anything but a bit of costume jewelry. It seems like someone as rich as this would have better pieces, if not real jewels, at least a bigger collection of fakes."

So, we headed downstairs, leaving Timmy to poke under beds and into the backs of dresser drawers. May led the way to the library where she had scoped out the liquor. Aunt May was as reliable as a dowser for finding the nearest drink.

The library was a large room. Well, compared to my place, the bathrooms in Opal's house were large rooms. However, this looked like a room straight out of an English country house, ceilings higher than the roof of my place. Bookcases flanked three sides of the room, well-spaced to allow art to nestle in between floor to ceiling, dark, obviously expensive wood shelves. A stand-alone rolling ladder lingered in front of one, should one wish a book from an upper shelf. A thick oriental rug filled the center of the room, leaving a space between carpet and wall to allow said ladder to roll unimpeded. Large, comfy chairs clustered around small tables. Near the door was a small, but serviceable bar with a small, but serviceable collection of bottles. The glasses were a bit dusty, but skillfully shaped and large enough to allow for respectable drinks.

"A little dust doesn't matter," said Beau, giving three glasses a quick wipe. "I'll just make them a bit on the strong side so the alcohol can disinfect."

"As if you need an excuse to make your drink a little strong," I said.

"I suppose you want me to water yours down," he said.

There was no need to reply. A glare sufficed. We took our drinks and settled into chairs, looking around the library. There was an impressive collection of literature. However, I noticed that the arrangement of books tended more toward the aesthetic than the utilitarian. Not grouped by subject matter, author, or any other property of content that I could discern, the books seemed to be grouped by size and color. I hazarded a guess.

"Aunt May, Opal was not much of a reader, was she?"

May shook her head as she looked around. "No. I am certain she could read and would read, should the need arise, but it was not a recreation that drew her interest. Her reading was driven by necessity rather than desire. What drove her desires was ..."

"Then why maintain such a large library?" Beau asked, forestalling an exploration of Opal's desires which, although I am certain would be interesting, would also be extensive and we had limited time. "I didn't come as often as you, Aunt May, but I do not recall a single time we even entered this room."

"It has the feeling of a stage set," I said. "Come into the library and we will discuss it."

Aunt May inclined her head. "There is some truth to that. She told me that it often put new gentlemen at ease, being in such a male-themed room. They could examine books and make some semi-knowledgeable comment to reduce their anxiety about why they were really here. However, what I particularly notice is the quality and quantity of beverage offerings."

"What do you mean?" asked Beau. "This liquor isn't very good, but it's not bad. I would have thought she could have afforded better."

Aunt May smiled. "Exactly. Opal had very refined tastes and had the resources to indulge them." She waved a hand toward the bar. "This could not have been for her, but I have not seen another bar and I have looked."

Aunt May fell silent, sipping her drink and looking around the room. Her gaze fell on the floor in front of one of the bookcases. She glanced at us. "I was noticing the rug in front of that bookcase," she said.

I looked at the bookcase she had been studying. It was at the far end of the room, near the desk. The rug in front of it was unspectacular, hardly worth considering. I looked at Aunt May, questioning.

"There are not rugs in front of the other book cases. They would impede the rolling ladder."

I looked and saw she was right. I still didn't see what difference it made. Aunt May stared at me, obviously expecting me to make some comment. She was seeing something that I wasn't. Neither of us expected Beau to channel inspiration, but Aunt May knew I could occasionally catch her drift. This time, however, she was drifting all alone. I shrugged and shook my head.

"And the rug is crooked," she coaxed.

Again I looked. She was correct. I got up and walked over to the bookcase and moved the rug. The floor under it had curving marks on it, as if ..."

"The bookcase," said Aunt May.

I suddenly looked at her. "Could it move? Can that really

happen? Like in the movies?"

Aunt May smiled. "Miss Milbank was a woman of means and mystery. It would not surprise me if she had constructed secret rooms. I believe we have found one."

"How absolutely enthralling," said Beau. "Our own mystery room. How do you think we get in?"

I shrugged. "If it's a secret room, I would guess she hid the way in."

"Look for a book that doesn't fit. One that doesn't look right. It's always a book." Beau was an aficionado of B movies.

I had my doubts, but turned to the bookcase. As with all the others, the books were arranged by size and color. Except for one. A thick, black volume stood out on a shelf containing a ten-book set of *A History of Indiana,* I peered at the title of the odd man out. *The Best American Mysteries of the Roaring Twenties,* and I had to smile. If you were going to have a secret door that opened by pulling on a book, this was the book to use. I pulled it off the shelf. Well, I tried. It wasn't actually a book. As I grabbed it, the false top folded in on itself, swiveled up, and became a handle. It was attached to the shelf at the bottom, so as I pulled, the entire bookcase slid toward me, clicking softly. It was obviously on a track and weighted so that even a man with my lack of physical abilities could move it with little effort. It came forward a couple of feet, then slid to the side, revealing a room.

This was obviously a work room. Part file room, part safe. Jeweler's cases lined one wall, full of big, gaudy pieces. I know nothing about jewels, but I know shiny and these were all kinds of shiny. Three file cabinets with five drawers each were labeled: Holdings, Gentlemen, and Potential. Pulling open a drawer at random, I saw over fifty thick, three-sided folders, each labeled with a number, but no name. Looking in one of the folders, I saw two thumb drives, several pictures, an audio tape and several printed pages. A desk in the corner had a few folders open on it, several piles of papers and envelopes, and a small picture of a much younger Opal, smiling as she looked across a wide expanse of canyon. Next to the desk was a small, but extremely well-stocked bar.

Beau and Aunt May had headed that way. This bar had the good stuff. I cannot name or afford excellent spirits, but I certainly can appreciate them. Beau brought me a lovely crystal glass and the fumes that rose from it made my mouth water. I wanted to gulp, but I am not such a boor that I will besmirch excellence. I inhaled. I sipped. I melted into a chair thoughtfully placed next to the desk. Screw the stuff. I wanted to spend the rest of our time right here, indulging.

Beau smiled at me. I smiled back. Everything was lovely. Beau sat in the desk chair and his eyes began to wander around the desk. They stopped. "Aunt May," he said. "There's an envelope here with your name on it."

Aunt May refilled her glass and came over. I stood and let her sit. She opened the envelope. Inside was a single piece of paper and an index card to which was taped a small key. On the card was written, "Be sure to bring the box."

"What box?" asked Beau.

"You have as much information as I," replied Aunt May. "Perhaps the letter will explain."

She took out the letter and read it. I didn't want to be rude and read over her shoulder, but I was very curious. Unfortunately, I had not brought my glasses and nearsightedness enforced manners. I could see there were only a few short paragraphs. Aunt May finished reading, folded the paper, and put it back in the envelope. Then she gave a little sigh, looking beyond this world while a small smile played across her face. She hadn't imbibed enough to blame liquor for the distance of her gaze, so I didn't want to intrude on this moment where I suspected that a friend's demise had reminded her of the ever-present lurking of mortality.

Beau, however, was more familiar and less patient. "Well?" he asked. "Don't keep us in suspense."

Aunt May shook her head to clear it, coming back to us. "Opal wrote this some time ago. It is an 'if you are reading this I must be dead' letter," she said. "She was giving instructions and explained what her gift to me was."

"What was it?" prodded Beau. "Did she tell you what box that key is for and where it is?"

Aunt May stood and went to the file cabinets. "She didn't write anything more about the key or the box. We don't have time to look for it. Remember, we must be out of here soon. Opal explained what I am to do and this takes priority. Would you bring me an empty file box from that stack in the corner, dear?"

Beau wasn't about to do anything until his curiosity was assuaged, so I grabbed one of the boxes and brought it to her. She opened the top drawer of the 'Gentlemen' cabinet and pulled out a green folder. Inside was a single sheet of paper.

"BB, I need you to help me, please," she said. "We need to gather some files. Start with the Holdings file cabinet. When I read a number, would you find the folder that has that number and put it in the box? I believe the folders will be in order, so it should not be too difficult. Then we will move to the next cabinet. We only need to take a few from each cabinet."

"Sure, Aunt May," I said. "But what is this all about?"

Aunt May smiled. "Opal left her money to the needy animals. They could not use what she left us. She has provided something more valuable and certainly more useful. She has bequeathed her power."

Beau was about to pop. This was beyond his reasoning and he knew something significant was going on but he had not one clue as to what it was. If Aunt May wasn't so small and his dear aunt, he would have shaken her. "What do you mean? Power? How can someone give you power from the grave? What can possibly be more valuable than her money? Look around! Think of what we could do if we had her money. Think of the things we could have."

Beau was almost in tears, mourning the loss of a fortune he never had. "What are you talking about Aunt May?"

Aunt May was used to Beau's outbursts. She had been studying the paper, ignoring him until he ran out of steam. When his torrent of words stopped and he stood gasping, she looked up, gave a small, tight smile and said, "Why, blackmail, of course, dear."

Chapter 4 - Making Our Exit

Beau opened his mouth to demand more information, but was interrupted by a very loud, sharp buzz coming from a speaker above the desk. I let out a little shriek. I attempt to be a manly man, but when surprised, the sounds I make seem to be channeled by an inner old-time house maid who has seen something that no refined lady should ever be allowed to see. Beau cocked his head and shot a reproachful look in my direction. It's not that he wasn't startled too, but there are so few times he can out butch me, he grabs any opportunity to be condescending. Aunt May was unperturbed. She was made of sterner stuff. Additionally, her delayed response was, I'm sure, aided by the regular application of spirits.

"That buzzer sounds all over the house when the front door opens," she said. "I have heard it many times. Opal did not believe in locking doors unless she was entertaining a caller, but she did not like surprises. Why don't you go see who it is, BB? Beauregard, help me gather the files. We have just four more from the Gentlemen cabinet and a few more from the Potential cabinet. Then we shall close up this room again."

"But the jewels," protested Beau.

Aunt May waved a hand dismissively. "They are fakes. Excellent costume jewelry, but nothing more. Opal explained that she never kept the presents given to her by her gentlemen friends. She had them copied, in case a gentleman ever wished to see her wearing his gift. But she would sell the real pieces. She believed in money, not things. 'Easier to transform into one's real wishes', is how she described it."

"But they are so pretty!" said Beau.

"Beauregard, please stop dithering and help me with the important work at hand. We must hurry and there is an unknown person in the house. So, to work. BB, seek and delay the intruder or expel him if you can. Time grows short and I grow thirsty."

I nodded and headed out to the foyer. No one—the door was closed, so it hadn't just blown open. I made a loop around the ground floor as quickly as I could. It was a really big house. I didn't go off into the garden or any of the storerooms. I just poked my head into the main rooms. I thought about calling out, but decided against it. Of all the people we had seen clustered at the gates, not a one was someone I wanted to talk to. There was also the possibility that this was some more pedestrian criminal, hoping to pick up something attractive. I might need to play intimidating and that's hard to do after announcing one's presence by yoo hooing in a decidedly wispy voice.

I headed upstairs. Down the hall was the costume room. I could hear Timmy's happy conversations with himself as he gathered glorious garments. I stuck my head through the door. Timmy peered out from behind a mountain of gowns he was carrying to a pile in the center of the room.

"I couldn't find more jewelry, but it doesn't matter. This collection is amazing! I wish I did drag regularly. This is a treasure trove. I also put aside some things that Cosmo and I can have some fun with. TiaRa is going to be over the moon. I'm sure she'll take some for her personal collection. What she doesn't want, Suave will love. I'm only taking the *crème de la crème* and the crème de la kink. There are some wonderful boas I couldn't pass up. Think I should take a selection of whips, too? There's plenty to choose from."

Now I appreciate fashion, but don't understand it. I could not choose between quality and crap if my life depended on it. That is why I stick to T-shirts and jeans for the most part. For work situations, I have button up shirts that others have chosen for me. If I want to expand my horizons beyond that, I must throw myself on the mercy of my friends. Thankfully, they have discovered there is no pleasure in making a fool of me by what they dress me in, because I don't get the joke. Timmy knew this, so his question was by way of sharing his joy, not an actual request for an opinion. My concern about the still missing interloper took precedence, so I pressed on.

"Have you seen or heard anyone since we went downstairs?"

He shook his head. "I heard a buzzer, but I figured that was you. Why? Is someone here?"

"I don't know. If you see anyone, give a shout."

"Will do." He dumped the gowns and went back for another load of treasures far more interesting than me.

I headed back down the hallway, looking into each room and finding stuff, but no people. At the end of the hall, double doors led to Opal's grand, private bedroom suite where I had found my BVM. Against one wall was an intricately carved mahogany wardrobe. I could see the raised carvings very well, because the door was open and a butt was sticking out. It looked to be a firm and well-formed butt, tightly wrapped in a pair of jeans that cost more than my monthly rent. It was also a butt that did not belong there. From inside the wardrobe came a chorus of banging and curses. The banging did not hint at hidden rhythmic talent. The cursing was well practiced, if lacking in innovation. I waited for a lull in the performance and spoke. "Excuse me, but what are you doing?"

The noise stopped. The butt disappeared, quickly replaced by the front of a young man who, although not bad looking, fairly dripped entitlement and a firm belief that he was far more appealing than he actually was. He looked familiar. Individual frats are difficult to distinguish. They all seem to come from the same factory and the same mold. Then it hit me. This was the boy who the police had chased away. Hmm, points for persistence if not intelligence. Something must be very important to him.

He tried deception and attitude, since those were comfortably familiar.

"I came by for my phone. Opal said I could pick it up. I have a key." Then he attempted a suspicious look and attack. "Who are you? And what are you doing here? Does Opal know you're here?"

I smiled and shook my head. It wasn't a bad bluff. It might have worked if I had no idea what was going on. "No, Opal does not know, since she's dead. But you know that, don't you? And I also believe you know you are not supposed to be here, because I saw you being chased away by a cop a couple of hours ago. So, let's try this again. What are you doing?"

He pushed his lower lip out, like a petulant little boy getting ready to throw a fit. "I came for my phone. She has it and I don't want anyone to take it. I want it and you aren't going to stop me."

He took a step toward me, muscles bunching and fists preparing for action. Hmm, he was not a lot bigger than me, but he was younger and I'm sure he was stronger, as I am usually very successful at avoiding anything arduous, while frats tend to flock to pastimes of the butch. Both he and I could tell I was outmatched, so I was getting ready to demonstrate my ability to hurry away, when Timmy showed up behind me, carrying a rather large and delightfully intimating bat. Evidently Opal liked to make sure she could keep the upper hand in any situation. Now, Timmy was a sweet young thing, but in his youth, before he found sobriety and his devoted husband Cosmo, he was a partier and was quite happy to show his gratitude to nearly anyone willing to provide party favors. Consequently, he had ended up in some dicey situations and had learned how to drop the veil of sanity and turn from lil cutie into a crazy queen, and more than happy to damage any and all who seemed a threat. It was a chilling transformation and the young man standing before us could see that crazy queen in Timmy's eyes, held in check for now, but excited at the possibility of coming out to play.

He was smart enough to see he was outmatched, so unbulked and pulled another familiar card out of his deck—sulky. He shrugged. Looked us both up and down. "I'm outta here. I'm not gonna hang out in a bedroom with a couple of fags." And he pushed past us and hurried down the stairs. A moment later, the buzzer that signaled the front door opening sounded.

I unclenched and smiled at Timmy. "Thanks. That could have been unpleasant."

Timmy smiled back. "What do you think he was looking for?"

"Dunno. He said his phone, but he was beating on something in that wardrobe and unless they've started keeping phones in metal boxes ..." I looked into the wardrobe. The kid had pulled away a stack of blankets and exposed a metal box about the size of a couple of shoe boxes stuck together.

"It's an ammo box from World War II," said Timmy.

I stared at him. "And how would you know that?"

"A guy I dated was a collector."

Another benefit of Timmy's many and varied flings, was a broad smattering of obscure knowledge, gleaned during the brief times when he was sober and had not yet departed in search of another drunken frolic. He pulled out the box and shook it.

"Should you be shaking an ammo box?" I asked.

"I don't think it's got ammo in it. Why keep bullets and bombs hidden in the bottom of your wardrobe? She wasn't a secret terrorist, was she?"

"How would I know? Seems to me one of the important parts of being a secret anything is not letting just anyone know what you are. Besides, I didn't really know her. If not ammo, then what?"

"Could be anything. People use them because they are strong. Probably has jewels or money or both." He shook it again. Something was definitely clattering around inside the box.

"Well, open it up. Let's see."

"Can't. See. It's got a lock. Do you have a key?"

"Nope. And I'm guessing there isn't one in the bedroom. That boy wasn't too bright, but he obviously knew there was something in here that had value and he would have known if she kept a key nearby. I'll bring it down to Aunt May. She just found a note from Opal and it mentioned a box. Maybe this is the one. I'll see what she thinks we should do with it."

"Sounds good. I'm finished going through the costume room. There's some great stuff. I called TiaRa. She was perturbed that I bothered her before sunset, but once I told her about the gowns, she rallied and got very excited. She called Suave and anything Tia doesn't want, Suave will take for the store. I'll start carrying the stuff downstairs. You help Aunt May and Beau get anything else they want. We need to get out of here pretty soon."

I headed out, carrying the metal box. Beau and Aunt May were sitting in the library, both sipping from rather large glasses, full, I was certain, of excellent liquor. The bookcase that hid the secret room was back in place and a box with several folders sat at Beau's feet.

"Find the culprit?" asked Beau.

I explained what had happened. "Do you think this is the box Opal was talking about?" I asked.

"Let's find out," said Aunt May, setting down her glass and opening the small purse she always carried. From it, she withdrew the index card with the key taped to it. "See if this fits."

I pulled the key from the card. It did fit and the top of the metal box swung open. Inside I saw several neat bundles of bills – large denomination bills. I pulled them out and placed them on the table. "Well, now we know what the boy was looking for and it wasn't a phone."

"That is one large pile of money," said Beau. "It must be over a hundred thousand dollars!"

Aunt May smiled. "How sweet of Opal. A going away present. Is there anything else?"

I looked. At the bottom of box was a large silver broach. I pulled it out. Beautiful and old, it was fashioned in the shape of a spider on a web. The body of the spider was a very large blob of blue-green glass. Around the edges of the web were smaller, green, blue, and purple stones like drops of dew.

Aunt May held out her hand and I gave it to her. "How sweet she was," smiled Aunt May. "I saw her wearing this once and admired it. She told me it had little value, being just some glass and silver plate, but was a favorite, as it was a present on a trip to New Mexico when she was young. She said it was the first gift a gentleman friend had purchased for her, so she felt it marked the beginning of her career." She admired it for a bit, then handed it back. "Well, I suppose we should be going. Has Timmy gathered all the goodies from upstairs?"

I nodded. I put the broach back in the box, but as I tilted the box, the light caught a small key hole at the bottom of the box. "Look. There's another door here. There's a secret compartment." I held it out to show Beau and Aunt May.

"Does the key fit that one, too?" asked Beau.

I tried it and shook my head. "Too small." I shook the box. I could hear something clumping inside. "Sounds like paper."

"Maybe it's more money."

"Maybe, but we aren't going to get it open quickly without a key and Ponce and his crew are sure to show up anytime now. Let's worry about it later."

"Agreed," said Aunt May. "Beauregard, bring the box and put it in the car. I will bring it home directly."

Beau emptied his glass and stood. "Aunt May, I cannot bear the thought of those beasts taking all that lovely jewelry in the next room."

"Do not worry, dear boy. I doubt very much that they will be clever enough to discern how to access that room."

Beau was unmoved. "I don't care. It may be glass, but it sparkles and that much glamour should not belong to anyone other than our own drag divas. At some point that room will be discovered and those jewels will be shipped off to some secondhand store for people who will not appreciate them like we will. I cannot bear for that to happen." Beau had obviously had enough to drink to become obdurate. Aunt May and I recognized the set to his jaw and exchanged a look. It would be easier to give in than argue.

"Fine Beau," I said. "You have ten minutes. Use one of the empty file boxes and take only as much as you think will fit into the ammo box once Aunt May has put the money in the bank. The box will keep things safe and is small enough that you won't give in to the temptation to grab simply everything.

Then put the box in the foyer with the gowns and things Timmy has brought down. We'll bring the ammo box with the money and the box of files and your box of jewels out to my car and put them in the trunk. I'll help Timmy load the truck. You take Aunt May home, unload the car and have a little lie down. We will meet at Hoosier Daddy later."

Beau nodded and started for the secret room. I headed out to the foyer where Timmy was adding to a large pile of assorted glitture. At the door to the library, I stopped and called back to Beau. "Take my Blessed Virgin Mary statue with you, too. I don't want her getting mixed in with the rest of the things. If TiaRa sees her, she will insist on having her and I will be forced to fight to the death. That piece of shell art is mine, all mine."

"Promise," called Beau, much more interested in the jewelry than my needs.

I decided to appeal to a higher authority. "Aunt May?" She looked up from her glass, looking a bit more glazed than usual. I suspected that the loss of a friend and the events of the day were taking their toll on her, as irrepressible as she was.

"Yes dear?"

"Please make sure Beau remembers my BVM." I pointed to the small statue that still stood on the table near where we had been sitting. "I will be forever crushed if it does not make it to my house. I already have decided on its place of honor, next to a lovely shell art lamp, complete with flamingo. They go together like holy water and communion wafers."

Aunt May nodded. "I shall make sure your Mary is with us when we leave."

"Thank you." I headed to the foyer, steeling myself for the oh-too-physical pursuits that awaited.

A short time later, all was ready. Timmy had helped load the truck, but insisted he had a previous engagement, so couldn't help unload. He gathered his acquisitions and put them into my car. I suspected his real motivation was a longing to model his new outfits for his amour Cosmo as soon as possible. So, Timmy, Aunt May, and Beau headed out the gate and I, after catching my breath in the truck, lying to myself that I would get to the gym more often, followed.

At the gate, the lawyer was blocking the path of Ponce and his goon. I slowed and called out, "It's all yours."

I didn't wait for an answer, but headed to Hoosier Daddy. I thought I was almost done. I just had to meet with TiaRa and Suave, then unload the truck and return it to work. Finally, home and a long, hot soak with several scented bath oils to sooth my overexcited brain and my protesting muscles. Then I could get on with my day off and all the nothing I had planned.

That's what I thought lay ahead – until someone stole the damn truck.

Chapter 5 - Recovered

I paced up and down across the street from Hoosier Daddy, waiting for the police, unable to keep from looking around, hoping that the missing truck would magically appear just down the block. Roger pulled up a few minutes later, rolled down his window and called, "Get in."

"I'm waiting for the police."

"I am aware of what you are doing. Get in."

"But ..."

"BB. There is, at this moment, a very disappointed young man not being pleasured by me because you lost a large truck. I would point out how hard it is to lose something that big that quickly, but I don't want to waste any more time. I would much rather not be here. Once more—get in or I shall bid you adieu."

I got in. Roger had been a friend for a long time, but only recently had I discovered that he ran a very discrete agency that specialized in fixing problems for an exclusive group of powerful gays around the world. The only reason I knew about the LnL (Limp n Limber) Detective Agency was because he had revealed his secret while we were trying to keep our friend Deb Eubank from being killed before she was elected judge. Since then, he occasionally hired me to do research. It paid well and I was willing, as long as no danger or anxiety-producing activities were involved.

"Where are we going?"

He gave me a withering look. "You misplaced a fourteen-foot truck. I thought I'd take you to it, instead of doing what—or actually, who, I was in the middle of doing."

"You found it!"

"Credit where credit is due. The police found it. Of course, it wasn't that hard. It's blocking an entire lane of the new parking garage."

"They haven't finished that yet. It's not open."

"The truck suffered very little damage when it pushed past the plastic traffic cones that were blocking the entrance. However, it set off an alarm. I heard the report on my scanner on the way over here. Since the call said there were gowns thrown everywhere and, as they put it, 'a whole shitload of faggy crap'. I figured it was your misplaced vehicle. I put in a call to my old friend Detective Crawford and got permission to take a look-see. If you claim it, don't file a report *and* clean up the mess, he doesn't have to do the paperwork and spend time and money investigating."

I nearly kissed Roger. I had no idea why anyone would take the truck and even less why they would go through the contents once they opened the doors and discovered what they had stolen. The things were flamboyant and wonderful for a drag queen, but not anything that would warrant a second look by anyone who didn't have a few wigs and baubles at home. I wasn't interested in the attire; I was just glad the truck was back with little or no damage. I was also very relieved that my shell art BVM was safely stashed at Beau's, waiting for me to bring her home and install her in the perfect place so she would bestow blessings upon me and mine. I'm sure Aunt May was equally glad that the ammo box of money and box of blackmail files were safe.

We turned into the parking structure. It was going to be opened in the next month, ending a long road with endless controversies about design and purpose and the battle for downtown parking versus the reliance on cars. Up a couple of ramps we found the truck. Most of the contents had been scattered around it. The gowns looked to be mussed and tossed in heaps, but otherwise unharmed. Several mid-sized pieces of décor had been smashed, probably on purpose.

Roger got out and looked at the mess—motioning me to stay back. He pulled out a camera and snapped several pictures. Then he looked in the cab. He pulled out his phone and made a few phone calls, which I didn't care to overhear. I was looking at the mess, torn between relief that the things had been found and dismay at the violation.

Roger hung up and came over. "The truck is undamaged. Whoever it was didn't want the truck. They wanted what was in it. It looks like they didn't find what they wanted."

"Why do you say that?"

He nodded to the mess. "They went through everything. If they had found it, they would have stopped looking. I called Timmy. He's not happy about another round with this stuff, but I offered him some cash and he caved. Cosmo is giving him a ride. You and Timmy clean up the mess, then drive back to Daddy's. Timmy will help get the things to Tia. You and Suave are on your own sneaking things into Suave Delights without Foxy seeing. Afterwards, take the truck back so you don't get fired again."

"What are you going to do?"

"I've got some things to check out. We'll meet back at Nacho's later. There's something going on and it isn't nice or friendly. I guess you didn't know who Opal Milbank was."

I shook my head. "Never heard of her before Beau showed up on my doorstep this morning, in tears because she was dead."

"Seems like a bit of the past is sticking an ugly hand out to grab at us. We all need to talk. Nacho is calling Beau and May. Try to stay calm. I know how easily your panties bunch up. It's gonna be bumpy for a bit."

I started to ask for more information, but I heard a car squealing up the ramp. We both tensed, then relaxed as Timmy's husband Cosmo pulled up. Timmy leaned over and gave Cosmo a kiss, then hopped out.

"Can I help?" called Cosmo.

Roger shook his head. "Cosmo, you are sweet and a monster in all things digital, but you are next to hopeless in handling delicate things."

Cosmo made a face. "I handle Timmy a lot and he hasn't complained."

"Timmy has been handled a lot by a lot and is not what I call delicate."

Timmy punched Roger in the arm. "I'm a sweet little flower and you know it."

Roger cocked an eyebrow. "Actually, I do *not* know about your petals, but if you are interested…"

Timmy punched him again. "Not going to happen. Never would. Never will. I have standards. Besides, I'm a married man." He fluttered his eyes at Cosmo. Timmy and Cosmo had crawled out of the bottle and into AA about the same time. Once they became sober enough to notice the world around them, they noticed each other and had been together ever since. They were almost cloyingly in love.

"Why don't you help BB? He can deal with your attitude." Roger turned to Cosmo. "You may be useful at our little meeting tonight at the Patio Café. Can you make it?"

Cosmo was a computer genius. His specialty was 3D modeling of characters for online role-playing games. He

44

shrugged. "Sure. I've got a project I'm in the middle of, but I can tie that up and head over. See you later." He called to Timmy, "See you soon, sweetie."

Timmy waved and waded into the piles behind the truck, immediately sorting, folding and stacking. Thank gawd, the enormity of the task began to shrink into the realm of possible. Roger headed back toward his car. "I've got to get over to talk with Crawford and explain things. He's done us a favor and I'll owe him. Make sure you don't leave a mess. And stay alert. We don't know what's going on. Do not leave the truck unguarded and watch out for strange men following you."

Timmy gave a giggle. "I am very used to having strange men follow me, but now I'm a ..."

"I know, I know. You're a married man and a virgin ... three times so far today." With that, Roger got into his car and drove away.

Chapter 6 - Meeting at Nacho's

It didn't take long to set everything right. When we arrived at Hoosier Daddy, a minor miracle occurred and I was again able to grab a parking place right across the street. This meant not only shorter trips, but less interaction with the churchies who were amassing their individual and group fervor in preparation for their evening prayer session. Upon seeing me, they went into overdrive like a brood of hens spotting a fresh handful of grubs. Some raised their voices to heaven, reading from whatever they were holding in screechy, impassioned voices. Others called out pleas to me to turn away from my sins. I was tempted to point out how much more pleasing they would be in the sight of their Lord if they threw away their current polyester fashion and put on some of these bits of lovely. However, engaging would only lead to further discussion with people whose thoughts, if they had any, held no interest for me.

After we brought TiaRa's treasures inside, Timmy went home and Suave came with me. We successfully got the goodies inside Suave Delights, which was attached to their old stone mansion, while Foxy was taking his afternoon respite, which I suspected was driven less by a desire to sleep than a need to allow the THC level in his bloodstream to drop. Suave stayed to rearrange the store in order to hide the fact that more inventory had been added.

I returned the truck and hurried home, collapsing onto the couch and refusing to move, while a cool drink helped the tension and confusion of the day's events slip away. Spot, my cat, recognized an opportunity and leapt to my chest. He is less than trim and makes deep breaths a challenge, but he is very insistent. I gave in. Lulled by his purring, I let myself drift away.

The phone woke me. It was Beau.

"Roger called and wants to meet at Nacho's ASAP."

"I'm busy right now."

"You're sleeping. I know you. Roger woke me up from a perfectly delightful nap. If I have to suffer, so do you. Not that an evening at Daddy's really counts as suffering."

Beau continued to talk, but I didn't pay much attention. He didn't require more than the occasional mmhmm. I struggled to sit up, no easy feat with a fluffy butterball on your chest, but I kept at it. Finally Spot leapt off my chest and huffed away. I looked around, trying to clear my mind. I was glad work was sporadic. How do other people work every day and still have a life? Well, I suppose my life is a little more nuanced than most. Nuanced. That's it. It may be a lie, but that's my story and I'm sticking to it. Beau intruded on my thoughts.

"I'll be by in five minutes. I still have your car. Roger said we had to bring the files. Aunt May didn't want to, but he talked her into it."

"All right, but make it fifteen. I have to fluff."

"Wasted effort, BB. Wasted."

"Fuck off. Hey, make sure you bring my BVM."

"Your what?"

"Blessed Virgin Mary. That shell art. It's the only thing that made this whole expedition worthwhile."

"You and your tacky treasures. You really need a course in décor. Homosexually impaired. That's what you are. See you soon. Be ready."

"Bring her or I'll send you back home. I have the perfect place ready for her and I will not have her besmirched by your blasphemy a second longer."

Beau sighed. "All right, I'll bring her, but she'll stay in the trunk. I refuse to spend an hour watching you decide on the perfect angle so the light hits her just right."

Aunt May was not a happy lady. "Young man, I simply do not believe I should give up these files. Opal left them for me, not anyone else."

This argument had been going on for too long. Only the easy accessibility of drinks made it bearable. I didn't see what the problem was, but Roger was not just suggesting. He was insisting and while Aunt May looked like a sweet old Southern lady, Roger was discovering her resolute backbone hidden beneath the soft folds of drink and drawl.

"It's too dangerous, May," said Roger. "Opal Milbank was involved with some very powerful people and powerful people have nasty playmates."

"You put me in mind of Roderick Habersham," said Aunt May. "He believed he could have his way with me, any way he wished, because I was a frail woman who would crumble before his manliness. He was a most attractive young man, attentive and quite well behaved when in public. I did wish to see what he could provide in private, but once we had retired to my boudoir and he had undressed me, he changed and became quite controlling. He did not think I would or could do anything to stop any and every desire he had, for fear of damage to myself or my reputation, being unaware of the unconventional strength of both. Well, I do not mind a bit of firmness, but when his interests extended to pain, I protested. He ignored my wishes and had the audacity to tell me to shut up or he would show me real pain. He was cruel, but, as is so often the case, he was also stupid. My hands were particularly strong that year, as the pecan crop had been plentiful and I had been cracking the nuts for weeks. At that point, I could scoop up a bunch in each hand and produce a rain of shells and a handful of nuts. Have you ever tasted fresh pecans? They are a particular delight. It is a taste I can still recall with ease."

Aunt May lost a bit of focus, chewing on a piece of ice from her drink, but quite clearly tasting a pecan from her youth. Beau cleared his throat.

"Aunt May, you were saying," he prodded.

She gave a slight shake of her head, returning from her memories, put down her glass, and patted her lips with a lace hanky. She continued, "Well, I slumped back until that boy was close enough and then I grabbed and gave him the twisting squeeze that shelled so many pecans. No shells dropped, but Roderick did. He dropped to the floor and was still emptying the contents and I believe the lining of his stomach when I finished dressing and went downstairs. I heard he entered the priesthood sometime later. And while I am not as fit as I once was, I think I can say without the sin of pride that I have learned a bit more about keeping myself safe over the years."

"I'm not saying you can't defend yourself, Aunt May," said Roger. "But the contents of those files ..."

"Have been given to me to use as I see fit," interrupted Aunt May.

At this point, Nacho rolled up to the table, leaning on the heavy, wooden walking stick and blew a cloud of noxious smoke from the gut-wrenching, ever-present cigar. "You can't keep 'em at your house, May," Nacho stated. "Somethin' that stinks is in the wind and it ain't just the guys at this table."

Nacho ran the Patio Café through the combined talents of excellent cooking, a preternatural ability to sense any untoward activity, and the ability and willingness to physically remove anything or anybody who misbehaved. "It don't matter if you can defend yourself against a man or two. That Milbank dame was the only thing standing between some very nasty people and a very large pile of cash. I still haven't found out what they are planning, but it was big enough that she approached me for advice. That was only last week and now she's dead."

"You knew her?" I asked.

Nacho glared at me. "BB, ain't I suggested to you before that you not question what and who I know?"

I decided that studying my drink was very important. "Sorry Nacho," I mumbled.

Nacho nodded. "Better. What I *will* say is that she reached out to share her suspicions about a bit of hanky panky going on. Someone or some group of someones were planning something unpleasant that was worth a pile of money, if they could get away with it. She didn't have details, but she had hints. She was sure it wasn't any penny ante game. It was millions. That's why she came to me."

While defending Deb from an unknown killer last year, we had learned something of Nacho's connections to TaDah! the Twinkie Army Destroying All Hypocrites, a secret organization dedicated to protecting gays and bringing down closeted power brokers who publicly railed against and privately rolled against those who embraced outside the dominate pairing paradigm. TaDah! had information gathering down to an art form, but only used its resources to protect and defend. Evidently, Opal also knew of Nacho's connections to TaDah!.

Nacho continued. "Some of these people probably figured out she had suspicions. It's a good bet they suspected she had some details. Now she's dead and they're gonna come looking for anything she left behind. They'll do anything to destroy it, just to make sure they ain't exposed. They ain't gonna find it at her place and they know you pulled some stuff outta there. So, they're gonna come looking for what you've got. Remember your fire last year. That was just to scare you. If you're a threat, you don't know what ..."

Aunt May broke in. "All right your honor. I bow to your insistence that these may not be safe at our home. However, the information was given to me to do with what I feel is proper. I know you have an affinity for gathering information."

"You won't be turning them over for anything more than safe keeping," said Nacho. "I promise not to do any digging through your drawers without your permission."

Aunt May gave a nod of assent. "Then, I thank you. Opal has left a folder with an explanation of what each file contains. I shall keep that and study it, but the rest shall remain with you. Perhaps you can help with something else while you have them."

"What's that?"

"Several of the folders have these." May reached into one of the folders and pulled out a thumb drive. "I assume they are computer related. However, I plugged one into my nephew's computer and was unable to see anything."

Cosmo spoke up. He and Timmy had been sitting quietly,

observing the conversation, content to sip their sparkling waters and listen. But computers were his specialty. "The drives are probably encrypted," he said.

"Young man, I am afraid that means nothing to me," said Aunt May.

"Hidden," explained Cosmo. "Maybe the information is scrambled and needs to be unscrambled before you can read it. There is probably a password. I have a few programs that may do the trick."

Aunt May nodded. "Opal was very technologically savvy," she said. "It would be like her to do something like that. If I gave you one of these things, could you see if you can make sense of what is on it?"

"Sure," said Cosmo. "I can try."

Aunt May handed the drive to Cosmo. "I must ask you to be very careful with this and not make any copies. I do not know what is on it, but I am certain it is potentially explosive."

"Promise," said Cosmo. "If I can open it, I'll just look at enough to make sure it is readable. Then I'll bring it back to you."

Aunt May nodded. "Thank you. I entrust you with this and Nacho, I will leave the rest with you."

"Thanks May," said Nacho. "Roger, grab those files. Let's get them in the vault."

"Vault?" I asked. I was one of the privileged few who had seen Nacho's office, but I hadn't seen anything that looked like a vault.

Nacho turned and glowered at me. It was a frightening thing. "BB, you are *not* asking me about something you have no business knowing, are you?"

Nacho had secrets ... lots of secrets. Anyone who knew

anything about Nacho knew that dangerous mystery was as much a part of Nacho as delicious tidbits, flowery muumuus, and smelly cigars. However, anyone with any sense also knew that poking around under Nacho's skirts was a bad idea, sure to end in tears, and only just tears if you were lucky.

I quickly shook my head. "Perish the thought. You just took me by surprise." I looked around for a diversion. Thankfully, the universe provided. TiaRa del Fuego was coming out onto the patio and she had fire in her eyes and purpose in her step ... unusual for TiaRa, who generally glided a bit above the realm of us mere mortals.

Chapter 7 - Dick Hobbies

"Dumplings! Opportunity has knocked and we must all pull together to round the bases to the end zone. It is for the children. Our children!" TiaRa could raise a song to sublime heights and MC a show that ran smoothly despite meltdowns and madness, but was not skilled at metaphor and had neither interest nor knowledge of sports. When she was truly excited, which was rarely, having been stunned once too often, she did not make much sense, but she did make her intentions clear.

"What's up, Tia?" asked Beau.

"Mr. Dick is retiring!" said Tia.

I shot a warning glare at Beau. "Too easy," I said. "And you know who she's talking about."

Hoosier Daddy was at the end of a half block of connected storefronts. An alley ran behind the block and another alley cut the block in half. On the other end of the half block was the small storefront church and its small, but growing congregation of born-again hate farmers who carefully studied their bible to find justification for attacking anyone who wasn't just like them. Being so near to our little cesspool of sin seemed to feed their souls. We found them a lumpy mixture of amusing and annoying. The other half block was completely taken up by a regional bank which strenuously ignored everything that happened on our half of the block.

In between Daddy's and the church was a wonderful hobby, craft, and game store. Dick Hobbies had been started many years ago by Harold K. Dick, a friendly, nearsighted man who had come into a fortune early in life. His grandfather was Otis Boykin, who had been one of the most famous Black inventors—resistors for missiles and pacemakers among other essential items. His mother did not follow in her father's learned footsteps. She wandered off to a commune in the early sixties and had a child—Harold, with a man named Dick who promptly lived up to his name and deserted. His mother dropped Harold off with his grandfather and disappeared into the counter culture, reemerging only occasionally to ask for money. When his grandfather died, he left most of his fortune to Harold, who had inherited a love of tinkering from his grandfather and an inability to create anything useful from his mother. His sole talent was in the construction of small versions of larger things. He built models and became infatuated with miniatures. As he had no need of money, he opened a hobby shop where he could indulge his interests in buying and building all manner of little things.

Dick Hobbies was known throughout the miniature world as a big player. When the half block of stores came up for sale, he purchased it. Of course, his first tenant was a gay bar. What other enterprise could be more appropriate next to Dick Hobbies than Hoosier Daddy? The shop at the far end of the block never seemed to stick around for long. Harold didn't mind. When it was rented, he had a little extra money, which he didn't need. When yet another enterprise went belly up, he used the space for storage.

The churchies had been there longer than most. I don't know how they were managing to make the rent. Harold charged a fair, but not cheap rent. He had been taught by his grandfather to keep charity and business separate. He didn't really care who he rented to, as long as they didn't damage the property and they paid their rent on time. Beyond that, Harold mostly focused on his latest project, which usually involved recreating some famous dwelling in miniature.

The churchies might have been more irritating to him than most. I'm sure they spent time trying to convert him. When that failed, they must have been smart enough not to condemn him. They might bite, but not the hand that fed them—or at least rented to them. I still didn't understand how Felcher had made the move from an abandoned auto-parts store to Magawatta. His congregation did not look large or rich. I never saw many people around the place, beyond the pickets harassing the gay boys and girls aiming for Daddy's. Perhaps they had some secret source of income. We all hoped that they would run out of funds soon and wander off to pastures far, far away and the little storefront would become home to yet another about-to-fail business.

"What difference does it make if Harry Dick retires?" asked Beau. "I'm glad for him, but I don't see it as cause for excitement. Miniatures bore me."

"His retirement is the cause," said Tia. "However, the result is that he is going to sell."

"Are you thinking about trying to buy a hobby shop?" I asked. "I love you Tia, but I don't see you as the proprietress of such a place."

TiaRa shook her head. "Mr. Dick is not selling his store. He is selling the entire block. But what is more important is that he has contacted the owners of Daddy's. He doesn't want to list it and allow a developer to tear down this block and put up one more hideous complex that tries to be *très chique* by slapping on a different exterior material every ten feet. So, if we can raise the money, he will sell it directly to the bar."

"Do the owners have any interest in expanding the bar?" I

asked. "It's not like Daddy's is bulging at the seams."

"As opposed to your jeans," said Beau.

"Pot, meet kettle," I said, then turned my attention back to TiaRa. "And do they have the resources? You know them better than I do, but I've never got the feeling that they were rolling in cash."

TiaRa waved away my objections. "Of course they have neither interest nor funding to expand the bar. I wouldn't wish them to. Part of the charm of Daddy's is the intimacy."

Daddy's is large black box with Day-Glo paint splashed randomly on the walls, with a small bar for ancients appended at the front, more passageway than room. Nacho Mama's Patio Café perched out the back like a hump. I could think of many words to describe Daddy's, but none were charm or intimate. "Then why the interest?" I asked.

"The children," said TiaRa. "All the young gaybe babies. The transaware. The baby dykes. The hidden and frightened who know or suspect they are different and have nowhere to turn except to inner sorrow. We must create a youth center to allow those who are questioning to have a place to discover answers and realize they are not alone, but are part of. Part of a community with a proud past and a glorious future. There will be places to safely socialize. Information for their questions. Professionals to help with school, family, social, and more. It will be a place of learning, recreation, safety, and fun. A place like we never had. And it is up to us to create it.

TiaRa del Fuego usually was untroubled by activities of the mundane world. Beyond planning shows and acquiring outfits, she rarely expressed more than polite interest in anything. I had seen her enthused about a new act or new man, but rarely, and never to such an extent. She was nearly vibrating with excitement. There was something very important to her here. I had a feeling we were touching a raw spot from her mysterious, misty past.

Aunt May looked up from her drink, unaware of the undercurrents of the conversation. "When I was a young woman, I started a youth center. It was, however, for a much younger clientele. There was a particularly virulent influenza one year that took a great toll on new mothers. There were an inordinate number of virile young men left bereaved and with child or children. They were overwhelmed, poor dears. I felt I had to do something to ease their suffering."

She patted her mouth with her hankie, then took another sip, looking back. "I raised the money and hired a staff of able young women to care for the children. I myself have never been good with children. I am afraid I do not have the patience, the skill set, or the desire to acquire either. However, I *was* able to offer succor to the fathers. While they were offered sympathy in full measure by many, it was viewed as unseemly in the eyes of most to offer to meet their more private needs. But these were young men in the very prime of their sexual potency and they were absolutely hungering for a diversion from their grief. So, on a regular basis I would call each one in for counseling and training in fatherhood. I recall Wilber Heckman, not altogether an attractive man, but possessed of a most remarkable ..."

Beau reached over and touched her hand. Aunt May sometimes got lost in her memories and needed a call from shore to come back to the present. "Aunt May, TiaRa was telling us about her inspiration."

May smiled and reached for her glass. "Oh yes, my dear. Forgive me. Please do go on."

We turned our attention back to Tia. "Please, Tia dear," I said. "Explain to us mere mortals what you are planning and why. If the owners don't want to expand the bar and don't have the money to buy the block, then they will rent from whoever does buy the block. I don't see what we have to do with that or what any of it has to do with underage drinkers."

"It is for the children," proclaimed Tia. "We have a chance to provide a place where anyone who feels a little different can come. Certainly, here in Indiana difference can mean death. And their hope of a promised land should not be a dark and slightly besoiled bar, no matter how wonderful the entertainment. We have a chance to provide a place of welcome for those beginning to question and their friends. And if that were not reason enough, the alternative is too horrible to imagine."

"What do you mean?" asked Beau.

"Mr. Dick has made the same offer to the other tenants of the block."

"You don't mean?"

TiaRa nodded. "The church at the end of the block has told Mr. Dick that they are interested in expanding. They have mentioned an interest in opening a school. They told Mr. Dick they are confident they can move forward quickly and are pressuring him to give them first place in line. They claim to have powerful friends and are hinting at a threat. I believe the group is headed by the antiques dealer near city hall."

"Do you mean Matt Ponce?" I asked.

"I believe that is the name," said TiaRa. "He and his brother plan to use this as a model school and to get state money to form a network of charter schools throughout the state."

Aunt May sniffed. "I sincerely doubt they will be welcoming to children of all interests."

"Certainly not," said TiaRa. "The owners told me the church plans to have a no-gays policy but to offer remedial classes for those whose parents think their children might be gayly inclined, to make sure they don't turn ..." She hesitated and shuddered, "queer."

Beau said, "We've got to stop them somehow. On top of what they are doing with that school, there's no way they'll let Daddy's stay. They'll raise the rent until it's impossible or just evict us outright. We have to do something."

"But what?" I asked. "I don't know how much a block costs, but there's no way we have enough money."

"I know how to raise a substantial sum," announced TiaRa. "The solution is one word." She paused, waiting for one of us to ask.

I stepped up. "And what is that magical word, Miss del Fuego?"

She smiled her most glamorous smile and spoke the word as if it were an incantation, "Cotillion."

Chapter 8 - The Legendary Cotillion

"I remember my cotillion," said Aunt May. "Jacob Buckalew was my escort. All the girls had escorts to protect their honor before their presentation. Jacob was surprisingly tall for his age. His hormones had a tight grip upon his body, but his mind was still struggling between duty and desire. Being young, he actually believed I was a fragile flower of the South ... in private as well as public. He was so absolutely immune to my hints that I suspected he was utterly unschooled in the changes coursing through his body and had not yet embarked on a course of self-study. I wondered if his interests lay more with his fellow escorts, until I accidentally spilled a cup of punch in his lap and as I was busily mopping it up, it arose that his interest could be unfurled. I was able to lead him to an upstairs linen closet and ..."

"What's a cotillion?" I asked. "It lurks in my memory near square dance."

"Ah BB," sighed Beau, thrilled to be able to waltz out a bit of his arcane knowledge, "it is a rite of passage. The cotillion dates back to the eighteenth century, where it did resemble a square dance. However, in the South, the cotillion is the grand display of what the children have learned at their etiquette classes. It is their first taste of being adults."

"Like a debutante ball?" I asked.

"That is for older youths," said Aunt May. "The cotillion is for younger—those younger than sixteen."

"That means you and Jacob were ..."

Aunt May nodded. "We had each celebrated our fifteenth birthdays the previous week." She took a sip of her glass. "I viewed him as my own present to myself. Unfortunately, as it was a new experience for him, the unwrapping lasted longer than the present." She turned her attention to TiaRa. "But what does children's etiquette have to do with saving the bar?"

At this point, Roger returned to the table, Nacho clumping close behind. "All tucked away, Aunt May," Roger said. "You'll have access whenever you wish. Either Nacho or I can fetch anything at any time. We both have access, but no one else can get anywhere near it without losing an essential body part." He sat down, leaned back in his chair and took a pull on his beer. Then he noticed that all eyes were on Tia. "What's up?" he asked.

We quickly brought Nacho and Roger up to speed. TiaRa did not enjoy having her grand reveal interrupted. She was used to being the center of attention. It was not narcissism; she was just usually the most interesting thing going on in our world. Sometimes Nacho came close, but Nacho eschewed the spotlight, whereas TiaRa del Fuego did not so much seek it, as she allowed it to be drawn to her, as sin to a satyr. However, she was a patient mistress, realizing that background information was necessary to make her proclamation clear, so she stood still until our eyes returned once more to rest upon her.

"A cotillion," repeated Tia. "A grand cotillion. The likes of which has never been seen. As you know, I have no small reputation outside of Magawatta and Suave also toured extensively. Together, we know some of the greatest performers in the world of drag. Now, every performer worth her salt has at least one baby that she has been nurturing, tutoring in the ways of the wiles. I propose that we bring them all together to show off their protégés. Not a competition, but a celebration. Of course, with just a touch of competition to encourage donations."

"Buying the whole damn block is gonna take more than a drag show at a seedy bar," said Nacho. "Miss Tia, you know I respect you and the shows you stage, but this is a small town and it ain't got the deep pockets to raise a couple or three million bucks."

"Maybe Foxy has that kind of money, but I don't know," I said.

Foxy KitTan was the richest person we knew, having sold controlling interest in the Pie Hole, a chain of pie and coffee restaurants he had started, when they went international. He still had an ethical veto over major corporate decisions, but had little to do with the company now, focusing instead on bringing taste and glamour to our little town and heaping happiness upon his beloved Suave, while convivially complaining about her ongoing pursuit of an infinite collection of wonderful little things.

TiaRa waved away our objections along with the foul smoke of Nacho's cigar. "The cotillion will be held in Magawatta, but the invitees, both performers and patrons, shall travel here. Do not worry, pumpkins. Your Tia is not without connections. We shall have a select group of glitterati from the world over." Tia, always looking at a point a bit above where we mere mortals groveled, raised her eyes higher. "It shall be an event unequaled. We shall limit it to the world's best performers, each presenting their favorite child. The attendees will donate to the protégé they feel is best. This will bring out the competitive edge of the divas. Each will want their baby to win. It will be a celebration and a competition *and* a way to help the upcoming gaybe babies. Legendary!

That is what we shall call it—the Legendary Cotillion."

Roger shook his head. "I don't doubt you can pull in a great bill, but Nacho's right. We can't have it at Daddy's. Nacho makes the best nachos in the world, but this place is a pit. That's why they allow people like BB in. There's no reputation to sully."

"That's where we need Foxy," said Beau. "He can pull off any level of glamour and richness. He's opened hundreds of Pie Holes around the world and while this is a bit different than opening a pie and coffee restaurant, he's learned every trick in the book. Plus, he's been in boardrooms around the world. He knows piles of rich people and how to handle them.

"Remember when he threw that fundraiser for Deb when she was running for judge?" I asked. "It worked out wonderfully, even though someone was trying to kill the guest of honor."

"Dumplings, you are correct," said TiaRa. "I feel certain our Foxy can help create a perfect event. I shall provide the perfect entertainment, as that is where my talents are strongest. He shall provide the wealthy audience."

TiaRa hosted the weekly Parade of Gowns drag show every Sunday evening at Hoosier Daddy, which was an essential slice of excellence that made our lives worth living. We gathered every week to soak in the talent, dish about our weekly exploits, drink a bit too much, and stuff ourselves between sets at Nacho Mama's Patio Café where Nacho provided the world's best nachos.

"Better do it quickly," said Roger. "You know those churchies will pull every underhanded trick they can to buy the block. Felcher is nothing if he isn't mean. It wouldn't surprise me if they try to offer more to Dick to make him decide early. If they get this block, Daddy's will be gone faster than a promise on a first date."

"What I'm wonderin'," said Nacho, "is why here? If they got

money, why squat in a crappy rented storefront? If they don't, then how can they play at all? Something's up."

"You're right," said Roger. "Maybe I'll have Cosmo take a peek at their records."

"How could Cosmo ..." I began, but a double-barreled glare from both Roger and Nacho silenced me. There was very little about computers and online juggling Cosmo didn't know about. He was mostly interested in online games and creating characters for clients, but evidently, he also occasionally did work for Roger's LnL Detectives.

Nacho nodded. "I'll see what my sources can dig up."

Roger stood, "Well then, let's get to it."

Nacho put a hand on his shoulder. "Hold on. We got something else to talk about. Aunt May? Do you know what's in those files I made you stash here?"

Aunt May took a sip from her drink and smiled. "I have not yet had time to give them more than a cursory glance, however Opal provided a brief summary in her letter to me. In short, they are a collection of her most effective blackmail files. I do not believe they are the type that would be used to force a person to hand over their life savings. I know I certainly am not the type to ask for such a thing. However, should one wish an audience with someone who might otherwise be too busy or to encourage a seemingly intractable someone to consider a new point of view, then they could be of great use. I recall one of my gentleman friends, Horatio Willikins (married to Olethea Wallinford, a very religious woman) had a real devotion to wearing my used undergarments. Once a week, he would come over and—"

"Aunt May," Beau touched her arm, bringing her back to us.

"Ah yes, apologies. As I was saying, it appears at first glance that the information would be inconvenient, either financially or to the reputation of her gentlemen. I have not had time to study the files, but I believe Opal chose the twenty or so most influential men from her admirers."

Nacho nodded. "The lady was a friend. She got us out of a couple of major scrapes and provided some important info once or twice on the QT. She didn't want anything for the help. Just wanted to lend a hand. I don't know how she knew to come to me, but she did. So, I'm a bit concerned about what got left behind. I also got questions about her dyin'. She was old, but with all the electronic gizmos she kept around, you'd think she'da been able to call for help. Roger, can you look into that?"

Roger nodded. I didn't even bother to mention that the house would certainly be at least protected by a security system and probably by a guard of Matt Ponce's choosing. Roger would have taken offense if I even hinted that such things might cause him a problem. "I'll take a look at the files you left behind, too. There might be some that she thought wouldn't be useful for you, but might have some potential for me or Nacho at some point in the future."

"Leave some behind," said Nacho. "If anyone does figure out how to get into that room, it would be swell if they didn't suspect some are missing." Nacho turned to the kitchen. "OK. I think that's it for now. I'll bring out a plate of nachos for those of you hanging around. I gotta get back to work."

Roger said, "Color me gone. Sooner I get there, sooner I can scope the place out. See you later. BB, call me when you get home. Cosmo should have a list of people for you to research by then." Most of my work for Roger involved digging through various databases to find out about people of interest to him.

TiaRa turned to go. "I must set the wheels in motion. This shall be my grandest show. We shall invite the reigning queens from all over the world and their single finest baby to perform. The audience will be a select and extremely wealthy cadre. We shall have a bidding war for the best performance. All the divas will be working the crowd to make sure it is their protégé who wins. I am certain we will be able to raise all the money needed to purchase the block, save Daddy's, and open our Center for Questioning Youth. And each of you will help, for I cannot think of a group who questions their own youth more on a daily basis."

Tia and Roger went out together. Cosmo and Timmy said their goodbyes, obviously planning to continue their nuzzling, and Jackie, the current studlet-in-waiting brought out our nachos. Aunt May, Beau and I ordered more drinks and dove into the heavenly munchies while Aunt May regaled us with stories of past adventures with the young men of Honeysuckle Springs.

Chapter 9 - Home Again, Home Again

Since I was driving, I felt it best to limit the liquid part of my consumption and focused on the nachos. Aunt May neither drove nor ever limited her drinking and Beau was happy to attempt to match her. So, it was up to me to drop them home and find parking near my little house. At least I was clearheaded enough to be able to consider where to place my newly acquired treasure, the shell art BVM, which I clutched tightly to my chest as I mounted my porch steps, warily watching for any holy statuary thieves lurking in the bushes. There were none. However, my door was open. Not just open, but kicked in. At least, I assumed that is what had happened. Magawatta is a college town. Things like kicked-in doors were not a regular occurrence. However, the fact that the door was swinging open and had splintered around the handle, plus my lightning-fast mind and experience watching TV shows gave me a pretty good idea of what had happened.

I paused on the porch, unsure what to do. I felt violated and desperately wanted to burst through the door and see what damage had been wrought. On the other hand, what if the kicker-inners were still inside? Frozen in indecision, I held my breath and listened. There were none of the bangings I would have expected if someone who would kick in a door on a quiet street was poking around. This was not a subtle crime. I heard an angry meow from inside. Spot, my large mutt of a cat, was displeased. Spot was often displeased, but he was also rather timid, preferring to hide rather than attack. If he was making his displeasure known, I was pretty sure there was no one else inside. So, clutching my Virgin Mary to my chest in hopes that she would provide some kind of protection, should it be needed, I crept through the open door.

Now, I am not obsessively tidy. Cluttered but not disgusting is my general level of acceptable. The house was not how I had left it. It was trashed but not trashed for the sake of trashing. No, this was a purposeful trashing. Someone had been looking for something. I was helped in this surmise by the note. Not actually a note, but a message scrawled across one wall with marker—"Where's Mary?"

I looked around, fright bubbling through my shock, not able to focus. Everything from the shelves had been tossed toward the center of the room, chairs upended, furniture toppled. An angry meow brought me back to focus.

Spot was standing on the kitchen table, tail swishing back and forth. I walked over and reached out to stroke him. He batted at my hand. Not unusual. He's not the friendliest animal. I avoided his claws and covered his face with my hand, his preferred method of attention. The contact with another living thing helped. I uprighted one of the kitchen chairs and sat, putting my BVM on the floor. Spot leapt from the table onto my lap. This was completely out of character. Spot did not sit in laps. He disdained behaving like a cat, preferring to wait until I was lying down so he could sit on my chest, proclaiming ownership. So even this old barn cat was well and truly freaked. I didn't feel like such a wimp.

It finally occurred to me that I needed help. I pulled out my phone and called Roger. I could call the police, but if I didn't call Roger first, he would be upset. For the police, this would be just another call. Roger .... well ...

I dialed.

"I'm busy, call back." Roger was never into polite and with me, he knew that filters weren't necessary.

Before he hung up, I said, "Someone broke in and ..."

Roger's voice changed. "Are you sure they've gone?"

"I'm ... I'm pretty sure. Spot isn't hiding and I don't see anyone."

Roger interrupted my babbling. "Don't touch anything. Don't call anyone. Stand very still. I'll call Petunia and head over there. We'll be there very soon. Don't move."

So I sat, patting Spot and staring into space. I didn't want to look at anything, because everywhere was destruction, so I channeled my ability to ignore what disturbed me.

A few minutes later, Roger burst through the door, took a step inside and stopped. He ignored me and scanned the room, cataloging everything. Then he turned to the door and examined the damage. While he was doing that, I heard heavy steps outside. It was Petunia, Roger's assistant and enforcer. Petunia had much in common with a brick wall, except no wall could glower in a way that would strike terror in anyone, of any size, living or dead. Petunia could. Petunia was one of those people you instinctively stepped back from and went to great lengths not to displease.

She pushed past Roger, glanced around, then punched Roger on the shoulder. He grunted. I would have passed out. "Roger, you tool. BB's shook."

Roger glanced at me and shrugged. "He'll get over it." Then he went back to examining the message scrawled on the wall.

Petunia punched him again and walked over to me. "Put the cat down," she ordered. I did. I always did what Petunia ordered, or even hinted at.

"Stand up." I did.

Suddenly, I was wrapped tightly in arms that were thick as tree trunks and solid as iron bars. I thought about resisting, but the idea quickly passed as I realized how ridiculous it was. So, I allowed myself to be squeezed by those massive arms and some of my horror slipped away.

"BB," Petunia spoke quietly into my ear. "We are now going to walk outside. Do not look at anything. We are going outside and I am going to take you to Beau's house where you will stay tonight. We will take care of this. Do you understand?"

I couldn't talk, but I nodded. We headed for the door. I halted. "Spot?" I asked.

Petunia continued to move me out the door. "We will take care of Spot. We'll take care of everything. We won't throw away anything. We'll just straighten up and try to figure out what happened. Now, come on."

Beau and Aunt May lived down the block, so we walked. I had no strength, but Petunia could have easily picked me up and tucked me under one arm. Instead, she forced me to walk, probably figuring a bit of movement would be good for keeping my focus on the solid ground beneath my feet. She held tight and kept me moving. I don't know if I have ever walked so far being held as tightly by a member of the opposite sex since I was a baby being held by my mother. But, just as it must have been then, the contact was calming and reassuring. We arrived at Beau's house. Roger must have called ahead because both Beau and Aunt May were there and waiting for me.

"You're up in the blue room, dear," said Aunt May. She led me upstairs and sat me on the bed, put a very large drink in my hand and set another on the bedside table. "Now drink that down. It will help you to sleep. You call if you need anything."

I was done. I followed directions. By the time I was half finished with the drink, the events of the evening and the shock took over and I lay back. Today had been far too full for this little boy. Tomorrow would be soon enough to face whatever came next. Sleepy bye time.

Chapter 10 - Friday Morning

The next morning, I stumbled downstairs and found a simple, but very delightful surprise laid out on the table. Beau had gone out for bagels and an assortment was arrayed. He had also picked up doughnuts from Cresent Doughnuts. Aunt May had made a large French press of very strong coffee and then retired to her room. All these yummies lined the edges of the table. In the middle, was the ammo box, now empty of its pile of money and home to the baubles Beau had gathered the day before. The box was lying on its side while a small mountain of très lovely jewelry was spilled out over the tablecloth.

"Sweetness, solids, bitters, and jewels," announced Beau. "The perfect beginning of a day to close the door on too much trauma."

Beau does know how to make me happy. I sat down, reached for a doughnut and did what I do best. A couple of cuppas later, while toying with jewels fit for the grandest of queens, I was willing to let my mind wander to the events of last night.

"Have we heard from Roger?" I asked.

Beau nodded. "He wants you to meet him at his office."

"Office?" I didn't know Roger had an office, but Roger operated LnL on a need-to-know basis. Beau shrugged. He knew less about LnL than I did. "I need to go back home first and change." I hesitated. "Do you know how bad it is? Did he give you any hint?"

"Nacho had some of his people clean it up. Roger said that they didn't try to decipher your decorating scheme, just straightened up and fixed most of the damage. I believe what he said was, 'BB should be able to handle it without pooping his pants or starting to cry.'."

"Such a big, caring heart on that asshole," I said.

Beau grinned. "You love us. You know you do."

I didn't answer. Instead, I picked up a bagel and munching, toyed with some more of the lovely jewelry. "I can't tell real from fake, but these sure put a twinkle in my eye."

"You are such a cheap date, BB. However, these are excellent fakes, Aunt May told me, that they would fool nearly anyone who wasn't a pro examining them with a jeweler's loupe." He pulled a tiara from the pile. "I can't imagine someone other than a drag queen wearing this."

I pulled at a necklace of diamonds, featuring a large green stone on a pendant. "God, if this were real and I wanted to wear it, I'd have to get breasts just to frame it right."

Beau nearly sprayed coffee at me. He was barely able to get his mouthful down without choking and glared at me. "It would be a crime to frame that piece with any kind of breast you could manage. Surgery will never progress that far."

I held the stone against my hand. "But someone actually gave this to Opal. I wonder what she provided in return."

"My guess is silence. I don't mean she threatened to alert the press, but that she was quiet while pretending to hang on to every word while he babbled on and on about whatever was important to him."

I shrugged. "I've been silent during plenty of male ramblings and no one has ever offered me a so much as a gum ball."

"You don't have a high enough class of talkers. No one cares if you're listening, what you hear, or if you might repeat what you've heard—even if they thought you could remember it."

"Someone cares about what I've had," I sniffed. "Do remember that someone or someones destroyed my house just yesterday looking for my BVM."

"OK, so one time you have something of value and it's something you just got. Speaking of which, you better get moving. Roger is not a patient man."

"Right." I began to stand.

"And put that necklace back. Don't think you are going anywhere with my jewels."

I didn't want his jewels, but the opportunity to fuck with Beau was just too tempting. I held the necklace up to my chest. "I don't know. After my traumatic experience, I think the only thing that can make life worth living again would be a lovely gift from a dear friend." I batted my eyes at him.

Beau made a grab for the piece, but I leaned back. "You have so much and I have so little." I tried, poorly, to imitate his Southern accent. "And a gentleman such as yourself, Mr. Beauregard, could bring such happiness into a poor, damaged girl's life by simply ..."

Beau lunged across the table and grabbed the necklace. "Fuck off BB. These jewels are mine, all mine."

"Actually, dear boy, they are ours," said Aunt May coming into the room. "And that is only until the auction. TiaRa asked, and I have agreed, that offering them at auction after the Legendary Cotillion would not only be a lovely gesture, but might push our fundraising over the top. I assume you would prefer having a place to meet with your friends, over being covered in jewels, but forced to sit at home. So put those things away."

Beau sighed. "My greatest hope is that there will be a few lovely bits left over that I can call my own."

"That may happen, dear," said Aunt May, "but for now, you don't want to damage anything. As I said, put them away."

Beau pulled the ammo box over and began to gently put the pieces back in, carefully winding them around themselves to prevent tangling.

"I guess I should get over to Roger's," I said. "Thanks for being my safe harbor in my hour of need."

Aunt May waved away my thanks. Beau stood and gave me a hug. "Any time—well, any time after you've had your house invaded. If not, I'll put it on your tab."

That didn't deserve an answer, given the number of times Beau had passed out on my couch. I headed home.

The short walk helped settle the meal, although it also gave me time to grow some swell anxiety about what I was going to find. The previous night was a bit of a blur, but it was not a gauzy "love is in the air" kind of montage. It was a series of jagged, unpleasant images of destruction. I got to my front door, noting that Roger had already had it replaced. I've got to hand it to Roger. He may be bad on paying his part of a bill when we're out dining, but when things really matter, he doesn't play poor. He had popped for a new door and one of Nacho's network of helpers had installed it. Of course, I didn't have a key, but as soon as I rattled the door, it was opened by Petunia.

Now Petunia is menacing at the best of times and I usually gave her a wide berth. However, when coming into a house that has been broken into, menacing is very comforting to have nearby. She held out a key ring.

"Door knob and dead bolt. Use them both, whether you are inside or outside. Use them both." She glared at me. "Do I need to say that a third time or can you imagine what will happen if I check and both are not locked?"

"Use them both. Always." I pride myself on being able to follow orders given to me by people who can do great damage without much effort.

"Do you have any doubts that I will be checking at random times to make sure you are following these orders?"

I did not and said so.

"Good. Then come in."

I did, stepping in and looking around. I was amazed. Nacho and Roger's elves had been busy. Everything that could be straightened easily had been. The collections of knickknacks that I continually rearranged, as if getting all in the exactly proper place would open a portal to another dimension where all was glorious, were put in boxes near the shelving units. I suppose the elves had known they would only incur scorn if they tried to decide the proper places to put everything.

The wall that had been defaced was repaired and repainted.

In fact, the entire place had additionally been cleaned and smelled fresher and looked more dust free than it had in ... well, than it ever had.

I didn't quite twirl around like a princess, but I took it all in, the tightness that was hiding near my stomach relaxing. On a chair near where Petunia stood, Spot sat, purring as if he was a normal cat, instead of glowering at me for not immediately feeding him. He reached up and rubbed against Petunia's hand, something he never did to me.

I sat, looking around at the marvel.

Petunia growled. "How soon they forget. What did I just tell you?"

"Oh, right." I leapt up and locked the door and fastened the deadbolt. I knew we were leaving in a minute and we were safe with Petunia there, but I also knew that arguing would be painful as well as futile. "I'll go change and then we can go to Rogers, OK?"

Petunia nodded and sat. Spot leapt onto her lap, stretched out, and began to purr. Again, something he never did with me.

"Do not be jealous of a cat's feelings," I thought heading back to my room. I changed quickly and returned to the living room.

"Where's my BVM?" I asked, realizing it wasn't in sight.

"Roger has it," answered Petunia. "Someone wants it, so we figured it was worth protecting until we know what's going on. Don't worry. He's not into women at all and not too hot on virgins, so she'll be safe." She stood. "Let's get going. There are things to do."

I followed her out to her car, carefully and obviously locking both locks under her watchful eye.

Chapter 11 - Meeting at Roger's

Petunia drove. That was a good idea, since I didn't know where we were going. Of course, she had a truck. I felt testosterone flowing into me just by sitting in it, which helped assuage the looming worry that had been buzzing around my head since yesterday morning. Yesterday, the relaxing day off that never happened. Instead, yesterday was a montage of discomfort and anxiety. I had been pressed into service as a mover. I had borrowed, lost, and then found my boss's truck. I'd learned far too much about a recently deceased, blackmailing lady from the previous century. Daddy's, my home away from home, was in imminent danger of being bought by a bunch of fag-hating born-agains who wanted to show their love by closing down the bar that was the center of our social life. Then, to put a cherry atop the turd sandwich of a day, my house had been broken into and trashed. A note defacing my wall suggested that those responsible would be back for another go at stealing my BVM. All in all, it had not been a stellar day.

I had suspected Roger had an office or storehouse somewhere, but as I said, Roger operated LnL Dicks on a need-to-know basis. Prior to this, I guess I had not been in the need-to-know category. When dealing with Roger and Nacho, I am happy to remain ignorant. Knowledge does not impart power in this case—it imparts danger. It seemed another ring of secrecy was about to be revealed—sigh.

Petunia pulled up near a warehouse where the railroad tracks used to run. The place had been divided into offices, none of which looked like they were still in business. Parking near a dumpster, we walked across the horribly mangled parking lot. Next to one metal door was a small, chipped plaque that stated, "Gladstone Boil Sucking—By appointment only". It was an old favorite, disgusting joke. The door was battered and looked like it was barely hanging on to its hinges. Petunia pressed her palm against the door, near the handle and waited. After a beep, she rotated her hand and with a sound I imagined a bank vault would make, the door slid back and then open, revealing that it was actually several inches thick, looked like it could withstand a direct hit by a tank and swung on huge metal hinges. We walked into a very comfortable room that looked a lot like Roger's apartment, but there were no windows and the quiet was complete. You don't get that kind of quiet unless there are many layers of soundproofing and other things between you and everywhere else. Behind us, the door hissed closed and locked itself with a series of metal sliding into metal sounds.

OK, this was new and disturbing. I guessed I was going to learn some more things I would rather not have, which would probably end up imperiling me at some point. I knew that declining the offer of information was not an option. I looked for a drink and a comfy chair. That was the best I could hope for.

Roger was on the phone and waved me to a couch. Cosmo sat at a desk surrounded by stacks of computer related things, very few of which I understood or wanted to understand. He looked up and gave a nod, having done his standard mind meld with the realm digital. Petunia leaned against a wall and became as still as an ancient suit of armor—but ready to spring to life the instant she was needed. The only normal person in the room was a lady, a little old for college, but young enough to pass through campus unnoticed. Her age would not set her apart, but her presence undoubtedly would. She was stunning. Not I'm a rock star so look at me and worship me stunning, but absolutely comfortable in her body, celebrating who she was and what she did, stunning.

I wanted to know her, to talk with her, to spend time with her. Satisfaction rolled off her and surrounded her like an aura. She was sitting on a couch, sipping a glass of juice and taking small bites from a croissant. It seemed as if her whole life had been leading up to that act and she was relishing every sip of juice, every nibble of croissant and every look around the office, with no desire to be anywhere else or do anything else. I sat and she flashed me a smile that I felt more than saw. It settled my nervous worry. Everything was OK. She gestured to the food on the table and asked in a throaty voice, "Care for a little yummy while Roger freaks out about whatever?"

It was the perfect thing to say. I relaxed even more. I wasn't into girls *in that way*, but I wanted to be around this lady as much as I could for as long as I could, if that were five minutes or five years.

"Er ... ummm ... thanks." Ever the debonair speaker, I reached for a croissant and managed to pour some juice without spilling it. "I'm BB."

She laughed. "I know. You had a bit of a night. I'm here to help look into things. I'm Wanda. I've worked with Roger before, but mostly I work with Nacho."

One of Nacho's secrets to which I was privy was that he was a field commander of the Twinkie Army Destroying All Hypocrites so hazarded a guess. "You're part of TaDah!?"

She inclined her head, not affirming, but definitely not denying.

"I don't believe I've ever met a woman Twink before," I said.

Wanda winked. "Gender is irrelevant, unless you are in bed and deciding what goes where." She took a long look at me, realizing that I was more than mildly interested in considering what went where and said, "And I never mix business with pleasure." Then winked again. She made me tingle.

At this point, Roger came over and sat down, putting my BVM on the table. I picked up the shell art creation and examined her for damage, but Mary was as pristine as ever.

"Take it home," said Roger. "I don't see anything special about it. Maybe if it's back at your house, they'll try again and we can ask them what's so interesting when we catch them."

Roger grabbed a couple of croissants, put some mystery meat between them, crushed them together and took a bite. I knew he was able to eat properly. I had seen him do so, but it gave him pleasure to channel his inner brute. All the better if he offends. I ignored him.

"I've talked with Nacho. I've also talked with our friendly detective, Crawford. Crawford isn't interested in combing through your stuff unless you want to file a report. Somehow, he got the impression that the whole thing was something I caused, or at least had set in motion, and he didn't want to waste time trying to get a straight answer out of me."

I was not sure what the history between Roger and Crawford was, but they seemed to have a grudging, very grudging, respect for each other. Crawford apparently allowed Roger a lot of leeway on quasi-police matters and Roger probably provided Crawford information that he obtained through his private channels. As long as it wasn't illegal and saved Crawford paperwork, he generally allowed Roger to follow his instincts.

"I see you've met Wanda," said Roger. "She's on loan from Nacho, because I have some intelligence gathering that needs to be done and sending you to look for intelligence is like sending a blind man out to find a candle ... you have no concept of it. However, first things first." Roger called out, "Cosmo, unplug yourself, come over here, and tell us what you've found."

Cosmo wandered over. His eyes brightened when he saw the platter of food and applied himself to it with the intensity he brought to all things. Cosmo looked every bit the nerd and that was appropriate. He claimed that his time with Timmy had made him much more social. However, it was clear that his comfort level with things digital was much greater than fleshier alternatives, Timmy being his one exception. He talked while he ate.

"I've been looking at the thumb drive Aunt May left with Nacho. Most of the time, when you plug in a thumb drive, it automatically opens and the computer reads it. If you are trying to protect what's on the drive from prying eyes, you put in a program that either messes with the data or messes with the computer. I've got a machine that can take a look without loading any of the programs. It takes a while, but I'm getting there. At this point, it looks like there are large files on the drive. That means video or audio, not just text." He grabbed a couple of munchies and headed back to his digital playground.

Roger turned to me. "I'm intrigued by the message on your Mary."

I looked at the back and again smiled at the inscription, "Oh Sweet Mary. Require my obedience and when I deviate, punish me."

I looked up at Roger. "Well, it sounds religious, but given that it was at Opal's and having seen some of her accoutrements, there could definitely be a secondary meaning."

Roger grinned. "You think? I wonder who our subservient Eppie J. might be."

"The signature? No idea. He's probably dead," I said. "Opal

was, shall I say, active for quite some time."

"Keep your eyes out for any possibilities while you are at work," said Roger.

"At work?" I asked. "Remember, I don't do dangerous and people who steal trucks and break into houses are not my cup of tea."

"You don't drink tea," said Roger. "And you'd be useless against anyone dangerous. You proved that yet again last night."

I didn't see any reason to protest. I have some pride, but wasn't about to argue that I should be chasing down bad guys. "So, what do you want from me?"

"I want you to do what you do best—sit on your ass and read. We have three, maybe four incidents that both Nacho and I think are related. Your truck was stolen, but nothing was taken. Your house was vandalized and we know what they wanted, but we don't know why and we don't know who. Finally, I'd like to know how it is that a little storefront church has the will and the wherewithal to buy a block of downtown Magawatta."

"What do the churchies have to do with stealing the truck or breaking into my house?" I asked.

"Maybe nothing," replied Roger. "I don't like them, but that doesn't mean much. However, Nacho has heard some rumors about them and their charter school plans that need to be checked out."

"Charter schools?"

"You know that it's getting easier to start a school and get state money to send your kid to a charter school, right? It's a way for parents to control the minds of their little dears, plus the charter schools aren't closely regulated, so all kinds of interesting frauds are possible. There's money to be made,

84

but it takes money and connections to get started and we are wondering where the Hateful Redeemer Mission is getting theirs."

"I can do some digging. They're a nonprofit, so I can see who's on their board."

"Good start. Look for any connections to Opal, too."

"How come?"

"I don't like coincidences and all this seemed to start with the surprise death of Ms. Milbank."

"Surprise? She was old."

"Old but spry. Something we can all aspire to. Nacho had been hearing whispers about her getting in the way of someone with a plan and a lot of oommph. Remember, she came to see Nacho and Nacho was quietly poking around. Now she's dead. That's one of several things that need looking into. There's also that kid you found rifling through her bedroom."

"Yea, but he was trying to get that money. That's why he came back and I figure he, or someone he knew, stole the truck because he thought the ammo box would be in it. We're just lucky that Aunt May and Beau took it to their house."

"That's your assumption. You're a good friend, BB, but your knowledge of what evil lurks in the minds of men is as thin as a politician's pledge of honesty. That boy obviously had poked around a bit when he was poking around her, if you catch my drift. We don't know if he was looking for something specific or what he found. I don't think he has the smarts or the skills to steal a truck, so if that's the reason for your truck getting snatched, he had help. No matter what, he's got some tales to tell. He just needs a little encouragement. That's why Wanda's here."

I looked up and saw Wanda smiling at us. "Boys like to tell me things," she said. "I guess it's because I'm a good listener. Plus, they like to show off a bit and I let them. I happened to run into Thad last night and we hit it off. I'm going out with him tonight ... or in."

"That's fast," I said. "Not surprising, but fast."

Wanda just smiled.

"We'll let Wanda work on him for a couple of days," said Roger. "She'll get him to talk. If honey doesn't work, Wanda is also an excellent interrogator."

Wanda cracked her knuckles and a gleam in her eye sent a shiver down my spine. I felt a flash of pity for young Thaddeus, but then I thought about our interaction yesterday. Young, buff, and certain of his place in the pecking order of the world, like so many entitled children of the rich, it might be a life changing experience. Besides, I was not being asked for my opinion or counsel, so I kept my mouth shut.

"I also don't trust the way the place was cleaned out so quickly," said Roger. "I have a call in to Deb, our friendly neighborhood judge, about Gibson, the lawyer. He's the one who claims the house had to be cleaned out right away. Maybe he just wanted a chance to go looking through Opal's things. We also want to see what Ponce took out of the house. Petunia is going to ingratiate herself with the crew down at Matt Ponce's. He's known to be a dick, especially when he's been drinking, which is most days, so he's usually short staffed."

"A big dick *and* short staffed?" I said. "Seems like a contradiction."

"Shut up, BB. Your attempts at humor are at their best painful and you are not at your best. Focus on the churchies plus, if Aunt May will let you, take a look and see if there are any connections with the folders she got from Opal."

"That sounds interesting ... and safe," I said. "But what about my house? In case you forgot, someone broke in. They trashed my place, scared my cat, wanted to take my latest treasure, and for all I know, would have ravaged me. Who was it? What am I going to do? I don't do butch and I'm scared."

"I wouldn't expect you to be anything but. The job was done well. While they made a mess, they also were careful. No prints. Nothing identifying, unless you want to try to compare writing samples and that would involve getting a suspect to scrawl on a wall. To me, it looks like someone who knew what they were doing wanted it to look rough. They could have picked the lock, but they wanted to scare you. Of course, that means they don't know you, because if they did, they could have scared you by sending you a telegram that said Boo!

"Your wit never fails to disappoint," I said. "But what about it? I like my BVM, but I'm not going to risk my life for her. I'm also not going to hang around and wait for them to show up again so I can turn her over."

"Calm yourself. Nacho already sent Merle over."

"Merle?"

"Petunia's cousin. She's not so bright, but she bigger than Petunia. We gave her a case of beer and a bag of peanuts to sit on your porch for the next couple of days. No one will bother you."

"Will she need food or a place to sleep?"

Roger shook his head. "Merle's a special gal. She doesn't talk much. She doesn't eat much. She mostly sits and drinks beer. She'll sleep when she's tired, but she won't have to move to do that."

"What about the bathroom? I don't suppose she uses a bucket. You're making her sound like a farm animal."

"Naw, she'll let you know when she needs the bathroom or anything else. She probably won't talk to you. When you come up to the house the first time, you should probably tell her you're BB, or else she might try to stop you and that will hurt. After that, she'll remember. Just don't sneak up on her. Merle can move very fast when she wants to and Petunia says she learned everything she knows from Merle. The best I can figure is that Merle exists in an alternate reality and what we're seeing is just some kind of interface between that world and this one. But don't worry. With Merle there, you'll be safe."

I've known Roger for years and if anyone else had spun out a tale like this I wouldn't have believed them, but I was certain Roger was both serious and correct. My house was not going to be revisited by anyone attempting a break-in. Anyone who tried would be painfully unsuccessful.

"What I want to know," said Roger, "is what is so special about a particularly tacky piece of shell art that bears a slight resemblance to a white version of mama Jesus. Our best starting point is the signature—Eppie J. It would be swell if you ran into someone with that nickname on either the church roster or in Aunt May's collection of folders."

"I'll look. If the church roster is posted online, I'll find it, but I hope you aren't suggesting I check it out in person."

"As much as that would amuse me, no. I do not think you should sashay into the belly of the beast. If we need any on-site investigating, Aunt May would be better suited. She knows how to be subtle."

Roger stood. "Why don't you go home and spend a little time online. Cosmo made sure your computer is secure. Use my passwords and the investigative sites I subscribe to. Cosmo will give you a list. Do *not* leave that list lying around. After you are finished using it, burn the paper. Find anything you can about everyone on the board. Let me know."

It was obviously time to go. I looked around to see if Petunia or Wanda was getting up, but it looked like the message was for me. Nobody else was leaving and no one was offering a ride. I shrugged. It wasn't far. I could walk. I could even handle carrying my BVM. So, clutching Mary to my chest, I headed out, feeling ever so athletic for exercising when I didn't have to. Such commendable behavior should be rewarded. Perhaps a stop at Beau and May's for a Friday afternoon refresher was in order, just to prepare for a long afternoon at the keyboard.

Chapter 12 – Meeting With Foxy

I didn't make it to my computer. I was only on my second drink with Beau and Aunt May—a small one, if you must know—when TiaRa called.

"Pumpkin, where have you been? Foxy and I have been on the phones all morning and the absolute crème de la menthe of drag and wealth are all in. The mere idea that we may be able to provide a safe haven for youth in the midst of this homophobic hinterland and at the same time give a poke in the eye to a clump of holier than thous who somehow believe they have been told by God herself to hate little homos has brought out the best in simply everyone. We have sponsors, bidders, and performers jetting in from every corner of the globe to attend. Plans must be made and made quickly. These are not your everyday glitterati. These are people with culture, panache, and cash—not that I don't love you and your rustic ways. But what is acceptable for the denizens of Hoosier Daddy will not be borne by these people. You must come to Foxy's at once. Each one of us has to commit completely and glamorize as we have never glamorized before if we are to pull this off. And please do not make a tired remark about pulling off. I am far too weary to hear it."

I must admit, the pun had already begun its journey from my brain to my mouth with very few filters in between. So, I decided that acquiescence was the better course. "I'm on my way," I said. "Should I bring Beau and Aunt May?"

"While I do cherish them, I suggest you come alone. With Beau and dear Aunt May, several drinks will be required and our gathering will quickly veer toward a party. There is work to be done. So much work. Do hurry."

When TiaRa del Fuego commanded, I obeyed. I left my BVM with Beau and May, promising to come get her on my way home, found where I had parked my car (I had already done my exercise for the day and Tia was waiting) and headed out. In short order I was knocking at the door to Casa KitTan (emphasis on the Tan, my dear). Foxy and Suave were an inseparable couple who lived in a grand old limestone house complete with turrets and extensive porches. Suave ran Suave Delights, home of eclectic wonders, on the first floor and the top two floors were a wonder of design and technology—design being Suave's passion and technology being Foxy's amusement. Suave was arranging some of the new acquisitions, pleased to be free from the watchful eye and questioning of Foxy.

"He is upstairs," she said. "Please keep him up there. I still have not told him of the wonders we acquired yesterday and he has not been down here. If I manage to slip them into existing displays, he may never notice. So, up you go. Hurry, hurry and stay as long as you are able."

Upstairs I saw Foxy and TiaRa sitting beside an enormous table covered with cards, lists and notes. Two large whiteboards on wheels had been drawn up near the table. One was labeled Divas and the other Whales. Each had a line drawn down the middle with the left side labeled YES and the other labeled MAYBE. TiaRa was in the midst of a conversation.

"Of course, my dear, it would not be a truly legendary show without you." She listened to someone reeling off reasons why it was not possible. "Yes, I do understand. I could only hope. As it is, we will simply have to make due with Cherri La Bomb." A pause for screams from the phone. "Why yes, she said she absolutely had to come, but only if she could headline." Another pause, with crafty bartering evident, although I could not make out the words. Tia expelled a melodramatic sigh. "Well, I suppose I could break the evening in two and have her headline the first half. That is *if* you could somehow manage to make the trip." More words, but TiaRa knew where the conversation was going and paid little attention, waving me to a chair. "Delightful Queen Gloriousity. You shall be the crown jewel that I am sure will push our work over the top so we may open the center. We shall name a room after you and I promise I will send my most reliable and dear friend to fetch you and tend to your every need. Thank you, my dear, from me and from all the youths."

TiaRa ended the call and turned to us. She smiled. "That is the final rose in the bouquet. It shall be quintessential. Queen Fantasia Gloriousity of the Chicago court is known worldwide and will attend. BB, it will be your duty to keep her happy. She can be a bit difficult, but I assure you, she is worth it." TiaRa turned to Foxy. "I have every confidence you will hook all the whales needed. What worries me is where we hold the Cotillion. It must be grand, yet there is no place grand enough in Magawatta that would not look askance at our performers."

Foxy waved a hand. "Taken care of, my dear. Taken care of. I have reached out to a dear friend who has access to the Ontario Mansion and I have persuaded him to allow access for the entire week before the Cotillion."

"He owns that fabulous old eyesore?" asked Tia.

"Heavens no," said Foxy, lifting an ornate silver statue of a frog with gleaming emerald eyes from the table. He fiddled with the base and a sudden flame burst from the frog's mouth. Foxy then withdrew a thick joint from the pocket of his red-velvet smoking jacket, lit it and inhaled deeply. As he passed the joint to me, he exhaled a cloud of the finest domestic bud. It tasted as good as it smelled. Some of the tension from the day's travails began to leak away.

Passing the joint to TiaRa, I asked Foxy, "What's the Ontario Mansion?"

"A sumptuous palace. An oddity spectacular in both architecture and history. I am amazed you have never heard of it. You can see it from the road just south of town."

"I don't go that direction except when I have to go to the dump. It gets redneckie very quickly and I begin feeling obviously gay and nelly."

"Oh, BB, you must not let fear drive your life or your direction. Keep your eyes open, but do not deprive yourself of an experience because of fear. I learned that at a very young age. You have the option of hiding your nelly, but I was never afforded the option of hiding my Blackness, so I embraced it, and let me tell you, coming from the Bayou country, there were far more opportunities for fear, should I have chosen that direction. However, we were discussing the Ontario Mansion."

"Why is it called Ontario?"

"It was built by Mary Jane Ontario, one of the heirs to the Valentine drug fortune. While old man Valentine paid for the library on campus, where I believe you occasionally work, Mary Jane was a child of the sixties and indulged heavily in drugs and fantasy. She married a man who owned a radical bookstore that was firebombed by a Klansman, then divorced him and married his brother. With the first husband, she built a huge mansion of stone, replete with turrets and a multitude of rooms for a steady stream of guests and parties. With the second, she bought a commune in the woods of the next county over. There she lived until her money ran out and she retired to a more sedate and parochial life somewhere in the Midwest, no one is sure exactly where."

I smiled. "I doubt she is all that staid. You can take the girl out of Magawatta, but can you ever take the Magawatta out of the girl?"

Foxy smiled. "True, my dear boy, true. However, she has never been seen again. The land of the commune was mostly sold to pay debts and finance her disappearance, although I believe some of the original members still squat in the woods."

"Literally?"

"Perhaps. I have never been, but I assume the facilities are rudimentary at best."

"And the mansion? Who bought that?"

"Ah, another interesting chapter. It languished on the market for many years. No one had interest or financing to repair and remodel it enough to make it useful or even livable. Evidently, Mary Jane did not place a high priority on maintenance and even at its best, the place was more suited to parties, orgies, and visiting counterculturists than a home. However, several years ago a developer bought the place for a song and raised quite a large sum with plans to create a conference center for high priced, executive self-actualization sessions. He had broken off from one of the popular initial-based self-help groups."

"Initial-based?"

"Organizations teetering on the edge of cultism that proclaim their brand with initials—often of their founder."

"Ah. I went to one of those once. Three days to get started with indoctrination and a whole lifestyle to follow. When they found out I didn't have my own money or any rich friends I could suck in for more seminars, they lost interest in me."

Foxy nodded. "Just right. I have been pursued by several, but am immune. They sell happiness and contentment. I have already found both, so have no need. However, this guru-to-be had a slick delivery and extensive plans. He convinced quite a few locals that they lacked meaning and purpose and he could provide both. The building and grounds were wonderfully remodeled. Great sums were raised. Then, he emptied the bank accounts, went to Florida, visited several plastic surgeons, and disappeared into one of the gated communities filled with similar moral giants under an assumed name. There are still warrants out for him, should he ever resurface. The estate was plunged into a legal limbo from which it has yet to emerge."

"And you bought it? When? You didn't buy it just for this, did you? I know you have money Foxy, but you don't have enough to buy a huge estate just for this, do you?"

"No, no, no, dear boy. Heaven forfend! The Ontario Mansion is not for sale and I would not want it even if it was. I would not take it if it was given for free. Think of what Suave would do if she was able to purchase furniture for such an enormous edifice. No, a dear friend is one of the parties involved with attempting to untangle the legalities of the mess left behind. He has the responsibility of maintaining the building, but has little hope of ever receiving any compensation, as he is at the end of a rather long line of creditors. I offered to clean and do any minor repairs needed, in return for access for the weekend of the festivities. The week before, we shall also have access as I have the place cleaned. It is certainly grand enough for the show and what is better, there are guest rooms for all the performers."

TiaRa clapped her hands. "You are a master, a true master, Foxy. I have been unable to think of a solution for accommodations. I can hardly ask this royalty to pay for their own rooms, but the cost would be too great to house them in a hotel and they would rebel if we tried to put them in people's spare rooms. I have been to BB's house and the idea of putting a queen into his place ... well, it is too much, or too little."

"My house isn't that bad," I protested.

"For you, BB, it is perfect. But these are ..."

"I know. I know. Royalty."

"It is my pleasure," said Foxy. "My friend owes me a favor. I was once able to facilitate an overnight slumber party there, including an invitation for him, for a fraternity pledge party that required the potential inductees to engage in a series of increasingly challenging acts. At least challenging to their self-perceived heterosexuality. My friend discovered that once enough liquor was added to the mix, the boys needed only the slightest push to jump to the other side of the line. He still talks about it in near religious tones."

"Well, you have, once more, risen above and beyond to save the day."

Foxy waved away the compliment. "I only wish I was in a position to purchase the block outright and save all the work you are doing, although I do, of course, rejoice in anticipation of seeing the show."

"Could you afford it, Foxy?" I asked. "I don't mean to be nosy, but I figured you could buy a block of downtown Magawatta with pocket change."

Foxy smiled and shook his head. "You have an exaggerated view of the amount of change in my pocket. I usually could and would purchase the block to protect our favorite watering hole. However, there is currently some nefariousness afoot. You are aware that when I sold control of the Pie Hole, I insisted on what I call an ethical veto. I can overrule any action of the board, should I believe it runs contrary to the core values of the company. For example, more profits could be had if the company paid minimum wage instead of a living wage. However, it makes more fiscal sense in the long run to pay people decently so they stay. Customers and workers develop relationships, which builds loyalty. Plus, we have never had a problem hiring people, even in the tightest of labor markets. Without my ethical veto, the corporation would have chosen short term profit over long-term value."

"That makes sense," I said. "So, what's the problem?"

"It has come to my attention that a hidden group has been buying up stock on the sly and they are planning an attempt to overthrow the former agreement allowing me veto power. It will fail in the long run, but it will damage the sparkling image of the Pie Hole. That damage will linger and I cannot allow it. I have had to put most of my assets into purchasing stock, to deny the evil doers access. That is the only reason I am not currently able to save Hoosier Daddy and launch the youth center. I believe some of those I have invited either know who is behind the perfidy or may be part of the treachery themselves. Once I have uncovered and expelled the conspirators, I will be able to be of much greater help."

"You have done more than enough," said TiaRa. "Now it is up to us to put on a show that sparkles like the stars above."

"I'm not sure how I can help," I said. "My design skills are not exactly ..."

TiaRa held a finger to my lips. "BB, as much as I love you, I would ask that you not utter the word design. You might soil it. No BB. Nacho has reached out to some associates who are skilled in creating illusions. You will be essential in your area of expertise—errands. You are willing to take orders and are most reliable on follow through. Both quite necessary and surprisingly rare skills."

"So, I'm a gopher? Nacho and Roger have me doing research and I *do* have a couple of jobs which expect me to show up occasionally. They are very handy to help keep a roof over my head and food in my belly."

"I am most certain you will be able to juggle all your balls. You have great experience at it. Everyone says so."

"Hmmm. That sounds suspiciously like a crack."

TiaRa patted my cheek. "Never. I am simply echoing what I have heard with the addition of my utmost confidence in your abilities." She handed me a list. "Here are all the performers. I need you to provide a list of options for flights. Give them prices for business class and coach. None of them will leave before noon. The Legendary Cotillion will be on Saturday, so plan on Friday flights. They will book their own flights, but you will need to provide them the information. We have so little time, so please do not delay. Then, if Nacho has work for you, do not let me keep you from it. Foxy and I will work out the particulars and let you know when you are needed again. So fly, kitten, fly."

I knew better than to argue with TiaRa del Fuego when she was on a mission. With a pleading look toward Foxy, in hopes he would try to keep Tia's demands on me within the bounds of humanly possible. I went off to do as I was commanded, first for TiaRa, then for Nacho. I knew I had better be able to report some results by the time I arrived at Hoosier Daddy if I had any hopes of being served.

Chapter 13 - To Work

I headed home, swinging by Beau's to pick up my BVM. In the plus column of working for Roger is that he is subscribed to just about every invasive service that can dig into just about anything about anyone that is online. That's most of the information in the world. I wonder what the archaeologists who dig up our civilization will think if they can't decode our digital storage. Will they think that most communication stopped around the turn of the century?

I had a tinge of fear as I parked, remembering what had been waiting for me last night. However, like an Easter Island monolith, sitting comfortably on a chair that seemed unequal to the task of holding her up, was, I assumed, Petunia's cousin Merle. She didn't move. The only indication that she was awake or alive was her left hand, which clutched a baseball. She would give the ball a squeeze and it would emit a little gasp. I hadn't known it was possible to squeeze a baseball that hard. Then she would release her grip on the orb, glance at it, as if considering whether to toss it to her other hand or at someone or something, then give it another squeeze. I vaguely wondered what would happen if she squeezed a crowbar. It would probably conform to the shape of her hand.

As I headed up the walk, she stretched out a foot, blocking the doorway. She had a baseball cap pulled low over her eyes. On front was stitched, "Make Assholes Groan Again." In a bored, but inescapably dangerous voice she said, "No deliveries. No surveys. No visitors. Go on by or I'll have to get up and you and I don't want that."

The tone was threatening enough that I nearly turned and left, but then I remembered that it was my house. "Well, it's just that..." I began.

Merle pushed the bill of the cap up, opened one eye, and shot a menacing look at me. It stopped me. I'm grateful she didn't open both eyes. I might have soiled myself. Courage is not high on my what-I'm-known-for list. I took a step back, but I remembered that Roger told me to identify myself.

"I'm BB," I said, hoping that would not anger her.

It did not. Her face lost its evil stone-goddess quality and a smile spread across her face. No, it did not crack her cheek.

"Well, isn't that fine," she said. "I hear you had a visitation of assholes. You just set your mind at ease, pooky. If they want to try it again, I'll be happy to make them regret it. Go on in. Door's open."

She moved her foot out of the way and I opened the door. "Thank you for this. Can I bring you anything? Or do anything for you? I'm a little shaken."

"I'm good. Petunia will bring me by some food later. I'm on a special diet. I have a cooler with drinks right here. If I need to use the facilities, I'll call out. Don't you worry bambino. I'll be right here day and night until we figure out who needs to be twisted for messing with your stuff."

"You're welcome to stretch out on the couch if you get tired."

"Naw. I learned to sleep sitting up in short spurts. Just ignore me. Best thing you can do is get to work on whatever Roger and Nacho told you to do."

I nodded and went in. Spot required me to do my penance for

not allowing him to sit on my chest today. I fed him kitty treats and gently spanked his butt until he was bored with me. Then I went to the computer and slipped into research mode. First, I dealt with the travel information for TiaRa's divas. That didn't take long. Then I turned to digging into the board of the churchies. It was comforting to follow digital trails. So much easier, less stressful, and less dangerous than what had been thrown my way since Beau came banging on my door the day before.

I started with the organizational papers for the church. That listed the board of directors—doesn't matter if a corporation is a for profit company or a church (that can make plenty of profit, but instead of profits going to the members, the profit generally comes *from* the members), there is a board of directors. That storefront church might have seemed small, but it had a big board of directors. As I started to dig into who they were, a pattern began to emerge. Most were not from Magawatta, but almost all were rich, very rich. Most were heads of companies. This was strange. Strange things ask to be looked into, so I did. I started digging into who these people were and what might connect them and any hint of why they were interested in a little church down the block from a gay bar. Time passes quickly when following link upon link. It quickly got too complicated to keep in my head, so there were soon stickers and papers large and small all around. Several hours passed quickly and my bladder suggested I take a break.

Having lowered my liquid levels, I figured it might be time to replenish them, so I called Beau.

"Come over," he said. "Aunt May and I were just making cocktails." Beau and Aunt May were always just making or just finishing cocktails.

"I have to tell Roger what I've found so far. Then I'll be over."

I gathered my notes and put them in a bit of order. My phone rang. The screen said the caller was Karl's Pizza Ditch. Intrigued, I answered.

"Whatcha find out?" Nacho's voice was unmistakable.

"Well, there seems to be a big board of directors and they aren't the regulars that have been picketing Hoosier Daddy, from what I've found out so far they are ..."

"I know," interrupted Nacho. "Rich bastards from all over the state and a few from out of state."

"If you knew, why did you have me look?"

"I'm interested in Magawatta connections. Who stands out that's local?"

"Well, now that you mention it ..."

"Don't fuck with me, BB. This ain't your Sunday afternoon tea party. I got things to do. I know something big and bad is being planned. That's what that Milbank broad was tellin' me. What I need to know is why here? What is it about Magawatta? Why does it start with that block?"

I was stumped. "I don't know. I haven't found ..."

"What have you been doin' all afternoon? Sitting on your thumb to see how far you can stick it in and find out what kind of plum you pull out? I'll give you a tip. Don't eat it."

I was a bit defensive. "If you'd have told me what you knew ..."

"If I told you everything I know, it would take years and then I'd have to kill you. Did you find out *anything* useful?"

"Well, I found out two interesting tidbits. At least I think they're interesting."

"Tick tock, BB. Don't make me ask again."

"Well, the first is that both the Ponce brothers are on the board. That's pretty weird, because even though Peter makes a big show of being way religious, I always figured it was a political decision. I'm pretty sure he goes to one of those mega-churches in Indy. More people get to see him being holier than thou. Matt is not known to be a churchie. In fact, he's known to be decidedly unchurchie, at least in behavior."

Nacho grunted. Since there was no demeaning remark, I took this to mean that the information was at least somewhat useful. "And the second?"

"The mayor and most of the planning commission are on the board. There aren't that many people on the board from Magawatta and the ones that are, seem to have pull, but not so much money. I still haven't been able to look into everyone. Like I said, it's a big board."

"Hmmm. Maybe you ain't so useless. I'll let Roger know and I'll throw in a plate of nachos next time you come in."

With that, Nacho hung up. In the world of Nacho, I had just received about the highest compliment possible—a free plate of nachos. Time to celebrate. I headed over to Beau's house, waving to Merle as I passed her. She didn't respond. I'm not sure if she was asleep, dead, or not into waving. The only indication that she was still among the living was her left hand which kept its rhythmic squeeze and release on the baseball clutched there. She was starting to make Petunia seem absolutely jolly. Odd family. I wonder what family reunions were like. I didn't want to get close enough to find out. They might involve ritual sacrifice and I didn't want to be selected as the chosen one.

Chapter 14 - Lester the Old Queen

After drinks, Beau and Aunt May needed a little lie down. I headed to Hoosier Daddy, a bit early, but Roger had called and wanted to meet and share before the Patio Café got busy. I passed through the curtains at the end of the bar, stepping onto the patio. It was nearly empty. However, at our usual table sat a stranger. Well, not a total stranger. I recognized him as one of the ancient gays that were permanent fixtures at the bar up front. I had never talked to any of them and never had the inclination to. There was a little too much of a "here is your future, beware" vibe to them. I hesitated. I really didn't want to sit with him, but that *was* our table. He saw me, raised his glass, and motioned for me to join him.

"Don't worry. I don't bite. At least not unless you want me to," he said, cackling a bit. "I want a word with you."

I still hesitated.

"Oh, come on. You aren't scared of an old queen, are you?" He raised an eyebrow and pursed his lips. "I have some information, BB."

I sat. "You know me?"

"I know who you are. I know you're looking into Opal's death."

That surprised me. He shook his head. "No one pays any attention to the ancients at the bar. You just walk by. But we aren't all just rummies. And none of us have always been old. I sit up there because I like to watch the comings and goings and I don't like the noise in the big room." He stuck out his hand, not to shake, but to be kissed. "My name's Lester. Lester the old queen. And if you're sweet to an old queen, you might learn something sweet."

I was intrigued and a little embarrassed. He was right. I never paid attention to the old men who sat at the front bar. When you first walked into Hoosier Daddy, there was a very small entry room. Usually, you passed through that and went into the bar, but on nights with a cover charge, the door to the bar could be blocked by a bouncer who collected money and stopped any frat boys who wanted to see how the other half lived. Through the door was the long bar, more hallway than room, where the ancients sat, perched on their stools, leaning on the bar, each with a never-empty glass. At the end of the bar, by turning right and stepping through the curtains, you were in Nacho Mama's Patio Café. If you continued straight ahead, you ended up in the cavernous main room, replete with a real seventies disco floor that featured scuffed translucent panels with flashing lights beneath. At the far end was a stage where either a DJ or performers held forth. I usually walked by the ancients as my eyes adjusted to the darkened bar and turned right onto the patio. If it was a night when TiaRa was hosting her Parade of Gowns drag show and I was running late, I would go through to the big room. I never considered the old men sitting at the bar. It hadn't occurred to me that, even though I didn't look at them, they might be watching me and everyone else coming and going. There was a big mirror behind the bar, so they could see everything. Now that I considered it, I realized that there was a lot to see and learn by sitting there. Hmmm. I kissed his hand.

Lester nodded. He winked. I could tell he had followed my train of thought all the way to my realization.

"You're a lot more sober than I thought," I admitted.

Lester smiled. "Used to be, the bar was the only place that it was safe to be who I was. I got used to it. I like to people watch. When you've been around as long as I have, you can pick out who is interesting to watch. Your group ... I like to watch."

"Would you like to join us?"

"No. Too much intrigue for me. But I heard about Opal. I know you're looking into it and I have a tidbit."

"You knew Opal?"

"I've been in Magawatta for nearly fifty years. I know a lot of people." He held up a hand to stop the questions forming in my mind. "I don't want to talk about it. Like I said, I like to watch. But I liked Opal. She was a tough old broad. Like I'm a tough old queen. So, let me give you my tidbit and that's it. I don't want to be friends. I've had friends. I have some left."

"OK," I said. "What's the tidbit?"

"Land," said Lester. "Land in Brown County. Check out who's buying what." He stood up and headed back toward the bar. At the door he turned. "And look for High Hopes."

"What's that?" I asked.

"That's for you to find out. Give me a chance to be a little mysterious."

"Umm... OK. Thanks."

Lester winked. "And buy an old queen a drink once in a while. Like I said, I don't bite. Unless you want me to."

With that, he went back into the bar. I stared after him. As I stared, Roger came through the door.

"What are you staring at?" he asked, sitting down and handing me a drink. "And what did Lester want?"

"You know him?"

"Of course. Lester's been here forever. Used to teach geology. He knows more about this town than anyone I've ever talked to. Plus, he blends into the woodwork, but watches all the comings and goings at the bar."

"I've never noticed him."

"That doesn't surprise me. The things you don't notice outweigh the things you do by even more than your ever-increasing body mass."

Since he had just bought me a drink, I let the insult pass and told him what Lester had said. Nacho came out of the kitchen and set a plate of nachos in front of us. I dove in, while Roger shared Lester's insights with Nacho.

"They have the mayor and planning commission in Magawatta," said Roger. "I wonder who they have in Brown County."

"Don't know," I said. "I haven't found anyone yet. I'm not finished running down the board, but why would they need someone from Brown County? It's just one county over, and there's no opportunity for graft or grift. It's just got lots of trees and artists. Neither of those is particularly known as a source of wealth. Plus, the hippies and artists would raise a stink if you tried to cut many trees down. I don't think the trees would protest if someone tried to cut down the artists, but you can never be sure."

"There's gotta be something more," said Nacho. "Milbank was hinting about something statewide. I got the feeling we're just poking around the edges."

At this point, Roger's phone rang. "It's Beau," he told us, then spoke into the phone, "Sister Marguerite's House of Pain and Pleasure, try our new spanking spa, if you've been bad, it's the best!" A stream of words poured out the phone. I couldn't understand them, but it was clear that Beau was in full blown freak-out mode. Roger cut in. "Stay right there. Why'd they take Petunia in too?"

He listened again. "I'll go by the station first. Lock the door and don't answer it for anyone. Even the police. I'll send BB. If anyone else comes to the door, call out and tell them I'm on my way."

More hysteria. Roger cut in. "Stop. Sit. Pour yourself and Aunt May a drink and do not get up for anything. BB will let himself in."

Roger stood. "Someone broke in to Beau and May's house. That's despite the locks I installed. Of course, Beau forgot to turn on the security system. Good thing I had Petunia watching. She stopped the two heavies, but she was less than gentle. The cop who showed up didn't know Petunia, so brought her along with the two intruders. The intruders will be going to the hospital once the paramedics arrive. I've got to go. BB, you go to Beau and May's and try to get their freak-out watered down a bit. Here's a key to the new locks we installed. I'll be there once I spring Petunia. Come on!"

I looked sorrowfully at my plate of nachos. My very own, special plate of nachos. I knew better than to insult Nacho by asking for a doggie bag. Nacho's nachos were to be eaten hot, at the table or not at all. Ah well, the things we do for friends.

I stood, allowing Roger to push me out the door. Roger called back to Nacho, "I'll give you an update once I know. Got anyone at the hospital?"

Nacho nodded. "I'll make the call. We'll have a report on anything the shitbirds say."

With that, we were out the door and off to the rescue.

Chapter 15 – Attack on Beau and Aunt May

Aunt May was wound tightly. Each movement was very carefully accomplished. Her tone was steely and her words sharp. None of the soft, liquor-induced languor wrapped her actions or speech. This was probably the first time I had seen her completely sober. Every bit of alcohol had been driven out of her by a very intense, shocking event. Beau, on the other hand, had opted for the opposite reaction. He was blubbering in a small ball in the corner of the couch, one small step away from climbing under a blanket and shrieking like a small child.

"They were so big," he wailed. "They were just so big."

I assumed this was not a compliment.

"The men are gone, now, Beau. Petunia took care of them. You're safe."

"But they were just so big," he cried, rocking back and forth.

I knew Beau was not going to provide any useful information. I turned to Aunt May, who was sitting very straight in a chair, gently sipping a drink that looked and smelled like straight bourbon.

"Aunt May, what can I get you?" I asked.

"Nothing, dear. I only need a few minutes to calm myself. They were so rude. I am certain they intended to strike me."

She took another sip of her drink. "Had they asked, I would have provided whatever they wished, but these were ruffians of the worst type. They clearly had the upper hand, but wanted to insure we would not prevaricate or delay. I must assume that is because they did not want to cause any disturbance that could be heard outside the house."

Beau and Aunt May lived in an ornate eyesore of a house that had been built by another grand doyen of culture. When the city built the new police complex, they were unable to acquire the property, so had to build around it. That meant that the thieves had been bold enough to break in and attempt a robbery mere feet away from dozens of police on perhaps the most secure block in all Magawatta. They were either very bold or very stupid. Either way, they must have been very desperate to get what they came for.

"But what did they want?"

Aunt May shook her head. "I am not sure. Perhaps the money. One of them said, 'Where's the box?' They could have been after Opal's files, but I suspect they meant the dispatch box that originally held that money. However, our savior Petunia appeared and dealt with them before they explained further. Beyond a few grunts and cries of pain, they said nothing more before she knocked them unconscious. She was just in the process of waking up one of them to ascertain their motives when the police arrived. I tried to explain that Petunia was our savior, but they paid no attention and took everyone away."

"It was horrible," moaned Beau from the couch. "I swear, I saw my life pass before my eyes. I don't know if I will ever recover. BB, could you be a darling and get me another drink? This one did absolutely nothing to calm me."

Fully aware that Beau was capable of fetching his own drink, I rolled my eyes and decided to put up with him a bit longer. However, it would be rude to have them drink alone and as I had to fetch a glass and liquor for him, I decided it would be only polite to join them. At this point, Roger clumped up the porch steps and opened the door, calling out as he did so. Petunia followed him through the door. She was never what one would call chipper, but her time with the police had painted an extra scowl on her stone-like face.

Roger held out his hand. "Gimme the drink, BB. You've got places to be."

"But I just..."

"You just nothing. Detective Crawford gave us a few minutes alone with the two guests while they were waiting for the paramedics to show up and set the bone one of them broke chatting with Petunia. Since they already knew her, and knew how she behaved when they weren't helpful, the fellows were willing to answer a few questions. When I asked them about your break-in, they didn't know what I was talking about."

"Maybe they were lying."

Petunia shook her head. "No chance. I suggested it would be a bad idea to lie and that I would know. They believed me."

I couldn't argue with that. The mere thought of lying to Petunia made me squeeze my legs together protectively.

Roger continued. "What that means is that we have two break-ins by two different groups. At least one group doesn't know what the other is doing. Both are somehow connected to Opal. I've got a hunch that this business with the church is connected, too. Nacho is looking into the board members of the church who are local. So, the only thread that is still dangling is our new one, provided by Lester. Brown County land purchases. You have forty-five minutes before the Brown County offices close for the weekend. We need to know who has been buying land in Brown County. Tick tock, BB. Get home and get some information before those offices close."

I sighed. I wanted to argue that the chances of me finding anything useful in such a short time were between slim and none, but it was an argument I would lose and would waste time I didn't have. I handed Roger the drink, gave Beau and May quick hugs and headed home.

Chapter 16 - Brown County
Bureaucracy

It didn't take long to find something. However, it didn't take much longer to get stuck. Looking at property sales in Brown County showed that a surprising number of small parcels had been sold over the past few months. Most of Brown County is forest, so there weren't a lot of street addresses. Parcels were mostly listed by longitude and latitude. I was able to map most of the sales and a pattern began to emerge. Most of the sales were concentrated in one area. That seemed significant.

The next step was to find out who was buying the land. That's where I got stuck. A few of the purchases were made by individuals. Those I chalked up to legitimate sales—people buying their little bit of paradise for one dream or another, especially as those sales were spread throughout the county. However, most of the purchases that were close to each other were made by a collection of LLCs. Limited Liability Corporations can be formed in any state and to find out who owns each one takes time and money, even with Roger's invasive search tools. I dug into a couple and the contacts were different small law firms in different states. Either someone was making a real effort to keep hidden or I was running into a mountain of coincidences.

I had a flash of inspiration. There might be a way to get a quick answer if I called the Brown County recorder's office.

Since any property sale had to file paperwork with the recorder's office, maybe they could tell me who actually bought the properties. I looked up the number and called, hoping the office did not close early on Fridays.

"Recorder's office."

"Hooray. You're still there!"

"Well, of course we are. Our hours are clearly stated as 9 a.m. to 5 p.m. It is now 4:55, so how may I help you in the five minutes remaining?"

This was one very precise individual. His words matched his voice. He put me in mind of my high school math teacher, Mr. Rush. Unbidden, an argument with him over a tenth-grade math test pushed into my thoughts.

"Mister Singer, the answer is 3.1415, not 3.1. Your answer is incorrect and does not deserve partial credit. Scoring is in whole numbers. Only the answer was to have fractions."

I shook my head to clear it and get back to the task at hand. "My name is BB Singer. I live in Magawatta and I'm trying to find out about some recent land purchases."

"All that information is on our website. It is public information and I make sure that once the paperwork is filed, it is placed on the website. The web address is ..."

"Umm ... thanks. I have the address. I got the information that is on the site. What I'm looking for is something that is not on the site."

"What do you mean?"

"Well, in the past few months there have been quite a few land purchases near the Brown County State Forest."

"I am aware of that. As I said, the information is on the site."

"Yes, but a bunch of the purchases were made by businesses, not people. What I'm wondering is if those businesses were linked. If they were actually all just a couple of people using different business names to hide the fact that they were buying a lot of land."

"Young man, the purchasers of the land are listed on the web site. That is public knowledge. Beyond that ..."

"I know that, but I was hoping that in a county as small as yours, the actual people might have come into your office and you might have noticed that it was the same person and ..."

"That information is *not* public information and I do not feel it is appropriate to share any such information."

"Well, maybe someone else there saw something ..."

"There is no one else here for you to speak with. I am Elbert P. Adelston. I am the county recorder and will have been the county recorder for thirty-seven years come May and during that time, there has never been a hint of impropriety in this office. I certainly do not plan to allow any now. And speaking of now. It is now 5:02 p.m. and the office is closed. If you have any further questions, you may call after 9:00 a.m. on Monday. However, my answer will still be the same." With that, he hung up.

I stared at the phone. Nacho and Roger were not going to be happy. I had found a question, but not an answer. Something was up, but we already knew that. What that something actually was, I still had no clue and it was going to take a lot of digging to even begin to find out. Finding out anything useful before Mr. Dick made his decision on who got to buy the block might not be possible. The churchies were pushing him to accept their offer. He had told TiaRa that he would hold off until we saw what was raised by the Legendary Cotillion. That was next Saturday night. So, in ten days, unless a pile of money dropped into our laps or some dastardly secret about the church was uncovered, Hoosier Daddy was going to be closed and Nacho Mama's Patio Café would be cast adrift, and us along with it.

Sigh. When the going gets tough, the effete take a nap. So, I allowed Spot to assume his rightful place on my chest and did what I do best, hoping that my dreams would guide me to an answer.

I didn't get far in my dreams before my phone woke me. It was TiaRa.

"BB, you simply *must* give Aunt May a ride. I am completely at my wits end deciding what should go when. She is the only one who has experience with an actual cotillion and I must have authenticity."

"What goes where," I mumbled. Waking is not my strong suit.

"Whatever do you mean?" asked TiaRa.

"You said what goes when. The phrase is what goes where," I said, struggling to sit up, which is not an easy thing to do with an oversized cat sprawled on one's chest. Spot didn't want to move, so dug in. The pain was a great motivator. I managed to sit up, hoisting the angry cat onto the floor.

TiaRa was continuing to talk. "No. What goes when. I must decide the proper order of presentation and that will determine the placement of dressing rooms, design of the program and—why am I explaining, BB? I need you to fetch Aunt May and bring her here. I just called her and she feels a consult will be just the thing to turn her mind from her recent unpleasantness."

"Where?"

"Are you still fixated on my wording? I just explained it to you."

"No, where do you want me to bring her?"

"The Ontario Mansion, of course. That is where I am and

116

where decisions of when must be made and made quickly. Aunt May is needed and you are supposed to be my rock to help me through this très important event and you are hardly being rock-like. So hurry, BB. Hurry."

"I don't know where the Ontario Mansion is," I said.

TiaRa sighed. "I shall put Foxy on and he shall give directions. Then hurry. Aunt May is waiting for you. Oh, and stop by Suave's on your way. She has a few trinkets she has gathered to help with the ambiance. She will have more as we prepare. Maybe you should borrow a truck again."

"No way. Not after what happened last time. Brian was very understanding. I'm surprised he didn't fire me."

TiaRa tut tutted. "There's no time now. I'm sure you'll come up with a solution. Now fly. Fly."

She turned the phone over to Foxy, who gave me directions. I grabbed my keys and headed over to pick up Aunt May and then to Suave's. The *few* trinkets Suave had gathered filled my car, leaving barely enough room for Aunt May, who had to hold an enormous frosted-glass vase to keep it from breaking. Foxy's directions were easy to follow and we soon pulled up in front of a huge tumble of a house. No surprise in looking at it that the house and grounds had been designed by and for those who dabbled in various mind-altering, though perhaps not mind-expanding, drugs. TiaRa was standing in the door, waving us in. I took the vase from Aunt May and followed her inside the entry hall. I was planning to continue through to the main room, but TiaRa stopped me.

"Drive around to the back, BB. There is a loading dock and it is much closer to the rooms where the trinkets will go. If you unload here, you will merely block the passage and need to move everything again. Hurry dear. We'll bring Aunt May home when we have bathed in her wisdom."

Tia patted my cheek, threw an arm around Aunt May and

pulled her toward the main room, saying, "Now I must have your advice on simply everything. It is imperative that the presentation of the performers and their protégés is perfect."

I normally would have resented being ordered and ignored, but TiaRa was in such a high state of excitement and was so wholeheartedly throwing herself into this project only for the good of all that I shrugged and turned back to the car. Time to be a mover, even though I prefer to be a shaker. I unloaded the car and headed to Hoosier Daddy to seek solace in a plate of nachos and some liquid refreshment.

Chapter 17 – A Spot of Blackmail

Over the next two days I saw little of the gang of reprobates. Dustyn, my boss from the library, insisted I come in. He was in charge of special exhibits, which involved pulling some historical something from the archives with much fanfare and press and allowing mere mortals to take a gander. The underlying reason for these folderols was to impress existing and potential donors to whip out something themselves in order to ensure their place in history, or at least on a small plaque in one of the reading rooms. Dustyn was a professional homosexual who would dither for hours over which shade of puce would best highlight the current displays. He had multiple storage rooms filled with bolts of decorated fabric, reams of specialized paper, and countless lovely little things that ranged from crafty to horrendous. He constantly added to his collections and every new display was a torture of decision ... for him. My job was to sit and pretend to listen as he babbled on and on and on ... and then to agree with him when he decided and when he changed his mind and never, ever to offer an opinion or, much worse, disagree with him.

It was tiring, but paid pretty well. I didn't much care how the display turned out, which was fine, as Dustyn cared enough for both of us. I couldn't let my mind wander, because I had to interject agreeable noises and occasional comments at appropriate times. I rarely had to attend the openings, because Dustyn didn't want to share the spotlight he perceived as shining only on the genius of the display, not the object being displayed. My absence was fine with me.

All day Saturday and most of the day Sunday, I massaged Dustyn's ego. By 5 p.m. Sunday, all was done and I was allowed to leave. I hurried home to get ready. As no one had been seen lurking around my house since the break-in, Merle had given up her spot on my front porch. Instead, she and Petunia drove by both my house and Beau and May's every hour or so on an irregular schedule and parked for a bit. No one seemed to be watching either house or obviously planning anything devious. No one had received any threats, so Beau, Aunt May, and I were relaxing a bit.

We always met at Hoosier Daddy for TiaRa del Fuego's Parade of Gowns drag show on Sunday evenings. In between sets, we usually gossiped about the week's events, but that night we had a lot of updating to do. Any news on the investigation into the break-ins at my house and Beau and Aunt May's? What was happening with the Legendary Cotillion? It was less than a week away now. Any new affronts by the churchies or new evil doers?

After a weekend of Dustyn, it was a relief to aim my feet toward Hoosier Daddy. When I arrived, there was quite the scene. The churchies had changed tactics and instead of walking a circle to nowhere, they clustered right up to the red line that was the demarcation between their rented space and a charge of trespassing. They were hurling prayers and insults at everyone who went into the bar.

Never one to resist temptation, Roger had recruited Timmy and a few giggly boys who were having a Sunday afternoon frolic at the bar, to come outside. Someone had a boom box blaring what could only be soundtracks from old porno movies and the group was busily engaged in creating tableaus of wild group-sex acts. All were clothed, but the intent was clear. This, of course, stimulated the churchies, some outwardly and some, I'm sure, inwardly (although they would never admit it). Then Roger stepped away from his group and began tossing quarters toward the churchies.

"Yea, here's a donation. Mmmm ... pick that up. Ooo. Let me see those buns. Yea. Hot."

He and Timmy began to loudly rank members of the churchies and debate what perversion they were into.

The music, the simulated orgies, and the chanting and praying churchies were all winding up, up, up. While great theater, there was also a growing potential for stepping over the line, both literally and figuratively. However, Roger was a consummate leader. The song rose to a climax and ended. Roger applauded loudly and announced, "A wonderful performance by all! Let us retire to the bar where drinks are on me." He shot a look at the churchies. "All are welcome. Every single darling one of you."

He and Timmy then headed into Daddy's, leading the boys inside and leaving the churchies shaking in their morals.

I followed the crowd inside, aiming for Nacho's. However, as I went by the bar, I paid attention to the ancients perched on their stools. They weren't the somnambulant sots I had always assumed them to be as I hurried by. Most were watching in the mirror. I saw Lester watching me. I smiled and nodded. He saluted me with his glass. I leaned in and whispered in his ear, "Thanks for the tip. I'm not there yet, but I'm getting there."

Lester smiled and nodded. "Here's to the adventure of discovery."

I continued past the bar and turned right onto the Patio Café. At our table Aunt May and Beau sat, drinks at the ready, the box of folders we had brought from Opal's house sitting beside May. Cosmo, laptop open, was explaining what he had discovered.

"Once I cracked the encryption, it got interesting. See, each drive has a combination of numbers and letters as a name. I believe that will correspond with the name of your file folder." He pointed to the screen and the label of the folder Aunt May was holding.

"Now, on the drive are four folders. You only gave me one drive, but I would bet all of them are the same. There are documents, pictures, videos, and audio. The file names are usually just numbers that look like dates, but I bet the folders that you have explain what they are and why they are important."

Aunt May nodded. "And may I see one of the files?"

Cosmo looked a little uncomfortable. "I looked at a couple, just to see what was on the drive and make sure there wasn't further encryption. It's not exactly suitable for public viewing."

Beau laughed. "Even here? She must have some real filth. I always knew I liked Opal."

"You are, of course, correct," said Aunt May. "Do you think I should make copies? I am of two minds. I do not want to have anything fall into the wrong hands. However, I would hate to lose important information through an accident or desperate act."

Roger was fairly glowing from his interaction with the churchies and had been swapping brags with Timmy. "Leave it to Nacho," he said. "Nacho has resources more secure than most countries."

Aunt May nodded. "I believe you. Perhaps you would be willing to talk with Nacho about it."

"With your permission," said Roger, "we'll let Cosmo make a secure backup, with everything encrypted, but put the decrypted files in the folders on your drives. That way, you'll be able to look at them whenever you want."

"I am most grateful to both of you. The little I have seen so far has proven to be fascinating. I had no idea the scope of Opal's dealings. She had her finger in many pies."

"As it were," said Timmy.

Roger turned to me. "And speaking of sticking fingers in pies, have you found out anything more BB? We need to know what the churchies are up to. I can't believe Felcher has fallen into a pot of money because the Lord has smiled on him. Then there's Lester's lead about Brown County. You're up. Please tell me you have something useful to contribute."

I explained about the purchases I had discovered. However, what I had *not* found out quickly became apparent.

"So some group of someones is buying land in Brown County. You don't know who and you don't know why. Is that about it oh master of research?" asked Roger.

I nodded. "Maybe I can search all the different companies and see who the owners are. That's going to take a lot of time. I've started. They are in several states and a few are out of the country."

Aunt May set down her drink and patted her lips with her hanky. "Who did you say had been so unhelpful?"

"The county recorder. If he doesn't know all the people who made the purchases, I'm willing to bet he knows if most of the companies are fronted by one person."

"Makes sense," said Roger. "That's what I'd do. Form companies all over the place, but have one or two local attorneys to do the paperwork. I'd probably only use one, because in a small town, they'd be sure to talk, so it would be cheaper to stick with one."

"You mentioned a name," said Aunt May. "The name of the recorder."

"Oh, yeah. He was very proud of it. Elbert P. Adelston."

"That is very interesting." Aunt May reached into the file box that rested at her feet, sorted through it and pulled out a folder, which she lay on the table. "It seems that Opal has left us a file on Mr. Adelston."

Beau leaned forward and reached for the folder. "What's she got on him?"

Aunt May slapped Beau's hand. "Beauregard! Behave yourself as befits your upbringing. This is a man's life, not an afternoon soap opera."

"It's a man who is being a dick. Why did Opal leave us the files, if not to use them?"

"Beauregard. Sometimes you try my patience. Adherence to one's code is not a fault. And may I remind you again, Opal left the files to me and me alone, because she trusted that I would be judicious in the use of them."

"But Aunt May ..." Beau was fast becoming a petulant toddler.

"Hush," said Aunt May. She turned to me and held out her hand. "May I borrow your phone?"

I handed it over. Aunt May opened the file, scanned the pages, then dialed a number.

"Hello, Mr. Adelston? Ah, I am glad that you remember Mr. Singer, but as you can tell, I am certain, from my voice, I am not BB. I am a friend of his. I am also a friend of Opal Milbank. No, please do not hang up, Mr. Adelston, that would be regrettable. I promise I will not take up much of your time and I do apologize for calling you at home, but I felt it best to contact you when you were not in your office. So many people around. Things can be overheard. Things you might want to have kept private."

Aunt May listened unperturbed as the man shouted. She winked at me and whispered, "He is affronted, yet curious, otherwise he would have hung up." Finally the man's voice ebbed a bit and Aunt May spoke again.

"I don't know if you have heard, but Opal was found dead. And you see, Mr. Adelston, she was kind enough to leave me a small part of her estate. The part of her estate that contained certain files, you see. That is how I have your private number."

Again, the shouting could be heard. Aunt May smiled, holding the phone away from her ear until the man again calmed down.

"Now, Mr. Adelston, I have looked at the file Opal left for me that has your information. It is my belief that what a man and a woman, and whoever or whatever else they invite to participate, do in the privacy of their rooms is of no consequence. I do not believe in holding such pictures or files over someone's head or any other part of their anatomy. I am happy to destroy everything that is in your file and trouble you no more. However, I would ask a small favor in return. I only wish that you talk with BB and answer his questions. They are questions that will go a long way toward protecting a number of people. You see, Mr. Adelston, you will be doing a great service as well as, shall I say, wiping your own slate clean. Do that and I give you my word as a Southerner and a lady, that Opal's entire collection pertaining to you will be destroyed. I will personally burn or erase everything."

Aunt May listened for a moment. Then she nodded and said, "Thank you Mr. Adelston. You are truly doing a good thing." Then she handed the phone back to me. She reached into the file box and fished out a pad of paper and a pen, which she handed to me.

"Ask away BB," she said and picked up her drink.

It was a very different Adelston who was on the phone. He still sounded like he had a stick up his butt, but he was not holding back. I briefly wondered what the files had contained. I knew better than to ask him and I was pretty sure that Aunt May would never tell me, so I set aside my curiosity with a mental sigh. Not too large a one. I have found that most people's deepest secrets are disappointingly banal. The roots are entwined with a personal view of who they are and how others see them and the times I have been exposed to someone's deepest, darkest secrets, the biggest challenge was not to yawn or snort with derision. I looked up from my pad and saw everyone at the table staring at me, simply drooling with anticipation. I cleared my throat and said, "Excuse me just a minute, I need to go some place a little quieter." I picked up the pad and pen and found a small table at the corner of the patio and sat down, my back to the others. It was the only way to keep my head clear.

Our conversation was relatively short. Adelston had not wanted to volunteer insights, but that didn't mean he didn't have any. With the push provided by Aunt May, he opened his floodgates and let his insights pour out. The man had been the recorder for a long time and had developed a nose for things untoward and he had been smelling something for a while. It was only his personal code of ethics that kept him from sharing his concerns and now that he had decided to share ... Well, it seems that over a thousand acres of forest around the top of a mountain had been purchased over the past six months by a variety of companies, but all were represented by a single lawyer, a guy named Gibson. It didn't take long, but a picture was forming. Several pages of my pad were filled.

A hand gripped my shoulder, making me jump. I looked up. Roger. "Finish," he whispered. "We have to go. Wanda called."

I nodded. To Mr. Adelston, I said, "Thank you. Thank you very much. You must love Brown County."

"I've lived here all my life, so far," he replied. "I intend to live here my entire life."

"You've just saved an important part of it, I'm sure."

"I am glad. I wouldn't have done it if I had not been forced, but I am glad the lady forced me. Am I correct in trusting that she will honor her word and destroy the documents she has?"

"I trust Aunt May more than I trust myself," I said.

"Good. Then goodbye Mr. Singer. I hope you will not mind that I hope never to see or hear from you again."

Before I could reply, he hung up.

"Come on," said Roger. "Gotta run."

"But I've just ..."

Roger interrupted, "No time. We have places to be."

I stood and turned toward our table. "Let me just tell Aunt May ..."

Roger pushed me toward the door. "No time." He called over to the table, "Aunt May, something's come up. BB will report later, but it's all good. Have a drink on me."

Aunt May nodded her acquiescence. Beau waved and Roger pushed me through the door, through the bar, and out to the street. Ah well, no rest for the wicked.

Chapter 18 - Wanda

"What's the rush?" I asked as Roger steered me to his car.

"We have to get Petunia and Wanda's waiting."

"Waiting for what?"

"Tonight's the night she made her move on Thad Wroks."

"The frat thief? You said she was going to get him to talk."

"He wouldn't share when she tried the nice way, so she's been leading him into a trap. She just called. He's slightly drugged, a little bit handcuffed, and just needs a visit from Petunia to shake the information loose. Wanda could get it out of him, but I don't like him and I'd rather give him a jolt. Petunia gives better jolt."

"What am I supposed to do?"

"There's a laptop in the back seat. Bring it along. When he starts kicking out names, I want you to check them. He'll be scared, but he also may be stupid enough to lie. I want to make sure."

By this time, we pulled up in front of Petunia's. She was waiting outside. She climbed in and off we went. My phone rang. It was TiaRa.

"BB, where have you been?" she cried in my ear. "So much planning. So little time. We are beginning to prepare the rooms at the mansion. Foxy's teams have been in all weekend, cleaning and fluffing. The mansion gleams. Now we need you to help transport. I have a show later and want to begin before I go to Daddy's."

"Sorry Tia. I was shanghaied by Roger. I will dedicate my tomorrow to you."

Tia sniffed, only partially mollified. "So on top of everything else, you'll miss the show tonight?"

"I wasn't intending to, Tia. You know it's the highlight of my week. But Roger ..."

Tia sighed. "I know how pushy that man can be. Very well. Meet me at noon at Suave Delights. We have so little time to turn the Ontario Mansion into a performance space adequate to showcase the stellar performers and their chosen babies. There are bedrooms and dressing rooms to be prepared and rooms so that the moneyed guests can relax, to encourage them to dig deep and donate extravagantly. So much to do. So much."

"Tomorrow. I get off work at noon and I will go straight to you, I promise," I said. "I'll work 'til I drop."

"Very well," said Tia. "Tell Roger he is indebted to me for stealing you away."

Tia hung up as Roger stopped outside one of the newish condos that had been popping up like boils ever since the new mayor had declared the city open to any and all developers who were willing to grease some part of his anatomy.

Roger led the way to an upstairs unit, which featured a beautiful view of the wall of the condo next door. The lights were low. Music designed to muffle conversations was playing, but not quite loud enough to cover the tearful begging, occasionally interrupted by the slap of something hard on flesh, coming from the back room. We followed the sounds to a bedroom of sorts. It was not a cozy suite. Instead, the room seemed to have been decorated from the Bed, Bash, and Bemoan catalog. Wanda, dressed in a pink, frilly robe gaping open to reveal a shiny black Lycra body suit smiled and waved us in, with what looked to be a thin cane made from bamboo.

Thad Wroks was naked and bent over something that seemed a mix between a bed and a vaulting horse. His hands and ankles were securely tied. His butt was up in the air, showcasing a number of red stripes. He was crying. I almost felt sorry for him.

"He tried to slip something into my drink," said Wanda. "He was so pleased with himself that he didn't notice what I put in his. After a few minutes, he was very open to suggestions and when I suggested how much fun it would be to try out my new toy, he was all for it. I made sure all the knots were tight before I called. My happy potion started wearing off just a little while ago. So, I figure he's ready to meet Petunia."

Roger walked into Thad's line of sight.

"Oh thank god," the boy moaned. "This crazy bitch drugged me and when I woke up, I was ..."

Then Petunia, a grim mountain, stepped forward so he could gaze upon her powerful, unsmiling form. His mouth kept moving, but only random squeaks emerged. Petunia has that effect on people. I view her as a friend, but I am still very, very careful not to do anything that might anger her.

"Thad, meet Petunia," said Roger. "I'm going to ask you some questions. If I don't like your answers, then I'll have Petunia ask you. Here's a little hint." Roger winked and stage whispered. "I don't think you'll like it if Petunia has to ask the questions."

Petunia didn't say anything, but she took a deep breath and bulked up. I was in no danger, but I took an involuntary step backward and swung the laptop that I had tucked against my chest down to cover my crotch.

Roger reached out and patted Thad's head. He flinched. Thad was learning a lot about life. There are some places that even the white, wealthy, entitled male, who is convinced he is simply smarter and better than everyone else, should not tread. This is particularly the case when said male is neither smarter nor better. Thad was discovering what happened when one of his ilk crossed that line and came up against someone who was smarter and had a sense of decency and self-worth, so could not be ordered about or bought off.

"Let's start with an easy one," said Roger. "What were you looking for in Ms. Milbank's bedroom?"

"My phone," answered Thad.

Roger shook his head. "Wrong answer, young man." He turned his head to Petunia. "I think you should ask him. Would you like Wanda's cane?"

Petunia smiled. I had seen her smile before. I still gasped. Thad let out a yelp of fear. Petunia said, "I don't think so. It's a pretty thing and I'd hate to break it."

"Wait!" yelled Thad. "You're right. I wasn't looking for a phone. I was trying to get into this metal box she kept in that big closet thing.

"Whhhyyyyy?" Petunia asked, still smiling.

Thad was blubbering and crying. Snot was running down his face. He wasn't looking like a future captain of industry. "I knew she kept money and other stuff in there. I needed it to pay back ..." He hesitated.

"To pay back who?"

Thad was clearly torn. "I'm not supposed to say. He said he'd hurt me and he has some big guys who ..."

Roger interrupted. "Thad. Let me help you here. You are

between what is traditionally called a rock and a hard place. However, this mystery man's threat is not right here. Petunia, on the other hand, is close enough to reach out and touch you. And touch you she will, Thad—repeatedly. Not in a sweet or pleasurable way. So, your choice is between a possible problem at some point in the future and a certain and painful problem in the here and now. My guess is that you have made some poor choices in your past and they are catching up with you. But when dealing with such problems, it is best to deal with the most immediate ones first." He nodded at Petunia.

Roger reached out and put a gentle hand on Thad's butt. Thad jerked at the touch. He was beat. "Freddy," he said. "Freddy Flash. The guy that runs U-Betcha Pawn."

"See, that wasn't so hard," said Roger. "Why don't you tell us all about it? Then you can go home and all this unpleasantness will be over and done."

A little stirring of hope flickered across Thad's face. Then Petunia cracked her knuckles and he gasped and nodded. "See, I got a little behind."

As I was staring at his behind, a remark popped unbidden into my head, but I decided no one would appreciate my contribution.

"Behind in what?" asked Roger.

"Well, Freddy is kind of the go-to guy for some of us at the frat."

"Go to for what?"

"Whatever we need. You know. On the weekends, some of us like to party a bit. Plus, there's always a helping hand for babes who need a little extra encouragement to put out."

"Like what?" asked Roger.

"I don't know. I guess GHB or roofie."

"Very classy. But how can you get behind? I can't imagine a dealer letting you run a tab."

"No, but, well, I've been running short of money this semester. My dad's been serving me shit about not doing good enough in school, so he's cut my credit limit and has been watching my charges and I don't want him to be on me for everything I spend."

"So, you've been selling for Freddy. Is that it?"

Thad nodded. "He gives me a bunch. I sell it. Then I pay him. But for a couple of weeks, we had like really major parties at the house and I got pretty high and ..." Thad stopped talking.

"Did you lose it, spend it, or take it?"

Thad shrugged as well as he could, given his current position. "Not really sure, but all of a sudden I was in to Freddy for like five hundred bucks. I tried to make it up by helping out some guys at some other houses and things were going fine until ..."

"You did it again. Right?"

"Yea. I got high homecoming weekend and ... Well, all of a sudden, I was in for like two grand and Freddy came to talk to me with a couple of really big guys. And the big guys had big guns and ..." Thad was crying again. "I had to give them my laptop. I had the answers to all my midterms on that. I had paid a lot for those answers and if I couldn't get 'em back, I was gonna flunk. So, the next time I went to Opal's, I snatched a ring from one of her rooms. I said I was going to the bathroom and I slipped into one of those upstairs rooms. There was lots of stuff up there and I figured she wouldn't miss it, or if she did, she'd think she left it somewhere. So, I grabbed it and brought it to Freddy. He looked at it and said it was worth enough for my debt. I got my laptop back and from then on, he'd give me product whenever I could sneak something from Opal. I didn't do it much, but I noticed that the really best things, the things she wore most of the time, she kept in that metal box. She also kept money in there. That's where she went to get the money she gave me. So, when I heard she was dead, I figured I wasn't going to be getting anything from her anymore, so it was kind of like severance pay. A goodbye gift, you know?"

"OK Thad," said Roger, continuing to guide him through his confession. "Now, be honest. Was it you who first broke in and set off the alarm?"

Thad shook his head. "No way. Opal had alarms all over the place. There's no way I would have tried."

"I have to ask, Thad. How did you know she was dead? It hadn't been announced. Did you have something to do with her death?"

Thad tried to pull himself up, but the ropes stopped him. "No!" he said. "I wouldn't kill Opal. She was old, but she was pretty sweet. Besides, she paid me and I could snag stuff every once in a while. Even if I could, why would I?"

"So, who told you?"

"Actually, I got a call from Freddy. He told me she was dead and if I hustled my butt over there, I might be able to grab a bunch of stuff. She wasn't going to be needing it anymore and I could always use the extra cash, so I ..."

"I wonder how Freddy knew," said Roger.

"No idea," said Thad. "Freddy knows stuff. I'm not that smart, but I know better than to go asking what he knows or how."

Roger turned to me. "Look him up, would you?"

It didn't take long. Sheldon Flaxman, aka Freddy Flash, was the owner-manager of U-Betcha Pawn and owner of U-StashIt, a rundown storage place on the edge of town. I was amused by the URL for the place www.ustashit.com. It seemed more a cure for incontinence than a storage facility.

He had a few convictions. A couple for intent to sell and another for assault. I looked that one up. It seemed that our Freddy had been trying to collect on a debt and had used a briefcase that was at hand to help persuade the reluctant debtor. There was a picture of the victim. It wasn't pretty. Thad, as large and as dumb as he was, had made a good decision to keep on the good side of Mr. Flaxman. I reported all this to Roger.

Roger nodded. He turned to Petunia and Wanda. "I think we've milked this one for as much useful information as we can. I turn him back over to you."

Wanda stepped forward, cane in hand. Thad cringed. "Now listen, Thad," Wanda said. "I am going to let you go. But pay attention."

Thad was focused with all his being on Wanda.

"I will be watching you. Friends of mine will be watching you. We will all be making sure you never again take advantage of a woman. If you ever even think about it, look around. Anyone that you see and some that you don't see, may at that moment, be reporting back to me. And if I hear that you have as much as sneezed in a disrespectful manner toward a woman, Petunia and I and perhaps some friends who are really mean, will come for you. Do you understand?"

Thad nodded.

"Do you have any doubts that we will find out, even if you think you are alone, even if it is years from now in a completely different town?"

Thad shook his head.

"Then we are going to let you go so you can prove how much you have learned."

Wanda nodded at Petunia. Somehow, a large hunting knife appeared in Petunia's hand, which she raised high above

Thad. He let out a scream as her arm dropped. He was untouched, but the ropes that bound his hands were sliced in two. Again the knife rose and fell and his legs were free. Wanda tossed his clothes to him.

"I assume you can find your way home."

Thad nodded, dressing quickly and backing out of the apartment, mumbling promises to forever more be good.

Roger turned to me. "Well, this has been most entertaining. I believe we have a solid lead on who sent the hulks to rob Aunt May and Beau. We will follow that up. We still have no clue about your dance with desperadoes. They haven't returned, so we'll keep up regular drive-bys of your house and Aunt May's. How traumatized are you? Shall we return to the bar and catch the end of TiaRa's show or is da widdle man all tuckered out?"

"Home please. I have to be at work in the morning and Tia wants me to be a gopher at noon."

Roger nodded and looked toward Petunia and Wanda.

"Wanda, many thanks. A pleasure doing business with you, as always. Bill double. I know you'd have done it for free, but you deserve it. Petunia, ride?"

Petunia shook her head. "I'll hang here for a while."

Roger nodded and we headed out the door. My bed was calling me, after a few drinks had calmed me enough to edit out the painful visions I had witnessed while enhancing the views of a muscular body not yet gone to seed.

Chapter 19 - Monday at Foxy's

Monday morning arrived without emergency. It's the little things that make me grateful. I woke up without anyone wanting anything from me, except Spot, who required food and adoration, but repaid them with loud purring. I left home on time and got to work and actually spent the morning doing what I was paid to do—going through the detritus of someone's life and sorting it into give away, throw away, and auction off piles. There were a few interesting pieces. A few things required research. Magawatta is home to a large university which spends extravagant amounts on team bacchanalia in order to suck in large donations from old alumni wishing to recall, with advantages, their glory days. As a result, many estates have sports memorabilia that to me look like trash, but to collectors, are worth extraordinary amounts. I always check, ever since I tossed a pair of shoes once worn by a legendary coach who was later canned because of an inability to stifle his anger at—well pretty much anything. It was only because the trash had not been picked up that I still had my job.

The day was running smoothly. At noon I knocked off for the day and went to meet TiaRa at Suave's to help with the Legendary Cotillion. Foxy answered the door and waved me inside.

"The two of them are in the warehouse deciding what pieces

are necessary. Suave is about to transcend. The opportunity to decorate an entire mansion is nearly too wondrous to handle. She has hinted that we will need to purchase several new pieces, but I was most firm. Although I pretend not to see her new acquisitions, I know that anytime she uses the car, or worse, the truck, several new surprises are being surreptitiously secreted back there. I turn a half-blind eye to her acquisitions, but even with that cursory tally I have no doubt there is more than enough to exquisitely bedeck several mansions. Do come in. They shall be busy for a while before they need your willingness to carry, but I have need of your keen ear, mind, and talents now."

Foxy's languid voice washed over me like the thick cloud of cannabis wafting from his study. He handed me the large joint he was smoking, turned, and beckoned for me to follow. Sitting at the large table in the middle of the room, with a glorious cut crystal decanter of certainly expensive, amber liquid before him and a matching glass, well filled, in his hand, sat a bespectacled man in a rather pedestrian suit. He had the air of a school principal to him and I instinctively hid the joint behind my back.

"This," said Foxy, "is Dr. Hemworth Tarkington. He is a member of the state board of education."

The man reached out his hand to shake. I paused. The hand I should be reaching forward held Foxy's thick, aromatic joint. The rug we were standing on was, I'm certain, extremely valuable, so dropping the doobie was out of the question. I didn't think I could bring myself to switch the joint to another hand under the watchful eye of this man. I might not be in school any more, but the terror of authority figures still lurked on an instinctual level.

Thankfully Foxy noticed my hesitation and understood my reticence. He laughed and held out his hand. "Hemworth does not partake of anything but liquid entertainments, but he understands that in my house he will see a diversity of pleasures." I handed Foxy the joint, then reached out and shook hands with the man.

"Hemworth is a dear friend of many years," said Foxy. "He has been providing a brief, but informative tutelage in the concept of charter schools. I assume you will drink." He handed the joint back to me and went to the bar in the corner. Foxy had wonderful taste in most things and the money to indulge, which he did. "Please continue, Hemworth."

Dr. Tarkington had a professorial air. Lecturing at, rather than speaking to, seemed to be his preferred mode of communication. He cleared his throat, not because he needed to, but as an introduction.

"As I was telling Foxy, the idea behind charter schools is not problematic. It allows children with specialized interests to attend a school that focuses more on that interest—such as music, academics, or ... well, the possibilities are nearly endless. In theory, the state makes sure that an approved required curriculum is presented to all children, so they don't grow up lacking a solid foundation, but additionally, they can explore their particular interests. Of course, in the cases where the parents want a certain focus, such as religious upbringing, they can choose a charter school that has that bent without having to pay for private schooling. The state pays the charter school on a per student basis. The state actually pays less per student in a charter school than for a public school, so everybody wins. In theory."

"You keep saying in theory," I said. "Call me suspicious, but ..."

"A most excellent point," said Foxy, handing me my drink. "Many people whose focus is business, not education, have bellied up to the bar. The supervision is lax at best and there are many loopholes. Any school formed is monitored and cannot be a for-profit company. However, they can and do hire management companies that can and do make a profit. Also, while the growth in charter schools has been robust, the funding for oversight by the state has not."

"It's not that we don't try," said Dr. Tarkington. "We have so many things on our plate. And with the growth of online charter schools ..."

"Online?" I asked.

"Some schools do not have physical classrooms or have limited school buildings and conduct most of their classes online. Even something as basic as tracking whether or not students are actually attending classes in these schools is something we haven't figured out. It's pretty easy to take roll and prove attendance when the students are sitting in front of a teacher, but with these online schools ..."

"As I have told you," said Foxy with a smile, "business makes decisions differently than you or I. Good is a relative term. Good for you or me may mean a supportive atmosphere where students are challenged to learn and grow. Good for a business is higher income and lower costs. If one runs a business and can be relatively certain they will not be audited, it becomes a reasonable gamble to cut certain corners and inflate the numbers of students."

"And I'm guessing this has something to do with the charter school the churchies are planning," I said.

"They have already submitted an application," said Dr. Tarkington. "They intend to start an online charter school called the BASIC academy. This is to be their headquarters, drawing from students throughout Southern Indiana. In some areas, where the population is small and decidedly church-going, they may actually cause public schools to close. In addition, they have already put in applications for additional schools throughout the state. They have plans to enroll 30,000 students within the next two years. The state pays nearly $10,000 per student per year. That is $300,000,000 per year. And while it takes several months for the money to make its way through the state bureaucracy, it does eventually arrive and that is a substantial amount of money."

"Particularly if they cut the services they promise or inflate the number of students attending," said Foxy.

"But how could they be sure they won't get audited?" I asked. "If they do, people will go to jail, right?"

"Ah, that is where this scheme is particularly lovely," replied Foxy. "Let us imagine a school that is headed by someone who is an established teacher, albeit at an explicitly homophobic school."

"That seems like a requirement for anything run by the churchies," I said.

Foxy nodded. "Imagine, furthermore, that this teacher, now principal, is married to a governor-to-be who is also heir to a rather large fortune and is well connected throughout this very conservative state, so would be able to discourage audits as well as provide advance warning of any surprise visits by authorities."

"The fortune would be very handy when getting started," said Dr. Tarkington. "Before a school can be approved, it must have an established infrastructure—classrooms, or a computer network in the case of an online school, a curriculum, a cash reserve, and more. In addition, the application requires a substantial deposit. After a school opens, the law has not provided a good mechanism for oversight, but before it is approved, we are as careful as possible."

"And you, dear boy, provided the clues that led to uncovering this clever scheme," said Foxy. "The churchies have indeed hired a management company. It is in their filing with the state. Now, can you recall the members of the church's board who stood out as unusual and can you hazard a guess as to who is also on the board of the management company the school-to-be has hired?"

I smiled. "I'm guessing Peter Ponce. Gonna be governor, well connected, access to a big pot of money. I've read his mother still controls the fortune, but he and his brother have access as long as they stay on her good side. I've also heard that keeping mama happy is no trouble for Peter. He's a case study for Freudian analysis. And, as I remember, his beard, I mean wife, has taught art at a few anti-homo schools."

"You have correctly identified the culprit and have painted a wonderfully accurate portrait of Peter," said Foxy. "The Ponce brothers are essential to the plan, but many of the board members of the church and school are also in line for a piece of the pie. The story of the family fortune is actually a bit stranger than you know. It seems that Papa Ponce was a renown philanderer and Mama Ponce was, and is, the queen of control freaks. It was a battle of wills throughout their marriage, but she came from a wealthy family and understood wealth. She had made sure that all the businesses and all the money was in her name. One evening, she came home early from a society event with a headache and discovered him in the arms of another woman. She had the servants physically eject him from the house with the few clothes he managed to scoop up on his way out the door. He discovered that he had only a few dollars in a drawer in his office. Before she relented, the man nearly starved. She had Papa Ponce by the short hairs and decided to put him on a short leash. She forced him to sign a contract that if she ever found any evidence of his being unfaithful, the entire fortune, upon her death would be donated to the Little Sisters of Fallen Women, a lovely convent entirely staffed, as it were, by former sex workers. That would mean that not only would he be penniless for the rest of his days, but that his sons, who were his pride and joy, would also lose their inheritance. As it turned out, the man's spirit was broken and he died long before his wife. However, the contract is still in force."

"How did you ever discover all that?" asked Dr. Tarkington.

Foxy smiled. "Stories of large fortunes and odd restrictions are table talk with some of my friends. That particular story came by way of an attorney who drew up the document and earned him a round of drinks from all present."

"Well deserved," I said. "That is a truly wonderful story and it couldn't have happened to more deserving sons. So, if any proof of infidelity of the father comes to light?"

"The boys will lose millions," answered Foxy.

"I'll have to ask Aunt May if there are any files related to the Ponces."

"Peter may not need the fortune soon," said Foxy. "If the school scheme comes to fruition, he will be in a position to acquire his own fortune. As I said, he is not only on the board of Felcher's church. He is on the board of a new company, BASIC School Management, INC."

"What is the deal with Basic? I can see the school using that name, emphasizing a back-to-basics approach, but why the management company?"

"They are not emphasizing a return to basic education," said Dr. Tarkington. "It is an acronym. I have run into groups using it before. It stands for Becoming A Soldier In Christ. They are not interested in subtlety as to their purpose."

"Adorable," I said. "Can they really run a statewide school from just one storefront?"

"They can and I believe that is their intention," said Foxy. "It also provides a reason why they are interested in that specific location. It is close enough to downtown to make it look official with a very little bit of fluffing to the outside. It is far enough away from the state capitol to discourage officials from the state board of education from coming on many inspection trips. Finally, Magawatta, while small, does offer excellent internet connectivity because of the large school and its contracts with various national defense groups. In fact, that location just so happens to be right next to where the trunk line for the internet backbone that runs into campus is laid. It will not only be fast. It will be the first to be repaired should anything go wrong. They could easily run operations that span several states from that location. As they grow, they will have a reason to take over the entire block."

"Once they close Daddy's," I said.

"Precisely."

"Well, that explains why they want that block and why they want it to be in Magawatta," I said. "So, I guess the break-in at Aunt May and Beau's isn't connected. It was that pawn shop guy trying to get some of Opal's stash and he's got nothing to do with the churchies."

"What?" Foxy looked confused.

I filled him in on what we had found out the previous night. I gave an edited version, since Dr. Tarkington was there. I knew once I started describing the scene with Thad and how we had convinced him to talk, Foxy would want all the details. Foxy could tell there was more to the story than I was sharing, but understood what I was doing. I was sure that the next time Foxy got me alone, he would not be so reticent.

"Ah, Foxy," said Dr. Tarkington. "You never disappoint. I bring you tidbits and you serve up a full meal of mystery."

"But who is after my BVM?" I asked.

"BVM?" asked Dr. Tarkington.

I quickly described the delicious shell art Virgin Mary. If I had harbored any question about the good doctor's sexuality before, the enthusiasm with which he questioned me about every detail of the slice of kitsch I had found at Opal's, laid them to rest. When I mentioned the message on the back, he positively quivered. His excitement at the phrase "and when I deviate, punish me" revealed what particular offering from the buffet Dr. Tarkington went to for seconds and thirds.

"You must send me a picture," he said. "Several. I must know who this Eppie J. is, or was. If he had such a gem to give away, think about what else he might still have either in his collection, if he is still alive, or in his estate. It is so unfortunate how much is lost. A magnificent private collection, which took years to build is discovered by the family after a death, and too often they throw everything away and sometimes even burn it, hoping that word about dear Uncle Phillip never leaks out. Lost forever. I, myself, have rescued several collections by contacting relatives directly when I hear of an aficionado who has passed."

"I met Dr. Tarkington while I was on the hunt for a very specific bit of accoutrement which Suave had expressed an interest in exploring," explained Foxy. "While I do not share his dedication to the discipline, as it were, I admire both his knowledge and his ability to ferret out new information. But to your question. I am not yet convinced there is not a thread that runs through all these events. All roads lead to Opal and while she was an expert in compartmentalizing different areas of her life, I have not ruled out the possibility that these roads are connected. Do not forget the road that leads to Brown County. That was the road that Opal brought to Nacho's attention before her demise."

"There you are! We had almost given up hope!"

TiaRa was standing in the doorway. She shook her finger at Foxy. "BB has come to work with me to prepare the Ontario

Mansion for the Legendary Cotillion and instead, I find him up here while you ply him with smoke and drink. What condition do you plan to leave him in? Unable to help me? I warn you, Foxy. If BB is not up to the task, I will stop trying to convince Suave that she has enough furniture to accomplish the task and will, instead, encourage her to go on a buying spree that will leave you penniless and in need of several new storage facilities."

This was no idle threat. Suave and purchasing was like a mousetrap—ready to snap at anything at the slightest touch.

Foxy held up pleading hands. "Do forgive me, Ms. del Fuego. I meant no harm. I am certain BB is up to any task you send his way. I have been monitoring his intake carefully and what he has consumed should in no way impede him, but should only enhance his creativity." Foxy shot me a pleading glance, obviously hoping I would not let him down.

"We do not need his creativity," said TiaRa. "We need his strong back. Forgive me BB, but your aesthetic eye is not known for its focus and clarity."

I did not mind Tia slighting my creativity. I am aware of my limitations and trying to match design suggestions with either TiaRa or Suave would be at best embarrassing. I chose to focus on her comment about my strong back. It was a lie and we both knew it, but I loved her for making it and resolved to try to prove it partly true, even if tomorrow would be an excursion through pain.

"Lead on, Tia," I said. "I am ready to haul till I drop."

TiaRa smiled. "We have a wonderful selection picked out. We will use one of Foxy's trucks and it should only take a few trips."

That worried me. "A few" is a very squishy term. I am able to channel butch for only so long. "Perhaps I should call Nacho and get some help," I suggested, thinking of his cadre of

Twink soldiers and the visual treat of seeing them lift and carry while I mopped their sweaty brows and anything else that needed mopping.

"Pish posh," said TiaRa. "You'll do fine. We have been delayed long enough by Foxy. March! Now!"

I sighed. When TiaRa ordered, who was I to do anything but obey?

Chapter 20 - Mansion Fluffing

Loading the truck was not as painful as I had feared. The mansion evidently had furniture aplenty that passed muster for both TiaRa and Suave, which was impressive, as both are very particular. Most of what we brought were hangings and bits of fluff and sparkles to make the rooms for the performers special and the guest areas for the patrons feel extravagantly ostentatious, in order to encourage a loosening of the purse strings. Everything fit into one load and most of it was refreshingly light, so the task that I had feared would toy with my, admittedly low, tolerance for physical effort, was well within my capabilities. I felt useful and butch by the time the truck was unloaded and we began to put each item in its perfect spot. Foxy's team of cleaners had done a wonderful job and the Ontario Mansion gleamed. TiaRa focused on setting up rooms where each visiting queen and their star princess would be staying and Suave focused on the main room where the performance and milking of the whales would take place. I scurried back and forth, as each of them called me to move, alter, place, and otherwise be useful.

"We are lucky that each room is already so different," said TiaRa. "I'm told that the man who defrauded his investors also convinced decorators throughout the Midwest to design a single room and that all the rooms would be judged. The best room would win the contract to do the entire house. Dangling not only a large contract, but the opportunity to declare victory over their competition drove the designers to extravagant heights. When Mr. Flim Flam departed, all was left in place, as the designers could not prove ownership without a lengthy court case, so they got in line behind all the other victims. Their loss is our gain. Not only is each room splendid. Each is different. This will prevent arguments, with one diva claiming their room is of lower quality than another, claiming their room assignment is an affront. I have seen fights over the brand of cans of hairspray. Every room here is so different, yet all are so spectacular, that I do not expect a peep from any one of the queens."

"There will still be battles," said Suave, coming in from the main room. "Do remember that these are the absolute top tier of performers. There will be an undercurrent of candy-coated bitchiness that would bring nearly anyone to tears. I hope you are ready for them, TiaRa. These are not the amateurs from Sunday afternoons at Daddy's. These queens can peel paint from twenty yards with a word and a smile."

"My dear Suave," Tia replied. "I have come up from the trenches of a thousand shitty little clubs. Even though I have perched here in Magawatta, I do not measure my discipline by Magawatta standards. I am certain I will be able to hold my own. I just hope that the performers protect their young. While each performer will make sure her own protégé behaves, as misbehavior will be reflected in the donations each one receives, it is a near certainty that one or more of the ladies will launch an attack on another's child just before that princess is due to go on. Do remember, this is a cotillion. The competition is actually between the star pupils. The audience will contribute to the performers they feel are best. At the end of the evening, after a final round of donations for each of the new performers, a belle of the ball will be declared. The queens will be the entertainment in between, not the contestants. So, most of my patrolling will be for the protection of the princesses. Nacho has promised to provide escorts for all the protégés and the Twinks will be instructed to act as guardians."

"What about me and anyone else who is helping?" I asked. "If these are world-class tongue-lashers, who is going to protect us? I'm pretty sure that I'll screw up something or at least provide less than perfect service at some point. What do I do when Fantasia comes after me?"

TiaRa patted my cheek. "You will be fine BB. My advice to you and everyone else who will be providing the personal maid service for our performers, is to keep your eyes down, fulfill all requests, and when in doubt, say 'Yes ma'am, you are absolutely right, and have I mentioned how extraordinary you are looking?'. Try not to openly weep in front of them, because that will not inspire pity, but will only encourage them. And if all else fails, find me and I will address the issue."

"Who else have you press-ganged into service?" I asked.

"Several people have *volunteered*," replied TiaRa. "Beau and Aunt May, of course, were happy to do their part. A few fans and a few of the other performers from our weekly show stepped up. I am sure we will have a full complement of maids, Nacho's Twinks, and all the stage hands needed."

"Well, since you are so well supplied..." I began.

Tia fixed me with a glare. "No, BB. Do not go there. I have promised Fantasia that my absolutely most trustworthy and competent friend will be at her beck and call. And that is you. She must be handled delicately. Several of the whales are coming for the explicit purpose of seeing her, as she rarely tours anymore. She can be, in fact almost certainly will be, difficult, and you are the only one I trust to handle her."

I sighed. "I wish you didn't have such a high opinion of me."

She pinched my cheek, then lightly slapped it. "I do and I am certain you will do nothing to undermine my high regard."

She turned to Suave. "Let's check everything one more time for perfection that sparkles. The owners of Daddy's have volunteered their staff and equipment. They will move everything here on Thursday and Friday. The owners are making a great sacrifice. They will have minimal music in the big room on Thursday, Friday and Saturday. No DJ. No dancing. They will have a play list running through backup speakers for those desperate enough to put up with it. Mostly, they will offer drinks at the bar so people will have somewhere to go."

"Foxy is up to his ears in arrangements," said Suave. "Travel, accommodations, refreshments. He's in heaven. He loves the intricacies of putting together an event. He'd do it all the time if he could, but I will not allow it. Too much stress and I won't have him work himself into an early grave. However, upon occasion, it is just the thing to stir up his blood."

So, the two divas went through the entire mansion one more time, continually spitting out commands for new additions, changes, baubles, bangles, and beads. I dutifully wrote everything down, hoping I would not also be put in charge of accomplishing everything I wrote. A couple of hours later we were done and I went off to Daddy's to bemoan the extent of my efforts in hopes for a bit of sympathy and perhaps, a few drinks to shut me up. Then home, where hopefully the new locks and watchful eyes of Petunia and Merle would keep me safe.

Chapter 21 - Tuesday

No one attacked me or my house during the night. Spot woke me up when he felt it was time for me to be useful and feed him. I placated him and with a contented sigh savored my favorite coffee—Pierce Brothers air-roasted Fogbuster. So wonderfully strong, never bitter or burned, it soothed my troubled soul. It was turning out to be a delightful day with no demands or drama. Then Roger called.

"Nacho's. Twenty minutes. Call when you're here and I'll let you in."

I was tempted to point out that I had a life and it was early, but he had already hung up. I got dressed and headed over to Daddy's. The only way into Nacho Mama's Patio Café was by going through Hoosier Daddy. There was a back gate to the alley, but it was plastered with signs warning all never to approach it, much less open it. I was one of the few who had actually passed through that gate, a fact I occasionally tried to bring up in conversation to prove how far above mere mortals I floated. Thus far, no one had been impressed. Some bars open as early as 7 a.m. However, Hoosier Daddy attempted to hold on to the little scraps of class it had and did not open until eleven, allowing a small lunch crowd who came for whatever wonderful creation Nacho had prepared. The menu was a single item with the choice being to take it or leave it. If nothing else were planned that afternoon, one could accessorize with a drink and, occasionally, a new acquaintance to while away the hours. I texted my arrival and Roger let me in, leading the way through the empty bar, out to the Café, where Nacho, Cosmo, and Lester waited.

"About time," grumbled Nacho.

I ignored him.

Roger took the lead. "Cosmo has found something about the land sales in Brown County," he said. "Actually, he has found a couple of things. Walk us through it, Cosmo."

Cosmo interfaced best with computers. Having a group, even as small a group as this, outside of an AA meeting, was a bit intimidating. He shifted uncomfortably, looked down at the table, and began to mumble.

"Louder," growled Nacho. "Faster. I got a place to run and we have things to get done."

The pressure from Nacho only served to increase Cosmo's nervousness. Roger stood and laid hands on his shoulders and began to gently knead the muscles. "Just imagine we are robots or cyborgs or mannequins," he said soothingly. "Not humans. We just need you to feed us the information so we can function."

It worked. Cosmo took a deep breath and rolled his head, further loosening up his neck and shoulders. I am amazed at Roger's ability to know how to dig information from people. Last night, with Thad, he threatened. With me, he orders. With Cosmo ... I briefly wondered how I could get on the shoulder-massage list. I knew that asking would get me nowhere pleasant.

"I mapped the plots of land that have been purchased by the dummy corporations." Cosmo swiveled his laptop around to show a map. A large area in yellow indicated all the plots that had been purchased. In the center, a large patch of green indicated land that had not been sold.

"What's that?" I asked, pointing.

Lester laughed. "That, my young friend, is the High Hopes commune, or what is left of it."

Pausing briefly to bask in the young part of his "young friend" comment, I said, "I wonder why it wasn't sold. Who owns it?"

"That is where it gets interesting," said Cosmo. "I got into the recorder's system and found that there have been several searches for the owner. Each time the result was the same."

"Well, who is it?" I asked.

"Mary Jane Ontario," answered Cosmo.

"Ontario, as in the Ontario Mansion?"

"Exactly."

"But isn't she dead?"

Lester broke in. "She's gone, but not dead. There was a lot of heat on the family. She claimed the FBI was tracking her. Her first husband's store got firebombed by the Klan. Money was running out. It was a pretty wild time. Remember Patty Hearst?"

"Sure," I said. Weird stories of wayward richies were enticing and this was one of the best. "Newspaper heiress, kidnapped by some group of neo-revolutionaries, which she then joined and helped rob some banks, but she claimed she had been brainwashed. Most of the original group died in a battle with the LA police. Others were rounded up over the next year. There was some talk that during her time as a revolutionary member, she was hidden by several people and once she was arrested, all those hidden people were rounded up."

"Well," said Lester, "some of the core group who died in LA first met here in Magawatta. They went to school here. Then they went out to California and into history. It was a wild and scary time. Mary Jane had gone through two husbands and a fortune and was ready to disappear. So, she did."

"Should be easy enough to find," said Nacho. "Tax bills gotta be paid or the state takes it."

"No," said Cosmo. "The taxes are paid in advance for the next hundred years with a substantial additional amount to account for tax increases. The only way to sell that land is to get the deed signed by the owner and even I couldn't find her and you know I'm pretty good at digging. She's almost certainly alive, but I don't have a clue where."

"How did she do that?" I asked. "I thought she was broke."

"No idea," said Cosmo. "Someone must have given her a hunk of cash, but I can't find out who or why."

"I think a trip out to High Hopes is called for," said Roger, looking at me. "Perhaps there are a few old timers still crashing there who know."

Lester smiled and shook his head. "I used to know everyone out there. Most of them are gone. All the ones that remain are very suspicious of outsiders. However, their high morals can be bent a bit if you bring an offering."

"Offering?" I asked.

"Pot. The better, the better," said Lester. "Try to find an old timer named MoonStar. He's not much to look at now, but once upon a time ... He'll try to come across as a wise old guru, but he's mostly an old drunk in tie dye. However, he's been there forever. He has a place to crash for free and food stamps so he can eat. Plus, no one has kicked him out, so he's like a barnacle. Stuck to the side of the mountain. Tiring to listen to, but if you can weed through the crap, he may know something."

"I'm sure Foxy will donate some bud to the adventure," said Roger.

"There's one more confusing bit," said Cosmo. "You know

I've been decrypting those drives Aunt May left with me. Well, there are a lot of video files and I've translated a few. Pretty raunchy stuff. She must have had a couple of hidden cameras, I don't recognize most of the people, but I figure that they must be important, else why would she video them? The few I looked at, if it was me, I sure wouldn't want anyone to see me doing what they were doing."

"Lovely," said Nacho. "Nothing like a porn collection of fat, old rich dudes."

"There were a couple of files that were text," said Cosmo. "One of them looked like a table of contents—probably for the other drives. I didn't have time to look at it closely, but I noticed that there was one entry for High Hopes. Next to it was typed, 'Mary has the key.'."

"That would be Mary Jane Ontario, said Roger. "We've got to find that lady." He turned to me and pointed to the door. "Young man, get thee to the commune and find out what you can. I'll call Foxy and you can stop by to pick up supplies on the way out of town."

"Aren't you coming?" I protested.

Roger shook his head. "Petunia and I have a meeting with the two lunks who broke into Aunt May and Beau's house. First time we talked to them, the police were around, so we couldn't be persuasive enough to be sure they were telling all they knew. I have a feeling today's conversation may be a bit too physical for your tender eyes, so we'll take care of that while you take care of this. Git amovin'."

"What's the rush?" I asked. "These do not sound like people who are going to be doing much more than sitting around all day getting high."

"The sooner we find out about that piece of land, the sooner we figure out what's going on," said Roger. "Everything is moving too fast and this is a great big loose end which feels like it will take a while to track down, so hustle buns, BB."

I was going to protest some more, just for the principle of the thing, but Nacho slapped the table. "I gotta get ready for the lunch crowd. Time for all you little dicks to shuffle off."

When Nacho spoke, everyone listened. We all stood up and went on our appointed rounds.

Finding High Hopes was not simple. No signs. Just a lot of dirt roads branching off other dirt roads. I don't know if they were actively discouraging visitors or just didn't care. In the days before apps that gave guidance to the most rural areas just by inputting the latitude and longitude, I guess you had to know someone who would take you. I trusted my phone as it sent me down a series of ever more rutted paths. Brown County is mostly rural. It's very pretty, especially during the fall, when those who will drive long distances to see leaves in colors other than green flock to the area. Not having much interest in folk art, camping, or activities that involve walking up rugged hills, I had not been a frequent visitor. However, I had an assignment and not completing it would curry the displeasure of Roger, which I could deal with, and Nacho, which I could not.

The road ended in front of a ramshackle building of the sort put together by industrious hippies of bygone days, who demonstrated their freedom from repressive norms by embracing odd angles, natural materials, and macrame. Sections were unfinished, apparently when the builders wandered off to chase butterflies or a high. Nothing had been maintained. High Hopes had not withstood the passage of time very well, although it had not fallen down. There were a couple of cars of questionable functionality parked casually in the yard. A rusted bicycle leaned against the porch railing.

I got out, rubbing my butt to encourage blood flow and called out, as I didn't want to frighten the inhabitants and doubted there was such a thing as a doorbell.

After a bit, the door opened and a plump, balding no longer young man wearing drawstring pants, no shirt, bent wire rimmed glasses and a hazy smile came out, looked around, and stretched. He probably had been a cute young thing many years before and hadn't bothered to acquire any other skills. I had met others like him. As cuteness faded, they relied more and more on the hesitancy of others to send a brother off to find other places to crash. But eventually, hints to move on would become demands and they would attach themselves to another unwary soul. These once cute wastrels were terminally lazy and basically benign, but unwilling to contribute anything except opinions, of which they always had many.

"Hey man," he said. "Got any smokes?"

"Sorry," I said. "I don't smoke."

He looked vaguely perturbed and a glimmer of suspicion flickered in his face. I wasn't providing his needs, so I might be *bad*, in his dichotomous world of good and bad. I noticed I was losing him, so I said, "If you are MoonStar, I'm looking for some information and I do have some very good bud to share."

He immediately brightened. His personal pendulum of judgment had swung back to me being *good*.

"I'm MoonStar. What are you looking for? What kind of bud?"

I knew which question he was mostly interested in. I stepped up to the porch and pulled out the small baggie Foxy had provided. A thick joint nestled on top of gooey green buds. I had done this dance plenty of times. Don't start with questions. In fact, don't start with talking. Start with fire. I lit the joint, took a hit and passed it over. He took a hit. Held it without passing the joint back, greedy little bastard, took another hit, then passed it back. Now, as far as he was concerned, we were best friends. Now we could talk.

"I'm trying to find out about a commune that used to be out here," I said. "A friend told me that if anyone knew anything, it would be MoonStar."

The wastrel took another large hit and spread out his arms like a god embracing his creation. "You found me. You found it. High Hopes is all around us."

"Are there other people who live here?"

"Some people from time to time. Most of them have places in town for when the going gets too tough out here." He fixed me with a stoned, but meaningful look. "It takes a real commitment to stay out here all the time. You got to get real with yourself. Plus, you have to carry all the water from down the hill and we compost everything—and I mean everything." He gestured to an outhouse at the edge of the clearing. "Most people can't handle it."

"But you can?"

He grinned. "I'm here all the time. I haven't left except to go for food or smoke for a couple of years now. I've been coming around for a lot longer than that."

"So, do you own the place?"

"Shit man. Land can't be owned. It belongs to nature. To the world."

"But someone actually does hold the deed to this place. In fact, all the land around here has recently been sold. This is the only place that hasn't sold."

MoonStar nodded wisely, like he knew all of this. I had my doubts.

"The deed is still registered to Mary Jane Ontario, but no one knows where she is."

"Mary Jane," he said, obviously trying to pull something out of his memories. "Mary Jane, Mary Jane, Mary Jane." Then his face lit up. "She was the first goddess. She always said she had protected the land with a fence of solid gold. That's why it's so mellow out here. Nice old lady. A bit pushy, but she made sure we all ate and stayed high. She liked my music. I play guitar and mandolin. You wanna hear a song, man?"

I tried to keep him on track. "Mary Jane. That's right. Have you seen her recently?"

He shook his head. "No man. Not for years and years. She had the hots for me. 'Course I was a lot younger then. It was when I just showed up. She had the hots for most of the guys." He grinned. "Had most of the guys, if you know what I mean. Except her old man. She didn't like him much."

I nodded. He was on the right track now and I didn't want him veering off onto a side street of past conquests. "When did she leave?"

He shook his head again. "Long time ago. No one's seen her for years. She had a blow out with her old man and left. I was here when it happened. In fact, I was the one who was with her when her old man blew up. She grabbed her stuff and headed out, saying she was leaving and never coming back. And I called after her, 'What about me?' and she stopped and said, 'You'll always have High Hopes, MoonStar. You'll always have High Hopes.'."

He looked a bit sad, catching a fleeting memory of who he had been oh so many years ago, a cute young thing with his whole life ahead of him and girls and boys throwing themselves at him. He looked at me. "And that's why I've stayed. But I never heard from her again."

"Are you sure she didn't leave a deed to the property

somewhere?"

"Naw. I went through her stuff. I was looking for an address or something." He laughed. "Also looking to see if she left behind any money or weed, but no. Just some old clothes."

I figured that I had plumbed the very shallow depths of this guy. It was time to go. He noticed my leaving vibe and laid a friendly hand on my arm.

"Hey, how about another toke, man? I've got a killer bamboo bong. I made it myself."

I reached into my pocket for the baggie and as I pulled it out, a random thought floated through my brain. "Hey, when Mary Jane was still here, did she ever have a friend named Opal?"

MoonStar brightened. "For sure. I remember that lady. She was a lot classier than most of the people that came out here, but she could handle herself OK. Opal." He nodded with a smile. "Fun lady. She and Mary Jane were pretty tight. She came out every full moon. We had a special party on the full moon. You know, that's when the Earth's power is strongest." He was losing himself in the memory. "Some wild times man."

I handed him the baggie that Foxy had given me and thanked him. He went in search of his bong and I wandered off to my car, glad that my semi-hippie phase had not left me lost in the woods.

Chapter 23 - Antique Mall

I was on my way back to town when Roger texted.

"Meet me Ponce Antique Mall @3."

I pulled off the road. This was going to be an interesting conversation and I can concentrate on avoiding meth-soaked drivers or a conversation, but not both. Piloting two tons of metal on winding roads with the occasional stoner, trucker, or run-of-the-mill idiot is something I like to focus on when I'm doing it. Silly, but true.

"Why would you want to have anything to do with Matt Ponce? On his best days, he's an antisocial bully who enjoys a good fight. Going into his lair is all kinds of stupid."

"I'm going because he asked—nicely. And because he said he had some information about the church that might interest me. You're going because he said he had a couple of questions he wanted to ask you and if you weren't there to share, he wouldn't have anything to say."

"What about the lunks who threatened Aunt May? I thought you had an appointment with them."

"Still in the hospital. They just aren't making muscle like they used to. I don't want to talk to them while they're sedated. It won't be as fun. They won't be able to feel Petunia's persuasion. I don't want to talk to Freddy Flash until I get what I want from those two. So, time was hanging heavy on my hands when Matt Ponce called. And here we are. Or will be, once you get here."

"Matt has goons, too. Is Petunia going with us for protection?"

"Naw. We're just going to talk. Matt assured me that this is to be a friendly conversation. He isn't going to pull anything that close to city hall and in his place of business. Besides, ye of little faith, I am not exactly helpless in dangerous situations."

I sighed. Roger never took no for an answer, so I knew the only thing I was accomplishing was delaying the inevitable. "All right. I'll be there."

"Knew you would. Did you find out anything useful at High Hopes?"

"Not much. No one knows anything about the deed. No one has the money to be paying the taxes. The guy out there is certain that it was left to him and his ilk in perpetuity. Of course, he probably also believes in alien abduction and fairies."

"I believe in fairies. I see them all around. I don't even have to clap my hands."

"Ha. Ha. He also said that Opal used to come out to visit while Mary Jane Ontario was still there."

"Now that's interesting. Another connection to Opal. That lady certainly got around. All roads and all that. Well, we'll file that away. See you soon."

The drive back was uneventful and I got to the antique mall right before three. Ponce had taken over one of the buildings around the old railroad depot, buying it for a dollar because it was in need of major repairs. The train had stopped running in the late 1960s and the depot and its support buildings were abandoned soon after. Being a Tuesday afternoon, the place was not very busy, so parking was easy. I saw Roger hanging out near the front of the building and we went in together.

Most antique malls are basically indoor garage sales. People rent booths and sell whatever they have gathered. Some specialize in jewelry, fine china, or flags. Some are little more than barely cleaned off dumpster finds. Because of my latest part-time job with the auction company, I knew that Matt Ponce actually supplied most of the merchandise in most of the booths. He sorted his finds, putting the crap in some booths and the cream in others. It gave the impression that there were different sellers and some gave better deals, the holy grail of most shoppers. Matt's game was that he stuck the good knockoffs in with trash and people were so busy trying to sneak out their supposedly valuable discovery that they didn't notice the pieces were fakes. A real class operation. Chipped pieces were in booths in the basement where the lighting sucked. He had a whole collection of little scams. Nothing that would get him arrested. Just cheap little rip offs, which described the place and the person.

I followed Roger up the stairs to the office. The door was locked, so we knocked. Typical. A bit of a power play to make us request entry. A buzzer buzzed. A lock clicked and Roger opened the door. Matt sat behind a desk across the room. No surprise. Another cheap power play, making someone come to him. However, sitting in a chair to the side was his brother, the future governor—at least in his mind. This *was* a surprise. Peter had a well-known rule of not being anywhere behind closed doors with a woman who wasn't his wife.

I didn't know if the policy covered girly-boys. He didn't look powerful. He looked like an assistant manager of a regional bank's branch at a struggling mall. If the branch closed, he could earn some money as a model for the little plastic man on the top of a wedding cake. His face was working on a look that told you he was listening carefully and considering something weighty. It wasn't really succeeding.

"You've been sticking your nose into things at the church." Matt spoke up. "You're trying to fuck up our plan to buy that block. You better back the fuck down."

There were no chairs for us to sit on. Another feeble power play. Roger looked around and noticed a coffee table off to the side, in front of a sofa. It was covered with dishes and candlesticks that someone, without knowledge of taste or style, might think had value. He walked over to the table and tipped it, so that everything fell to the floor, picked up the table and placed it so that it faced both Ponce brothers. It was still a bit low, so Roger looked around and saw some ledger books on a shelf. He grabbed a few to lift us high enough so we would be at the same height as Matt's chair and sat down.

At the first crash of glassware, Matt had stood and balled his fists. His brother had put on an I-am-concerned face.

Roger looked at Matt. "Sit the fuck down, Matt," he said pleasantly. "I didn't come here to arm wrestle or measure dicks. I know who would win. I came because you said you had some information. I wouldn't be surprised if that was a lie, but if it wasn't, then start talking. If it was, BB and I will be leaving. Oh, and Mr. Dick offered the shop to us first. You and yours just stuck your noses in. I never had you figured for a churchie Matt, particularly the kind of churchie that Reverend Felcher attracts. And you," for the first time, Roger looked at Peter Ponce, who quickly looked at the floor, "I had you figured for a much more televised place of worship. You never struck me as someone who did anything that didn't sell your brand."

Peter didn't have a scripted reply to that. His mouth moved a few times without sound coming out. Then he stammered, "It's the children. Having the children of the church near those people ... they need protection ... sanctuary."

"Seems to me that it's you who are pushing them closer to us," said Roger. "Seems like you are gathering a whole bunch of kids and stashing them right next to all us nasty homos. If we are the predators you always claim us to be, isn't that school you have planned kind of like delivering the cow, or chicken if you want to hold on to your fantasies, to the butcher?"

Peter was shocked out of words. He did his goldfish impression for a bit and finally managed to squeak, "How did you find out about the ..."

"Shut the fuck up, both of you," roared Matt, slamming his fist down on the table. "Roger, you have been poking your dick where it don't belong. You been doing a lot more than poking and it's got to stop. You don't need to know any more about the church than this—we are connected. Very connected. I got muscle, plenty of it. I got my brother here to show you we got connections with deep pockets and plenty of pull in this state. Your little dick agency needs a license to operate. So does that queer bar. So does that greasy spoon you all hang out in."

He picked up a pencil, snapped it in half and threw down the pieces. "All three could be gone just that easy.

So, back the fuck down. We want that block and we're going to get that block. Your little fag corner is gonna be gone faster than a fart in a windstorm. You butt pirates are going to have to find some other place to be freaks. This is bigger than you think. Much bigger. And the people you are screwing with are bigger than you can imagine." He sneered. "You're just a pimple on the ass of a whale."

Roger stood. "Matt, you seem to be obsessed with all things ass. That doesn't surprise me. Like attracts like. However, this conversation is a waste of time. If we stay any longer, you're going to whip out your dick and start slapping things with it. While that might excite your brother, I might puke." He turned to me, "Come on, BB. Time to go."

"Just a minute," said Matt and pointed at me. "You were the one with the truck at the Milbank dame's house. You, those other fags, and that old hag took a bunch of things that should have been mine. While I was there, some kid came by looking for his phone. He told me there was a box full of money and jewels in her bedroom. Stupid shit thought I'd split it with him. But it wasn't there. You took it. That don't count as furnishings. That box and everything in it is mine. I want it and I want it now."

I started to explain that we had permission to take anything we wanted, but Roger put a hand on my shoulder to stop me. "Matt, go fuck yourself," he said. "If you have a problem don't talk to BB about it. Talk to the lawyer. He gets paid to explain things so simply that even an ignoramus like you should be able to understand."

With that, Roger turned and walked out and I followed close behind.

Matt called out. "That box is mine. I'll get it one way or another. No one rips me off and gets away with it."

Outside, Roger turned to me. "Good job, BB. You didn't cry and you didn't pee yourself. Let's swing by Daddy's. Nacho needs to hear about this."

"About what?" I asked.

"This has just gotten a whole lot more interesting. It's about more than a storefront. More than a block. It's certainly about more than some geegaws you got from a dead woman's house. This is a whole lot bigger. Peter Ponce would not have showed up and threatened us unless something very big was going on."

"But he didn't threaten us. Matt did."

"Matt did the talking, but Peter wouldn't have been there unless he wanted to show the power lined up on their side. He also wanted to make sure that Matt didn't talk too much. They wouldn't have shown the depth of their interest unless they knew we were getting close, so hang on sugar, there're some bumpy nights ahead."

"Fabulous," I sighed.

"Like I said, we need to go to Daddy's. I need to talk to Nacho and you need a drink or five."

Chapter 24 - Wednesday

The next morning, I went to work. Ed's Removal and Auction House was a refuge from all the craziness swirling around. I wasn't an essential cog. I could pack and unpack without much breakage and I occasionally had knowledge of some obscure item, which allowed me to put it in one of the lots for the auction without wasting time looking it up. It was fun to see the stuff that filled people's lives. Treasures they simply couldn't live without until they either weren't living or weren't cognizant. Then, what had been treasured became trash, until it was scooped up to begin life anew in someone else's collection of stuff.

It was pleasant enough work. There was no danger of large people attacking me, which was a definite plus. The time flew by and when I looked up, it was already two-thirty. I usually left between two and three. There were days when things were busy and I stayed later, but as I think Jesus said, "There will always be stuff," so there was no need to try to prove something to somebody by working late. I have spent years trying to rid myself of the deadly combination of Christian work ethic and Jewish guilt and I'm finally seeing some positive results. I finished the box I was working on, said goodbye, and headed out the door. I planned to walk. This is a new attempt at exercise for me. It makes me feel I am doing something to make my pants fit less snugly. There is a flaw to the plan, as Cresent Doughnuts is located near the halfway point. I am trying to convince myself that muscle weighs more than fat and since I am building muscle by walking ... However, Roger was waiting in his car. It looked like he had plans for me.

Roger rolled down the window. "Get in," he said. "We have a meeting. Actually, we have two."

"Who, where, and why?" I asked, getting in.

"The first is at Daddy's. We have an information exchange planned with Nacho. The next is with Freddy Flash."

"I have no problem going to Daddy's and seeing Nacho. I do have qualms about Mr. Flash. I thought his goons were still in the hospital and you weren't sure that they even were his goons. Besides, it sounds like he lives on the dangerous side of things and I know you have no illusions about my efficacy in a fight. Wouldn't Petunia be a better second?"

Roger snorted. "I don't want you there to fight. I want to demonstrate that I am there to talk, not fight, and the minute he sees you, he'll know I have no intention of fighting. Petunia would give the opposite impression. Besides, she's sleeping. She was up late last night. Went to the hospital dressed as a custodian and spent some time chatting with the goons. They were very interested in talking with her after she introduced herself."

"Introduced?"

Roger gave an evil smile. "Her introduction might have involved a few sharp objects. Late night in a hospital, the staff is short-handed, overburdened, and over-tired. She had a while to chat and made use of the time."

"I don't think I want to know."

"I am sure you don't and the specifics are not important. The goons confirmed that it was Freddy Flash who sent them and that the jewels and any piles of money were what they were after. After chatting with them, Petunia suggested that it would be a good idea for both of them to take in the sights of Chicago or some other city a distance away from Magawatta. She left them with enough money to shuffle off to Buffalo and mentioned how unhappy she would be if she discovered they did not follow her advice. I checked with the hospital this morning. They both had slipped away between shifts, leaving no forwarding address and lifting a few narcotics from the meds cart that was making the rounds."

By this time, we had parked down the street from the bar. I knew that protesting our meeting with Freddy Flash would be pointless, but the opportunity to relax beforehand and suck up a bit of liquid courage was appealing.

I followed Roger into Daddy's and headed out to the patio. Lester was on his regular stool at the front bar, noticing everybody who came in. It occurred to me that he probably knew more about the comings and goings of Daddy's than anyone except Nacho. How Nacho knew was a mystery that I didn't dare investigate. I caught Lester's eye in the mirror and with a nod invited him out to the patio. He winked and gave a slight shake. He seemed happy where he was, unnoticed, but noticing. On the patio, Beau and Aunt May were already at our table, sipping drinks. We tended to arrive early on Wednesdays, as that was the night TiaRa hosted her amateurs' show. Unless she insisted, we usually went home before the show started. While I heartily approve of people slipping into something more comfortable to body and proclivity and learning how to work it, the early attempts are often painful to watch.

Roger went back to talk with Nacho while I replenished my liquid levels with Aunt May and Beau. A couple of drinks into the conversation, Nacho clumped out to the table, Roger following close behind.

"Sounds like you were almost useful yesterday," Nacho said,

sitting down and holding a match to the ever-present cigar. "I got a couple more pieces of the puzzle. You didn't check out Gibson."

"Gibson?" I asked.

Aunt May patted her lips with her lace hanky. "I believe that was the name of the lawyer who handled Opal's estate. I remember being taken aback by how uncouth he was. That, in itself is unsurprising when dealing with an attorney, but for Opal to have entrusted her estate to such a person did seem out of character. However, as I was reviewing the folders she'd left for me, I discovered the reason. There are some graphic photos of Mr. Gibson. While his face is not appealing, when seeing him *au natural*, his face is not what draws the eye. I have seen longer implements and I have seen implements of greater girth, however, his combination of the two is quite unparalleled in my experience, which as you know is not insignificant. And while the pictures might cause some embarrassment should they be exposed, as it were, that would be balanced with the pride of letting the world know of his endowment. However, there were also some documents which exposed his part in a few questionable activities, which would be difficult to explain away at the very least, and might result in disbarment and even incarceration. I believe Mr. Gibson suspects I have those documents, but is not sure. If necessary, I believe I could persuade Mr. Gibson to provide information if you know what you need."

"Don't bother," said Nacho. "I didn't know what we were looking for, so I had some of my associates poke around. I got interested when you told me that the lawyer fronting for all those land purchases was Gibson."

I had missed that completely. At least I reported my conversation with Adelston, the recorder of Brown County with enough detail that Nacho had picked up on the name. I began to mumble an apology or excuse, but Nacho waved the cigar at me to shut me up. It worked because I immediately started to choke on the smoke.

"Gibson has been on our radar for a while. His name has cropped up a few times in sketchy circumstances. Kinda like dung beetles hang around shit. Where you find one, look around and you'll find the other. When you mentioned him, I had someone poke around on his server."

"How did you get access to his server?" I asked, then realized that I really didn't want to know how and Nacho wouldn't tell me. I shook my head quickly. "Sorry. Never mind. Stupid question."

Nacho continued as if I hadn't said anything. "Funny thing, he's also the attorney for the BASIC School Management company and the BASIC Charter Academy. Remember them?"

"That's the school that the churchies want to start," I said.

Nacho nodded. "Bingo. And you'll never guess what we found in a password-protected file in the directory for that school."

"How did you get into a password protected ..." I stopped. Again, a question I didn't want to know the answer to.

"Oh do tell," Beau said. "You know you want to." Beau must have started drinking early. He would never have been so flippant with Nacho otherwise. He was lucky. Nacho just shot him a glare that would have stunned an ox at fifty paces. Beau mumbled an apology.

"Plans for a great big campus stuck out there in the hills of Brown County." Buildings, dorms, and a great big wall around the entire place. Gonna cost millions."

"But can they do that?" I asked.

Nacho shrugged. "Probably. Zoning is pretty lax out there. Plus, as you found out, most of the people that need to approve it are on the church board."

174

"What's to say it's really going to be a school?" asked Beau. "It could be a training ground for soldiers for Christ. The wall could be to keep people out as much to keep students in."

"It's possible," said Nacho. "All we know for sure is that they are building something big once they get that final chunk of land."

"I still don't understand why they would plan it in Brown County," I said. "There are plenty of big parcels of land close to Magawatta. We're closer to the main power grid for utilities and internet. Brown County is barely wired for electricity. The whole Magawatta planning commission is on the board, so they could get nearly anything passed. Why Brown County?"

"Don't know," said Nacho. "We know where and have an idea of what. Now we have to find out why."

"I still want to know where Opal Milbank fits into all this," said Roger.

"And my BVM," I said. "Someone wanted it enough to break into my house."

"Oh screw your Virgin Mary," said Beau. "You didn't have thugs break down your door and threaten you. I still feel shaky."

"You'd feel less shaky if you stopped drinking so much," said Roger.

"It's drinking that is keeping me calm," replied Beau.

"Untwist your panties," said Nacho, standing up. "There's a good chance that was a whole different pile of shits. Sounds to me like they heard from the frat boy you had some things worth something and decided to take it. A whole lot more amateur than this school thing. But for now, I got a place to run. Just wanted you all to keep your eyes out for any information that might float by about the churchies' Brown

County plans."

With that, Nacho stomped off.

Roger looked at me. "Time for our next meeting," he said.

I really didn't want to go, but there was no helping it. I downed the rest of my drink, waved goodbye to Aunt May and Beau and followed Roger, off to what I imagined would be my death.

Chapter 25 - Freddy Flash

I thought we would be heading to the main location of U-Betcha Pawn, tucked between the post office and a car wash, down the block from a liquor store and a fast-food drive through that specialized in extra greasy burgers with a retro theme. However, Roger headed to the far west side of town, where a number of developments had erupted in the past few years. After passing through the half-wall, stone entrance which proudly proclaimed we were now traversing the paradise that was Meadow Pyle Estates, the roads became smooth and wide, with gentle curves. The houses were close together and looked like they had been stamped out in a factory and assembled in place. People were rarely seen except when making the walk from front door to car. It was the perfect place for an army of replicants to hide before arising to enslave the townsfolk.

But while the creepy community was well suited for robots, it did not seem like the kind of place someone named Freddy Flash, who ran a pawn shop and engaged in numerous illegal activities would hang his hat. I said as much to Roger.

"Looks can be deceiving, grasshopper," he said. "I believe that out here, Freddy blends into the beige landscape." He pulled into the driveway of a midsized house that looked exactly like the houses on either side. The rectangle of lawn was unnaturally green. Next to the door was a small, sad flower garden framing a 3-foot-high resin fountain which featured an angel pouring water from a never empty jug over a pile of equally plastic seashells. I had seen such things in home 'improvement' stores and often wondered if anyone actually bought such things. Here I had my answer.

Roger rang the bell. Immediately a loud, angry barking echoed from inside the house. I took a step back. Roger grabbed my elbow and pulled me back up beside him.

"It's fake." He pointed to the doorbell, which I saw had a small camera embedded above the button. "He's watching us. These doorbells come with a bunch of prerecorded sounds, so you can set them, just like the ringer on your phone."

As my heart rate returned to normal, the door was opened by a short balding man who turned and headed into the living room, calling out, "Close the door behind you. It locks on its own."

I'm not sure what I had expected from Freddy Flash. I guess a mix between a character from *The Godfather* and a seventies pimp. I was relieved, if a little disappointed. Freddy Flash looked like a cross between an accountant and a high school guidance counselor.

I was confused. This couldn't be the same person who had sent a couple of big, bad men to beat up and steal from Aunt May. This was not a drug dealer to college frat boys seeking date-rape drugs or a person who could scare the likes of Thad Wroks into doing his bidding. He was wearing a sweater with pockets. Horn-rimmed glasses that looked like they had been cool in the fifties, but were not being worn ironically or in an attempt to be retro. He stood in the middle of the room. Hands in his pockets, head cocked, studying us.

I looked around the room and was proud I didn't gasp or laugh. It looked like the decorator had a serious addiction to home decorating shows, online shopping networks, and the cheesiest of home décor stores. Everywhere I turned was something that hurt my sensibilities. There were wall decals proclaiming this to be the Crystal Palace. A gaudy faux-crystal chandelier hung from light-bedecked chains over a table. A more traditional looking, but still obviously plastic, crystal chandelier hung in the middle of the sitting room. Translucent tiles framed the kitchen countertops. Framed paintings of cute cats with Margaret Keene big eyes hung in lieu of art. I don't have a great deal of taste, but I knew that if Suave or Beau saw this, they would close their eyes tightly and exit quickly, hoping the sight had not blinded or permanently scarred them.

"It's my girlfriend's place," said Freddy. The explanation did not seem intended to excuse the taste as much as the femininity of the room. "She likes to decorate. She even has giant fake flowers glued to the wall over the bed. But she's gone during the day and the place can't be bugged. She's a private citizen with no connection to my business. Any surveillance in this neighborhood would stand out like big tits on a nun. Besides, my bully boys don't like it and I get more work done when they aren't around. But I made it clear that this is not a place for any kind of rough stuff. You understand?"

Roger nodded. "Sure. That's why I brought BB. Look at him. I wouldn't try anything violent with him around. He might break."

Freddy smiled and nodded. "So what do you want? I'm busy and I don't like chit chat."

"The thugs you sent to visit Aunt May and Beau limped out of town last night, but not before they pointed the finger at you."

Freddy shrugged. "Can't believe everything someone like that tells you. I'm glad they're gone. Once they meet Petunia, they'll always be rabbits, hesitating and looking over their shoulders. They were useful and you broke them." He looked at Roger. "I have more, plenty more. People expect it. There's a need in this business."

I couldn't stop myself. "Freddy Flash? You don't look like a Freddy Flash. How can you—" I ran out of words.

Freddy smiled. "Sheldon," he said. "Sheldon Flaxman. But in my business, a stage name and stage persona go a long way toward reducing the need for violence. Most of the job calls for an accountant, keeping track of incoming and outgoing money and merchandise. That's my training and that's what I'm good at. But Freddy Flash and the bully boys allow me to pay attention to what's important and keeps people from trying stupid stunts. Any other questions?"

Roger spoke up. "I appreciate your being forthright. Let me return the favor. I can't have Aunt May or Beau attacked again. Both Nacho and I have considerable resources, as you know. May and Beau are friends and we will protect them, whatever the cost."

Freddy, or Sheldon, didn't take his hands out of his pockets. He studied Roger silently.

"You are operating under false information," continued Roger. "The contents of that box is not worth what you are risking. I assume that the frat boy told you it was filled with expensive jewelry. You must know that one of the few things frat boys are good at, is lying. Another is making stupid mistakes. The jewels are all fakes. Good ones, but worth hundreds at most, certainly not thousands. The money that was in the box is now in the bank. It's just not worth what you are risking."

Freddy shook his head. "You don't understand—the situation or me. Do you think I'm stupid enough to sell stolen property? The return on something like that is never worthwhile. You can only do that kind of thing if you do a deal and then disappear. I have no desire to move all the time. I'm comfortable here."

"Then why are you ..."

"First, I'm not saying I'm behind this. But if I was, I wouldn't be doing it for the pieces themselves. A much more profitable and safer venture would be acquisition for a third party. And if that third party was well connected to various powers that exist within government and law enforcement, they could not only offer to provide money and protection but also threaten to act on one's lack of assistance. That combination of carrot and stick would be a powerful motivator. Of course, I am speaking hypothetically. I really have no idea what you are talking about. I don't believe I know these people you mentioned, but if I did and I had heard of any interest in their possessions by powerful people, I would advise them to leave that box on the porch, in plain sight and go away for a few hours, because powerful people often have more than one way to skin a cat and don't really care if the cat or the cat's friends don't like the skinning."

Roger didn't reply. He just stared at the man for a minute. Then he nodded slowly.

Freddy took his hands out of his pockets. He had a phone in one hand, which he glanced down at. "I need to take this call," he said. "This has been a most interesting chat, but I'll have to let you go now."

He gestured toward the door.

Without a word, Roger turned and went to the door. I followed. Freddy let us out, closing and locking the door behind us. We got in the car and backed out of the driveway.

"Do you believe him?" asked Roger.

"He reminds me of my Uncle Murray. Murray was a master of not saying things, but what he said was always the truth. He couldn't lie to save his life."

"So, he's been hired to get that box. There's something about that box or those fake jewels that someone wants."

"What do you think we should do? And, hey, what about my BVM? We didn't ask about the break-in at my house."

"It will take a couple of days for them to figure out another attack. I'll increase the drive-bys of May and Beau's house. I still don't think the two break-ins are connected. I think someone just has a hard on for the Blessed Virgin Mary. But when my people are watching May and Beau's, I'll have them swing by and make sure you haven't been violated. It's just down the block."

"That hardly seems like enough."

"You'll be fine. Come on. Let's go to Daddy's. A couple of drinks and you won't have a worry in the world."

I had my doubts that he was correct, but I was willing to try his solution, as long as he was paying.

Chapter 26 - Thursday

Far too early, I got a call from Suave.

"BB, I am afraid we need some help."

"Doing what?" Usually I would be catty, but Suave was not one of the gang. She and Foxy floated a bit above our humdrum lives, friendly visitors from above.

"We have some very early arrivals."

"Performers?" I asked. "They aren't supposed to be here until tomorrow."

"Well, these decided to drive so they could bring their entire wardrobe as well as their protégés. Once on the road they felt a bit anxious, so they didn't stop and drove all night. I just arrived at the mansion with some flowers and small pieces and found them hovering at the gate. We can't exactly leave them in the lobby. The poor dears have been driving for days and they are performing for free, to help the cause."

"I see what you mean. But what do you want me to do? TiaRa knows where everyone is supposed to sleep."

"Yes, TiaRa would be splendid at this moment, however, you know how she responds to mornings."

"Badly."

"To say the least. Still, I would disturb her, but she has turned her phone off. I know the room assignments and thankfully, we set up all the rooms yesterday so we could spend today making final touches to the main room and stage. However, we have no sustenance. No food. No drink. Would you be a dear and do a supply run?"

"For how many?"

"We don't know how many will show up today. At this point, there are five performers, each with a protégé. Perhaps you should plan for five more couples, just to be sure."

"I can get some things, but Suave, I don't have much ..."

She interrupted. "Oh do forgive me, dear boy. I forget the simplest things. You will not have to pay for it. Go to McCays. Just mention Foxy and tell them if they wish, they can call me for confirmation. In fact, I will call them right now and place an order. That way, you will not have to make decisions. I am an early bird, but as I recall, it takes you a bit in the morning to focus properly. Yes, just go pick it up and bring it here and you will have brought joy to many a queen. Come as quickly as you can, my dear."

"OK, Suave. I'll call when I'm on my way, just in case there are any changes in your plans.

"You are a dear," said Suave and hung up.

From that start, my day continued to involve patching one hole only to receive a frantic call from TiaRa or Suave or Roger to fetch, fix, or ferry. Despite the crazy cries for immediate attention, by midafternoon the mansion was sparkling and ready. The early arrivals had been comfortably put up in their rooms and the rooms of the yet-to-arrive were fully fluffed. I had garnered thanks from Suave and noncommittal grunts from Roger, which was his version of high praise. TiaRa had taken a few of the visiting royalty on a tour of Magawatta, with an aside to me, "Try to get some rest, dear. You are looking a tad bit haggard. Tomorrow Fantasia arrives and she can be quite demanding, so you'll need to be on your toes."

Joy. If today hadn't been up to the level of demands that I could expect from Fantasia, who would command me as her personal maid and servant, perhaps it was time to pray for an early death or at least a tiny little coma. The thought of a coma gave me an idea. Perhaps I should stop by to see my dear friends Beau and Aunt May. Like Pooh Bear, it was always time for a little taste of something when I went to visit them. In Pooh's case, it was honey. In our case, we generally sought something a bit more liquid.

I was heading toward their house, considering what sort of something would go well with an afternoon nap after too busy a morning and before a certain to be stressful day, when my phone rang. I sighed, thinking the trio must have discovered something else that absolutely *had* to be done and couldn't be done by anyone but me.

I was surprised that the number displayed was Foxy. Hmmm. Conversations with Foxy were always interesting. Visits with Foxy always involved quality consumables. I answered, actually hoping for a summons to visit.

"BB, dear boy, I fear you are dreadfully busy and being pulled in many directions at once." The dulcet tones filled my ear.

"It's been pretty wild," I said. "I think the worst is over, at least for today. I'm heading over to Beau's house to relax."

"Ah, you make my plea doubly difficult. However, you are the only one who I can trust and this is frightfully important and I *do* promise to reward you generously if you could find it in your heart to do one more service."

"Foxy, you have been more than generous more times than I can count. I'm tired, but for you ... Maybe I should ask what you need first."

"A pick up, my dear boy. That is all."

"I thought you had a truck for the store."

"Ah, no. I did not make myself clear. I will provide the car. It is the driver I need."

"Oh, sure. Where, when and who?"

"One of my closest, most dear friends is arriving shortly by air. He is attending the show on Saturday, but he is also here to help me. He will be staying with us. Unfortunately, I have just been detained. As I told you, a secretive cabal has been attempting a coup of my company and I have just discovered an opportunity to purchase a large block of stock. If I do not snap it up, the opposing forces will, so I must attend to this until the deal is consummated. However, the man who schooled me in business and helped me start the Pie Hole is due to arrive forthwith and I would not, cannot, leave him receptionless. Could you? Would you stand in my stead to greet him?"

"Sure Foxy. I'll go right now. What airline? What flight number? When does it arrive?"

"Oh dear boy. He is not flying commercial. And he is not flying into the Indianapolis Airport. He has his own plane and is landing in Magawatta. You know we have a small airport west of town. That is where he shall be and he shall be there within the half hour."

"OK. That's easier. I'll head out there now."

"No, no, BB. I could not ask him to ride in your car. I do not mean to criticize, but for this man, a car as utilitarian as yours would be a discomfort. You must swing by and pick up our car. It has been detailed just for this occasion and appropriate food and beverage have been laid in to make him comfortable. Additionally, the car is known to the ground crew, so you will not have to go to the parking lot. Drive directly to the gate marked "Planes". Ask where Aristide DeJoie's plane is landing and they shall point the way.

Aristide will also recognize the car. I will have texted him to expect you. Bring him here. By that time, all this bargaining will be over and we will be able to relax. You will enjoy meeting Aristide. Not only is he a most interesting person, he may well know who is behind this attack on my position. He is my most trusted friend and a trusted person in business is a rare find indeed. So, hurry, BB. Please. I will be in your debt."

Foxy did tend to be a bit on the long-winded side. By the time he had finished his explanation, I had arrived at Casa KitTan. I didn't mind doing a favor anyway, but the chance to drive Foxy's car was more than enough payback. I don't care much about cars, but Foxy had a fully restored 1966 Cadillac Fleetwood 75. It was a grand boat of a car, something like the *Queen Elizabeth* on wheels. I had never even been inside the thing. Foxy rarely took it out and it lived in style in its own garage, under a soft cover. Now, I was going to pilot the superb land yacht. It was a real indication of Foxy's trust in me, his desperation, and his regard for the man I was picking up, all coming together to give me the experience of a lifetime. I offered a little thank you to the powers of the universe, along with a small prayer that I didn't fuck up and put even the tiniest scratch on the magnificent machine.

Foxy met me at the door, phone in one hand and keys in the other. He didn't stop talking on the phone as he walked me to the garage, unveiled the car, and handed me the keys. He kissed his hand and laid his hand on my cheek. I'm not sure if it was a thank you, a blessing, or his own prayer that I brought his car and friend back safely, but at that moment, a new conversation broke out which grabbed his total attention, so with a nod of thanks, he turned and went back toward the house, while I got in the car. It started like a well-oiled whore and off I went to the small airport on the edge of town.

The trip was flawless. I arrived and was directed toward a plane that was just pulling to a stop. The door opened and a giant of a man leapt out as the stairs unfolded. He had a suitcase in his hand, which compared to his grand size, looked like an attaché, instead of the full-sized suitcase it was. Everything about this man was large. He seemed to glow with an unworldly power. I would have been intimidated, except he turned his smile on me and, like from some blessed guru, that smile filled me with a deep calm. All my worries fell away. It was as if I had known him all my life and seeing this radiant being again was the best thing that had ever happened.

His gigantic hand wrapped around mine. "You must be BB. Foxy texted me that you were doing me the honor of collecting me. I am Aristide and I am sure we will be great friends. So, let us get to my dear friend Foxy and see how we can sooth what is troubling his mind."

I stuttered a bit and finally got out a question. "Do you have any luggage?"

"Only this case and I will keep it with me. I will sit back here," he opened the back door and climbed in, "and you will take us to the man."

"Do we need to do anything about the plane? Close the door or anything?"

Aristide waved his hand as if it was inconsequential. "The crew will take care of everything. We need only concern ourselves with our journey." He pulled the door closed. I got back in the car and carefully drove back to town while Aristide hummed and glowed in the back.

We pulled up at Casa KitTan and Foxy was already out of the house, pulling open Aristide's door and sweeping him into an enormous hug. The two held onto each other as if they were brothers at arms who had been separated by the Great War. No words, I just looked on. There are moments when one can only be an outsider, but it is a privilege to be able to see that such affection is possible. It makes the world a bit warmer.

After several minutes, they broke the embrace and Foxy ushered us both into the house. I felt like I should leave them to their reunion, but Foxy would have none of it.

"I will be forever grateful, BB. You are the only person I could trust with such a precious friend. I am certain that you and Aristide are destined to know each other. While you possess enough differences to keep things interesting, you both have souls reliable and true, a rare thing in this world. Besides," here he gave his most seductive smile, "I have just acquired some Thai weed that was actually grown in the rain forest of Thailand, renowned for the richness of its soil. These plants are the product of selective breeding over decades and feature red and purple, crystal-covered hairs. Then, at the height of potency, they are harvested, hand wrapped to hold in the THC, and dipped in a secret mixture which, I am assured, includes a small amount of raw opium. The newly born Thai stick cures and further increases the potency. Only a small amount of this artisan delight is ever exported, but I have managed to procure some as a special welcome for Aristide and, as a thank you to you, I must insist that you join us."

It would be rude to turn down such an offer and I was raised not to be rude, so I agreed. Soon we were sitting in Foxy's comfortable smoking room. Aristide's things had been put away. Glasses of excellent liquor had been provided, and an ebony pipe, beautifully carved and inlaid with veins of silver and gold intertwined, was being passed. The first hit made lovely little explosions of pleasure ignite in my head and down my spine. The second made my entire being vibrate with utter contentment. I turned down the third pass, as I still had things to do next month and I was not sure I would be functional by then.

I sat, happily contemplating the flames of the candelabra on the table. Foxy spoke. "Aristide, it is always a treat to see you and I believe you will enjoy the show on Saturday. It should be exquisite. However, you know I have other things on my mind."

Aristide nodded. "I wondered if you would prefer waiting until we were alone."

"I thank you for your discretion, but BB is not only a trusted friend, but also is the researcher I rely upon when investigating matters I wish to remain private. You may speak freely in front of him. And BB?"

I pulled my attention away from the flickering flames. "Hmmm?"

"Please, my dear, this information is vital to me, so I beg you to pay the closest attention possible. In addition, it is not to be shared with anyone and I do mean *anyone*. I shall probably share it with Roger and Nacho, but do not presume that I have. Allow me to share what I wish, how I wish, and when I wish. If these strictures make you uncomfortable, please say so now and I will release you from your post."

It took a minute for Foxy's verbiage to filter through the Thai stick. I realized he and Aristide were looking at me, expecting an answer. I concentrated and reviewed the last few sentences and finally understood what they were waiting for. "Sure, Foxy," I said. "Mum's the word. All I ask is that if you do tell Roger or Nacho, don't tell them I knew about it first. That would be ..."

Foxy nodded and smiled, "Uncomfortable, yes, I understand." He turned to Aristide. "So, my friend. Have you discovered what someone could possibly offer that would make my dear investors consider removing me completely from the Pie Hole? What would reward them better than leaving me at the helm of my own ship? We have been and continue to be extraordinarily profitable. I only exercise control in extraordinary circumstances."

Aristide fixed Foxy with a stare. "I would never have believed it would be possible to overturn the management of the Pie Hole. I thought we had made it impossible, but in business, as you know, all things are possible. It still may fail, but whoever is behind it has found a perfect crowbar to separate you from your company."

"And what might that be?"

"Gold. A large, thick, undiscovered vein of gold in a nearby county. The land has been acquired. Officials who will look the other way in return for appropriate donations have been approached."

"Are you talking about Brown County?" I asked.

"That is the name I have heard."

"I've read about gold in Brown County, but it's just specks and flakes. People go up for a weekend vacation. They learn to pan, slog around in the creeks, and come back with a couple of bucks worth of gold for their trouble. I've been invited to go gold hunting a few times by people here on vacation, but I've never been tempted."

"What is being suggested," said Aristide, "is a far larger operation. It involves pit mining, where the top layer of ground is stripped away in order to expose the vein underneath. Truckloads of dirt are washed to claim any bits of gold trying to sneak off. The claim is that the gold is near the surface, so once the top layer of earth is scraped off, a plethora of nuggets (not flakes) that are easily captured and potentially worth billions are to be had for the taking. But in order to be allowed the opportunity to buy shares in the gold-mining operation, one must own sufficient shares in the Pie Hole and be willing to overturn your ethical veto clause."

"I simply do not understand the connection between my company and a gold mine," said Foxy.

"Money," replied Aristide. "The Pie Hole is undervalued. You have always insisted on more expensive processes."

"If I did not, the quality of the product would suffer. My insistence on quality has kept the Pie Hole a haven of delectability. You know that!"

"I do. However, you also know that if one sold the name, lowered the quality, and moved into markets you have eschewed, such as mass-produced snacks available at grocery stores, an enormous amount of money could be made for a few years, before the brand lost its shine. My sources tell me that there is a buyer lined up who intends to do just that. With the money made by selling the reputation of the Pie Hole, the start-up costs of the gold mine would be covered, with a hefty bonus for whoever is behind this plot."

"Hold on a minute," I said. "There's no way anyone could dig an open-pit mine in Brown County. It just can't happen. Brown County is nothing but artists and hippies and trees. If anyone starts ripping down beautiful vistas, there will be a revolution."

"That problem has been solved. The general public will see plans for a large school and retreat center. There will be a very tall wall all around the property, enclosing several acres, ostensibly to keep the students from getting lost or bothering the locals. However, once the wall is up, digging will begin in earnest."

I shook my head, trying to understand all this subterfuge, but I couldn't. "But that would mean that the churchies ..." I trailed off.

Foxy, however, understood the circuitous route that financial dealings often took. "I am impressed," he said. "A path very hard to trace, but each step follows the other most logically."

"Then please explain it to me," I said.

"It is the Ponce brothers. They are behind the land purchases in Brown County, the school, and the efforts of Reverend

Felcher's church. They convince their mother to invest in their school. She is a religious woman and will like the idea of a school that promotes good Christian values. The school will not take long to establish and promote, providing a ready supply of cash. This will allow them to pay back the mortgages they must have taken out to purchase the land in Brown County. I would guess that they have mortgaged themselves far beyond the extent allowed by any reasonable financial institution, so have reached out to, shall we say, unorthodox institutions.

"The mother provides enough money to start the school. The school provides enough money to hide the start of the mining operation. The sale of the Pie Hole provides the money to begin mining. The expansion of the school provides operating capital. And when the mine starts to produce gold, all are wealthy beyond their greediest dreams, while the school provides convenient cover, sheltering not only the work, but, I suspect, a great deal of the profits from taxes. The rich usually feel paying taxes is beneath them and heretical to their endeavors."

"And the need for that start-up money would come right about the time the sale of the Pie Hole would close," said Aristide, "if the current plot is successful."

Foxy shook his head in admiration. "Wheels within wheels. A truly devious plan." He looked at Aristide. "But how shall we stop it?"

Aristide took a sip from his drink. "It has been my experience," he said, "that plans with so many angles can often be toppled by knocking a single part out of alignment. What we must do is discover the most vulnerable point and see about tossing some sand in the gears. Then we can step back and watch the structure fall."

At this point, my phone rang. Roger. I picked up. "Yes, pumpkin, what do *you* have for me to do?"

"Get to Daddy's now. The cops are here. The sheriff is here. Indiana State Troopers are here. They claim some underage student got served and then was stopped for public intoxication walking home. They are threatening to haul everyone to jail and yank the liquor license. For now, the bar is closed to the public and the owners have to show up at a hearing first thing tomorrow."

"What can I ..."

"You can get your buns over here. Call Foxy and see if he'll come help. Tell him to bring his checkbook."

"I'm at Foxy's now. Hold on." I explained what was going on and Foxy agreed to gather what he could and meet us at Daddy's later.

I relayed this to Roger. "Great. I've got to get back to dealing with the cops. Wanna guess who's behind this?"

"Let me think ... would the name start with a P?"

"They're trying to take a bite out of the wrong ass. We have connections they haven't even thought about, but it's going to take some dancing to straighten things out."

"But the Legendary Cotillion is Saturday!"

"The Legendary Cotillion will go on as planned. Good thing everyone and everything is actually taking place at the Ontario Mansion. Everything will work out, but we need to circle the wagons. Get over here now."

He hung up.

Head spinning, I pointed myself toward Daddy's and the shit storm that lay ahead.

Chapter 27 – Thursday Night

It was not a group of happy campers that gathered around our table at Nacho Mama's Patio Café that evening. There had been many conversations with powers that were and lawyers and judges. The statement of the young man in question was in question. He was not available for questioning. No one could even find out his name. However, according to officialdom, he was sticking to his story and for now, that was all that mattered. No one was in jail, but the liquor license was suspended pending review. Everyone was grumpy, but Nacho was ready to rip someone apart.

"I sent out the word. This is a direct shot and we ain't gonna let it slide. I got our best working on it. Lawyers are challenging the suspension and all should be open by Sunday at the latest. We also are gonna find out everything about this kid. I wanna know his name, his address, his favorite fruit, and if he's a top, a bottom, or somewhere in between."

"I'm on it," said Roger. "First we have to find out who he is. Then we'll start digging. We'll know the last time he took a dump and how he liked the taste of it before I'm through."

I had brought everyone up to speed on Foxy's discoveries. Foxy had provided the necessary funds to pay fines, but had returned to Casa KitTan to work with Aristide on undermining the takeover of the Pie Hole.

"What are we going to do about tomorrow night?" asked TiaRa. "Only a few of the ladies have come today, but by tomorrow evening, all will have arrived and they will want to go out on the town."

"Won't they want to rest up before the show?" I asked.

TiaRa gave me a pitying look. "These are performers, BB. Being in the spotlight is as necessary to them as oxygen. While the Legendary Cotillion is Saturday, they are certain to be insulted if they are not pulled onto stage at the local bar on Friday and *begged* to do a number or two. In public they will behave, but if they spend the evening at the mansion with only the other divas to occupy their attentions, I fear the result will be a disaster. Hair will be pulled and blood spilled. On Saturday, they will come together for a grand cause, but tomorrow night they must be kept happy and, more importantly, kept at a distance from each other. If not, they will compare makeup, couture, and past successes and slights. Tomorrow night, each one of the *femme de chambre* must be absolutely attentive to the needs and wants of the performer to whom they have been assigned, so that each diva focuses on themselves, instead of on each other. That way, cat fights may be avoided, if the gods are with us."

"Femme de who?" asked Beau.

"Femme de chambre," repeated TiaRa. "It's French. It means lady's maid."

Tia tended to pick up words from other languages and use them whenever she could manage to sneak them into a conversation. I did not attribute it to false pride as much as a desire to add class to whatever adventure we were involved in.

Tia continued. "Each performer has been assigned a femme de chambre who's responsibility it is to keep that performer happy, to provide for every one of their wants. If you recall Beauregard, you have been assigned to Savanah Flambeau. She is a most agreeable Southern lady, so I am sure you will get along just fine. My only concern is that you and she might dip too deeply into your private stocks. So, you must promise me to exercise an amount of control both for yourself and her."

"I will do my best," said Beau, "as challenging as it may be."

"Maybe the lack of booze at the bar is a blessing," said Roger. "They might be able to control themselves a bit more."

Tia considered. "That may be true. So, are we agreed to go ahead with a celebration here sans alcohol?"

"I talked to the owners," said Nacho. "They'll be open. Said we could call it a fundraiser or a call for solidarity or whatever, but they ain't gonna let anybody keep them from being open. We just have to be sure no one sneaks in drinks. I've called in some Twinks to work the door to explain that this ain't a game. No liquor. No way."

"Then we will make sure we have primed our pumps sufficiently before attending," said Aunt May. "I have the honor of being your femme de chambre, TiaRa my dear. I thank you for putting such trust in an old woman and I promise to do my absolute best to help you in whichever way you require."

"I am certain you will be a perfect companion," said TiaRa. "I picked you because of your years of experience. Many of these girls are young and recently thrust into stardom. They have become used to having the world grovel at their feet. My usual methods of rough handling will simply not work with them. However, they all have been taught to respect their elders and I feel certain that if needed, you can channel a stern and commanding presence that will make them behave."

Aunt May smiled. "It would be my pleasure." She reached down to her purse. "I have something for you, my dear. Consider it a loan of prestige and luck for the evening. I considered surprising you with it on Saturday night, but it has unique colors and I did not want to put you in a position of having to choose between a gift and the couture you choose for the special evening." Aunt May pulled out the broach that Opal Milbank had left her. I had forgotten how splendid the old silver shone and made the spider on its web seem alive. Aunt May had obviously cleaned it and the small green, blue and purple stones sparkled, while the blue-green blob of glass that was the spider's body glowed.

TiaRa gazed at the lovely piece and slowly stroked the spider's body. She looked up at Aunt May with a special gleam in her eyes. "The Navajo believe that Spider Woman is the protector of humans. I am sure she will protect us all when I wear this."

"There's another belief," said Roger. "That Spider Woman uses her web to catch and eat misbehaving children. I have a feeling that will come in handy, too."

TiaRa slapped Roger's chest. "Leave it to you to know about methods of punishment." She turned to Aunt May. "Thank you, my dear. I look forward to working together as a team on Saturday."

"For now," grumbled Nacho, "why don't all of you get outta here. If there ain't any booze tomorrow night, there's gonna be a lot more eatin' going on, so I'll be up all night cooking. Just as well. I've got people poking around for information who are gonna be reporting back. We'll open the doors tomorrow at seven. Show up at six-thirty to help out. Until then, go waste someone else's time."

Nacho rolled away, leaning on the ever-present cane, went into the kitchen and slammed the door.

Roger stood. "Out the back gate" he said. "It locks behind you. BB, I suggest you get some sleep. Tia and I are going to be battling over who gets to use you all day long tomorrow."

Oh joy. A tug of war between two immovable forces of will. All the more reason to walk Aunt May and Beau home to prepare, or at least to drown any worries.

Chapter 28 - Friday Morning

The morning came too early, too fast, too many, too much, and too hard. Some of those, when shared with an appropriate someone, can signal the prelude to a day of delight. All of them together, each demanding unrewarded exertion from me and me alone, for and from a multitude of demanders, signaled a headache that just kept growing and a never ending, exponentially expanding potential for screw ups that would quickly bite me in the ass and result in oh so many more demands. Some days are full of birds and springtime. Some are all about pounding a stupid pipe or hammer or some other bit of heavy butchness all day long. I have never worked in a salt mine, but on days like this, I can imagine.

Performers began arriving early in the day. Some drove, most of them got lost. Indiana highways are not set up on a grid, as one would expect. Indiana is designed like spokes on a wheel, with Indianapolis at the center. This means the near-universal norm of even-numbered highways running East–West and odd-numbered highways running North–South sometimes holds true and sometimes doesn't. TiaRa had given out my number freely as the go-to person and early in the day I began receiving hysterical calls from queens lost in small Indiana towns, afraid to get out of their cars and ask the locals for directions.

Some flew. Of those, some were willing to take public or for-hire transport. Most insisted on personal transport. For those I had to either gather them myself or beg someone else to play fetch.

Once they made it to Magawatta, getting arrivals to the Ontario Mansion provided further entertainment. Once there, I was able to deliver them into the capable hands of the assigned femme de chambre, once I could locate and wake said femme.

Roger called regularly, sending me on errands. He was trying to find out about the underage boy who had allegedly been served. The names of underage law breakers were generally not readily available, but such hurdles had never stopped or even slowed Roger before. However, in this case, the name of the boy in question was eluding even his best efforts.

"That is telling," said Roger. "We are not seeking highly classified information. My contacts should be able to tell me anything I want to know about this boy. I usually would be able to tell you who he is, what he was drinking, what brand of underwear he was wearing—if any, and more. Someone is hiding his identity. That either means his family is rich, which I doubt, or this is a setup. I need you to dig and dig deep. Try listening to the recordings I always make of the police band."

"But that will take hours."

"Then you better get to it. The sooner you get started, the sooner you'll be finished. Call Cosmo, he records them digitally and I'm sure he can show you how to play them at faster than normal speed."

A call from Nacho interrupted Roger's directions. In my subservient world, Nacho trumps Roger. "Get your butt over here. I have some special ingredients coming in, but I don't have time to go pick 'em up and everyone here is busy."

I was about to mention that I was a little on the busy side myself, but I knew how that would fly. "I'll be there as soon as I can."

"Good. I also have a delivery to an attorney who does work for us on a hush-hush basis. I'll tell you who and what you'll be bringing when you get here."

"Don't the owners have lawyers working on it already?"

"This whole thing stinks. It should have been a slap on the wrist. A fine at most. Now we're being told that the paperwork has been misplaced. That means someone is stalling. This attorney has a bit more pull."

"Am I going to see Deb, our friendly lesbian judge?"

"BB, if I wanted to tell you the name, I would have said it. If I didn't, don't you think there might be a reason?"

"Oh, I..."

"Yea, you didn't think. That's your default setting. Maybe you should see about changing that. Now, stop fucking around and get over here. Come to the back gate and yell."

I headed to Nacho's. On the way, TiaRa called. "We have a few special diets that Nacho needs to know about for the dinner tonight."

"Tia, you are not seriously asking me to tell Nacho that a meal that has been cooking since last night must be altered or that additional meals must be made, are you? Please do not ask me to do that. For you, Nacho may do such a thing. For me, the best answer I could hope for would be a refusal with no physical damage. I doubt I can be that lucky."

"Oh, BB, you are such a marshmallow."

"No, Tia. You are the Sorceress of Song, the grand diva. You are one of the few people who Nacho will treat with more than disdain. I know Nacho is on our side and loves us, in a very gruff way, but I am certain that if you want such a change, you will have to request it yourself."

TiaRa gave a hearty, overburdened sigh. "Ah well, if you are not up to it, I suppose I will have to take it upon myself."

"Thank you. And if I might make one more request."

"Do you imagine I am just lolling around waiting for you to invent things for me to do? Most of the girls are here at the mansion and with each one, a new set of problems arises that only I seem to be able to handle."

"I'm sorry, Tia, but this is a small one. Could you wait thirty minutes before you call Nacho? I'm heading there right now. I'm supposed to run an errand and bring back a food order. I am willing to bet that your request will cause a bit of an explosion and if I have already come and gone, then I will not be delayed."

Again TiaRa sighed mightily, but she was a beneficent goddess. "All right. For you, BB. Don't forget that tonight you are scheduled to pick up Fantasia Gloriousity at the airport. She is due to arrive at five. You must be there in plenty of time. And, please, BB, be on your best behavior. Fantasia is doing this as a favor and she can be quite demanding, unlike the devil-may-care attitude you associate with me."

I saw no use in refuting that statement. I merely agreed to be at the airport at five, thanked Tia, and headed to Nacho's. There I picked up the list of things Nacho needed from the distributor. I also got a large legal envelope and instructions to drive to the back of the justice building and call a certain number, wait until a large deputy came out and said the phrase, "Tits is nice until you're sneakin' under a barbwire fence." If any of the words were said incorrectly or out of sequence, I was to drive away quickly and call Nacho. If the code phrase was delivered correctly, I was to thank the deputy, hand him the envelope, and drive away.

"Deliver the envelope first," said Nacho. "I don't need to tell you not to look inside, do I?"

I shook my head. Information around Nacho was strictly need-to-know and often involved things that were vaguely dangerous and unpleasant. I was glad Nacho existed. I was also glad that Nacho was well aware of my limitations and had never evidenced an inclination to attempt to extend them.

The envelope drop went as smoothly as the undraping of a fantasy lover. Heartbeat slowing a bit, I headed to the food importer's warehouse. There I was greeted effusively. Nacho was a good customer. Carp, the owner, was one of those crusty old guys who always had a smile and a story. He had a booth at the local farmer's market and was a regular stop when I shopped there.

"BB! You here to pick up the special things for Nacho?"

"I am."

"Hey, don't you know Foxy KitTan?"

"I do."

"I have a special order for him and I'm sure he'd appreciate getting it right away. I'd appreciate not having to wait for him."

"Well, today is kind of ..."

"Tell you what. I just got in an order of stuffed croissant, fresh baked. Some are filled with soft cheese. Some have meat. Some are dessert. How about one of each to sweeten the deal?" He uncovered a tray and heavenly scents wafted up to me.

It *was* past lunchtime and at the rate things were going, I wasn't going to get anything to eat. I was certainly not to get something as lovely as what lay before me.

Carp smiled and scooped three into a bag and handed the bag to me. Then he pointed at two boxes, one labeled "Foxy" and the other labeled "Nacho."

"You can stack them. Nothing will crush. Come by and see me next farmer's market. I'll save a half dozen ears of the best corn you've ever had in your mouth."

I had to smile. I also had to move my buns. There were many miles to go before the dinner tonight and then the no-booze celebration at Daddy's. I gathered my burdens and nodded a goodbye. I decided to swing by Nacho first and then go to Foxy's. With any luck, he'd invite me in and I could hide from the world for a little bit, while I ate my lunch.

Chapter 29 - Friday Lunch at Foxy's

My plan worked perfectly. I got to Nacho's before TiaRa's call, so it was a fast drop and dash. Roger called when I was on my way to Foxy's and told me that Cosmo had written a program that could listen through the recordings faster than any human and pull out all references to drunks.

"I'll let Cosmo see how small a pool it is to listen to. With any luck, I won't have to depend on you at all," said Roger. "I feel much safer when I'm relying on Cosmo to pay attention to detail."

I would be insulted, but my relief was greater than the dig.

The best part of the plan was that I hit Foxy's just as he was sitting down to lunch and he absolutely insisted I join him.

Foxy set a lovely table. Even lunch involved a main course, a couple of side dishes, and an oh-too-rich desert. The whole thing was accompanied by wine with the meal and a drink after, while Foxy decided what would be the perfect smoke to compliment the meal. I was well fed, well watered, and about to be well smoked and ready to face anything the afternoon threw at me, or so I thought, when the doorbell rang and Aristide arrived, with gleaming eyes and a smile that foretold of a juicy secret.

Aristide marched into the room, ignoring the impressive track of mud he left on Foxy's exquisite rug, flung himself into a sturdy armchair, and began to unlace his tall, muddy boots. "I have been shown the promised land," he declared.

"I trust you do not mean you have had a conversion experience or a near-fatal emergency," said Foxy.

Aristide's rolling laugh befitted his oversized body. "Neither, my friend. However, I *have* earned a glass of your very best cognac and I *do* mean your best and do not forget that I am quite aware of the contents of your special cabinet."

Foxy sighed. "Then you are also aware that there are very few people on this earth or any other to whom I would offer such a delicacy and there is, I thought up until this very moment, no one to whom I would proffer it without proof of a truly world-altering achievement. And yet ..."

Foxy stood and went to a small, carved cabinet on a side table, opened it, and withdrew a dusty bottle. He pulled a single, small, crystal glass from the cabinet and dusted it. He then uncorked the bottle and poured a small dollop into the glass. He took a deep breath from the open neck of the bottle, then pushed the cork back in and looked at the slightly lower level of its contents with a hint of sadness.

Bringing the glass to Aristide, he explained to me, "The cognac was bottled in 1859 and when I bought it at auction, my winning bid was over $150,000. I will not offer it to you, as you are in the midst of machinations and need a clear head. I will not join my friend as I do not feel my trials are resolved. At the end of this however, we shall all drink together, either to toast the end of something splendid or to celebrate. But for now, my dearest friend, it is for you alone to enjoy."

He handed the glass to Aristide, who, knowing full well what the drink represented to Foxy—his past successes and joys—held the glass to his nose and inhaled deeply. A smile spread across his face and he tipped the glass to let just a small drop of the liquid float on his tongue, then swallowed.

"I remember when you bought this bottle," he said. "It was the most expensive treat you had ever purchased and you did so after we allowed your vision to go public, a move that both secured your fortune and laid the groundwork for our current problems. It is an appropriate offering because I have found the beginning of a path out of our current brier patch. Having sworn an oath to secrecy, which I have every intention of breaking in just a moment, I have had the plot revealed to me."

He had our complete attention. As great as Foxy was at controlling a group during one of his stories, Aristide was obviously the master at whose feet Foxy had learned his craft. I was ready to jump out of my chair and shake the old man, but I looked over at Foxy. He was sitting, breathing deeply in order to calm himself. He obviously knew that begging for speed would only increase the wait. So, I wriggled in the chair and kept my mouth shut.

Aristide took another sip. He paused to savor the bouquet and taste. Finally, he set the glass down, looked at us and spoke. "There is indeed gold. I have seen it."

Foxy's face fell. "Then all is lost."

Aristide smiled and shook his head. "There is gold, but the conspirators do not own the land where it is located. They own the land adjacent where they feel certain there is also gold, although not so close to the surface. The only place where the gold is near the surface is on land they have not yet been able to purchase. And if they try to find gold on the land they own ..."

Foxy nodded, a smile spreading across his face. "Then the property they do not own becomes both exorbitantly expensive and a potential block of the entire project, as they will not be able to keep the mining secret and will have to satisfy the demands of the property owner."

"Who owns the property?" I asked.

"That is a mystery. I was told that all efforts to discover the current property owner have been unsuccessful."

"Where is it?"

"I am not familiar with the area. All I know is that we had to hike through brambles and muck for quite a distance. My guide said we had to go that way because we were actually trespassing and dared not be discovered. The undergrowth was quite thick. The only possible way to proceed was to walk through a creek that was nearly dry. My guide said it was called Plum Creek. And the only thing for miles around was ..."

I broke in, "... an old commune called High Hopes, right?"

Aristide's eyes widened. "You know of the place?"

"That's the land that Mary Jane Ontario owned. In fact, she owned most of the land all around there. Probably all the land that the conspirators have bought. She sold it and disappeared years ago. No one knows who has the deed to the land the commune sits on."

Foxy was calculating. "I believe we have a way to delay the reckoning, if not bury the plan altogether. Aristide, you can still talk freely with the guests I have invited, yes?"

"It is known that you and I are very close, so that anything I say will be taken with many grains of salt. However, what I say will be listened to."

"Then a question must arise in the minds of those considering selling my soul for pieces of gold. The question that must work its way into the conversation and consideration is: 'Where is the gold?'. How do we know there is gold in them thar hills when Indiana has been a territory since 1800, a state since 1816 and prospectors have been searching for gold since the 1830s? Flakes have been found, but never has there been any evidence of a vein."

"But, my dear Foxy. I have just this afternoon seen several large nuggets, a rocky vein with gold intertwined jutting out of the ground. My guide could easily take pictures of the nuggets. They have not done so to prevent others from ascertaining the location."

"No. Introduce doubt. Pictures can easily be faked. A piece of land can be salted."

"Salted?" I asked.

"A common practice by confidence men selling phony mines. Targeted people are invited to look at the mine and a quantity of the supposed treasure, be it gold or gems, is hidden in the dirt beforehand. The unfortunate sucker uncovers the treasure and is certain they are about to be rich. They invest and the mine turns out to be nothing but dirt."

"So, you want to warn the people that they are looking at salted earth, not a real mine, even though it sure sounds like it's real," I said.

Foxy nodded. "We do not know what is true. The conspirators have not been able to examine the land carefully. They don't own it. They haven't found gold on the property they do own. What we seek is delay. The guide is certain not to mention he took you, otherwise all will want a look. Why would someone want to risk losing the Pie Hole, which has provided solid profits for over two decades, on the assurances of an unknown group, that gold is where it has been long looked for, but never found?

"Their sales pitch has focused on how they will hide the excavations from the public. We need to introduce the question: 'What if there is nothing to excavate?'."

Aristide gave a rumbling laugh, then finished his glass. "A perfect delay, my friend, well conceived."

Foxy smiled and looked at me. "Now it is up to you and your friends to make the best of the delay and destroy the hopes, dreams, and plotting of those who have been buying the land. All our troubles seem to be knitted by the same hands. We only need to find the end of one of the lengths of yarn and give a good pull and all the different pieces will unravel. Aristide and I will do all we can from our vantage. I rely on you and your friends to exercise your prowess. Together, we may yet discover what is going on and stop the evil doers. Let us have a drink to toast our resolve."

Unfortunately, Beau chose that moment to call. He was at his hysterical best. "Aunt May! Have you seen her? Where is she?"

The best way to talk Beau down from one of his freak fits is a calm, soothing voice. Speak slowly. Try to engage his higher functions. Move him from reaction to consideration. I had learned this over many years and many tantrums.

"Hello, Beau. Where are you now?"

"What do you mean? What does that matter? Where is Aunt May? Is she there? Have you seen her?"

I took an audible deep breath and slowly let it out, subliminally encouraging Beau to do the same. "I haven't seen her lately, Beau. Where are you now?"

"I'm at home. Right here in the living room. I just woke up and she's not here. She's always here and I woke up and she's gone."

Another deep breath. "You took a nap?" On days that Beau didn't work, he and May often started drinking earlier in the day and by midmorning, a nap was necessary.

"Did Aunt May take a nap too?"

"Yes, I took a nap. May didn't. She was having coffee this morning and didn't join me, so she didn't need a nap. She said she was going to prepare something special for TiaRa."

Good, Beau's brain was kicking in. I could hear him becoming calmer as he considered.

"Maybe she's with TiaRa. You know today is a very busy day. The performers are all coming in for the show tomorrow."

"No, the reason I woke up is that TiaRa called, looking for May. That's why I got so scared. If she isn't here and she isn't with TiaRa and Nacho's is closed, where could she be?"

I could hear a bit of hysteria creeping back in at the corners. I had to squelch that quickly.

"Now Beau, I'm sure she's fine. Perhaps she's decided to go boy hunting. I'll tell you what. I'm supposed to go out to the mansion to help Tia, but on the way, I'll swing by a few of the campus bars. I'm sure I'll find her there and when I do, I'll give you a call. How's that sound?"

"You promise?"

"I promise. I'll even let her use my phone to call you if she's not busy with a boy."

Aunt May wouldn't carry a phone.

"I don't like how they feel," she would say. "And even more, I don't like the assumption that anyone can reach out and touch me anytime they want. I don't mind being touched, but I prefer it to be a mutual decision."

"Why don't you take another nap? Tonight, will be a late one with the dinner and then the celebration at Daddy's."

"Maybe you're right."

"I know I am. I'll call when I find Aunt May."

"Thanks BB. You're a pal."

I hung up and explained the situation to Foxy and Aristide. Foxy sent me off with a joint for later while the two of them focused on plans to sow doubt about the secret gold rush.

I headed toward the bars around campus. It was Friday afternoon, when any good student would be studying, so I knew the bars would be full.

Chapter 30 - Fantasia Gloriousity

Aunt May was usually at home or at Daddy's. However, occasionally the mood hit her to branch out. "It is not from lack of love, dear boy," she would say to Beau. "But I do still have needs and as much as you and your friends are dear to me, not a one of them has the slightest interest in such explorations." This was correct, but I wondered where she could find a suitable partner, outside of a retirement community. I once was both drunk enough and curious enough at the same time to ask. Unfortunately, the amount of liquor in my system that allowed me to ask also robbed me of my ability to be diplomatic in phrasing. I never thought that a person outside of a movie set actually threw a drink in another's face. I was wrong. After enough apologies, a towel, and a refilling of drinks, Aunt May deigned to answer.

"BB, I have no interest in pursuing an older man. They may have experience, but often their memories and member are not up to the task. I find one of the advantages of living in a university town is that one can often find young men caught in the uncomfortable tension between wishing to become a man and missing their mommy. If one picks the correct moment, it is possible to fulfill both of their needs as well as my own."

So, when I went looking for Aunt May, I did not make the rounds of the bars catering to the silver set. I aimed for student bars that sported tables and areas that allowed some distance from throbbing music and judgmental eyes, where a college boy might engage in conversation with an older woman. There she would sit quietly, with her drink and her little hat, until a lonely young man with too much to drink and unresolved mommy issues noticed her and came over to ask what she was doing. Far too often, she ended the afternoon with a new tale of ushering a boy into manhood. She was regularly more successful than me or Beau.

I had gone looking for her before and had a route pretty well scoped out. Some from Daddy's might want to try the same route in hopes of poaching a horny, but uncertain boy. That held no interest for me. While the body of the boys might be pleasant to look at, they always insisted on opening their mouths at some point, to express their important views of the world and over the years I have grown tired of the same old existential angst. So, when Beau asked for help, I started around the route. I was in the fourth stop, a place called Boo Boo's, replete with bad rip offs of the Hanna Barbera characters, when TiaRa called.

"BB, you must drop everything immediately and get to the airport. I have only just received word that Fantasia Gloriousity will arrive in forty-five minutes and you must be there to meet her or I am afraid of what she might do."

"No, Tia, you're wrong. I have the schedule right here. She sent me her ticket information and she doesn't arrive until tonight at five. I believe the actual time is 5:03."

"I am aware of her travel plans," said Tia. "However, Queen Gloriousity reads cards and sees prognostication in nearly everything around her. The tea leaves in her first cup of tea evidently told her she had to make haste and leave immediately to avoid calamity."

"I don't think that I can be there in time," I said. It takes longer than ..."

"You must, BB. You simply must. Fantasia Gloriousity has been part of the Chicago Royal Court for over two decades. She is not to be kept waiting. She expects to be treated as the queen she is. If you are not there to greet her, she may well turn right around and go back to Chicago! You know there are planes back and forth every thirty minutes. That's why she was able to switch flights to arrive so quickly. That is also why she could turn around and leave."

"But I'm looking for Aunt May and I ..."

"BB. Fantasia Gloriousity is the most important performer at the Legendary Cotillion. It is essential that she performs. My reputation here and throughout the entire country hangs in the balance. Royalty can be vicious and they do love to talk and I cannot, will not, be the subject of their disdain. I will call Roger and have him find Aunt May, but you must leave now and drive as if hell itself was chasing you. Do not fail me."

I sighed. TiaRa del Fuego had spoken. I had never heard her so desperate. Her usual demeanor was beneficent distance, floating somewhere between a mystic and a stoner who had taken far too many somethings and was lingering just this side of consciousness. "I'm leaving now. How will I recognize her?"

I had never heard TiaRa chuckle. However, I could hear one barely held beneath her reply.

"You'll know when you see her. I have no doubt. Now fly."

I had been commanded, so fly I did.

Traffic laws were broken, but Saint Lance, the patron saint of aging gays was looking out for me and all those tasked with enforcing such laws were busy elsewhere. I arrived at the edge of the waiting area just beyond security, out of breath, but only minutes after the appointed time. As I had hurried along toward the arriving passengers pouring out the security doors, I worried how I would pick out my charge. I had made a cardboard sign last night, but Tia's urgency had forestalled any thought of swinging by the house to pick it up. I didn't really relish the idea of standing in the waiting area as tired passengers walked past, calling out "Fantasia" or "Gloriousity". I wasn't sure which would be appropriate. I was certain that either choice would earn me odd looks and perhaps questions from various authority figures. However, as I panted to a stop I saw, standing like a pillar in midstream, immovable so that the current of people had to part around her, swathed in purple sequins topped with a cartwheel of a hat, beplumed with ostrich feathers, her arms across her ample chest, her face set in almighty fury and her eyes seething, seeking the peon who had so flagrantly besmirched her, an enormous wonder, who could be recognized as royalty from space. I hustled up to her and nodded my head, fighting down the urge to bow or fall to one knee and kiss her feet.

"Hi. I'm BB. Sorry I'm late. I only just got word that ..."

She held up a hand, stopping me.

"You are late. I was giving you until a count of twenty before I left."

I didn't ask what number she was on. She pointed to her bag, an enormous roll-on. I'm sure it exceeded the allowed size. I am also sure that such trivialities did not bother her. I took it. She started down the corridor and I followed.

"Is this it or do you have luggage, too?"

She stopped abruptly and turned, wrinkling her nose.

"What did you say your name was?"

"BB. BB Singer."

"Well, BB Singer. Do you know why I am here?"

"Sure. You're going to perform at the Legendary Cotillion."

"That is correct BB Singer. And do you know who I am?"

"Um ... Yes. You're Fantasia. From Chicago."

"BB Singer, I am Fantasia Gloriousity, one time queen and permanent member of the Royal Court. I am Fantasia Gloriousity, who has performed on the grandest stages of the world and had queens on their feet and kings on their knees hailing my performance and my style."

She flicked at the billows of sequins enfolding her bosom. "How could you possibly imagine that I would consider appearing for a performance in this ..." She again flicked a finger dismissively at the long, sequined gown and feather wrap. "... traveling garb or that my wardrobe could begin to fit into such a tiny minaudière?"

She turned without waiting for a reply, heading for baggage claim. I followed behind, envisioning the challenge ahead of keeping this being satisfied, until she had been returned to the lofty heights from whence she came. I was wondering if there was any way I could get out of being her maid and keeper. Anything less than death would not be an excuse for Her Highness, but perhaps something less permanent would work with TiaRa.

The drive back to Magawatta was tense and very quiet. Her Highness more than filled my passenger seat and her two trunks and three suitcases more than filled the trunk and back seat of my car. Of course, no assistance was offered, except occasional calls to caution that a particular suitcase must not be crushed. I managed not to infuriate her by keeping my thoughts, about packing less for a single performance to myself. Once underway, any attempt by me to engage in conversation was met with a glare and an emphatic "Hush!" before she turned again to the meditation playing on her phone, some quack revealer of ancient secrets who was channeling their knowledge to any and all who would listen and pay. Ms. Gloriousity was evidently a big fan and watched, mesmerized, repeating prayer after prayer to bring the inner light out. I personally thought she brought more than enough light to the surface, but my opinion was not sought.

I focused on the road, the traffic, and happy thoughts, while avoiding considerations of how much fun it was going to be, trying to keep this particular lump of charm happy and willing to perform for the next two days. "Remember the kids—the safe space for younguns who had nowhere else to turn in Indiana," I kept thinking to myself. Their road was harder than the slight inconvenience of being a peon for true royalty who was, I had to remind myself, also doing this out of a desire to help those newbies and was only charging expenses. I kept driving and kept my thoughts to myself, as the most Reverend Baba Bozoji droned on and on and on.

We arrived at the mansion and after getting Her Highness and her bags safely transported to her suite, bid farewell, explaining that TiaRa was looking forward to saying hello, but would await her call, in order to give Fantasia time to recover from her journey. I closed the door with a sigh of relief and started to turn, when the door was flung open.

"BB Singer! Wait!" she commanded. I thought that perhaps she was going to offer a tip or a word of thanks. Ha.

"I have forgotten to give you your most important charge. This is crucial. Are you listening?"

I managed not to roll my eyes and nodded.

"I never perform without the protection of my goddesses. You must acquire them for me."

"What?"

"My goddesses. I have five. Kali from the Hindus. Nana Buruku from West Africa, who gave birth to the moon. Virgin

Mary, the mother of the Christ child. Oya from Brazil who controls winds, lightening and violent storms. And the Haitian Maman Brigitte. You must find these five deities and assemble them on an alter in my dressing room before I shall go on."

I stared at her. "Where am I going to find ..."

She waved her hand. "That is your quest. You must succeed or I will not be able to perform. I always have these five near me, watching me ... guiding me."

"Why didn't you bring them with you?"

She looked at me like I had just squatted and deposited a load on the carpet. "Take apart my alter? Haul my goddesses around like they were so much baggage?!"

I was going to be holding back a lot of sighs and the next forty-eight hours were going to be very, very long. Maybe I could tap my boss Dustyn who worked at the Valentine Library on campus. They had quite extensive collections of all kinds of everything. However, self-obsessed was a charitable description of Dustyn. It would be interesting to put him and Fantasia in a room together and see who sucked up all the air first. Suave might have one of the deities in her shop. Foxy had interesting collections and I wouldn't be surprised if he had some voodoo statues. He was from the Bayou country of Louisiana. The Virgin Mary was no problem. I had the BVM from Opal's. If that wasn't grand enough for Her Highness, nothing would be. I was shaken from these thoughts by Fantasia waving a piece of paper in my face. I took it.

"Here are their names. Do not fail me."

"I don't suppose pictures of them would do?"

That stopped her. I could see her trying to decide if I was joking or not and if she should soil her hand by slapping me. She settled on a small shake of her head. "Not pictures, not paintings, not drawings. Three dimensional, well-crafted, and imbued with holy essence. Do not fail me BB Singer, or I shall not go on. Now, leave me. I must attend to my preparation."

She turned, muttering, "So much to do. So much. Ah … what I must put up with." She closed the door.

I headed toward my car, dialing Suave as I walked to see how easy this search would be, wondering how long before the next emergency summoned me.

Chapter 31 – Goddess of the Early Evening

Saint Lance smiled upon me once again. I didn't have to beg Dustyn. One call to Suave was all it took. She had lovely wood carvings of Kali and Oya. Foxy surprised me by announcing he was a collector and had several versions of both Nana Buruku and Maman Brigitte. The Haitian Maman Brigitte statue gave me the willies. He had several of Nana Buruku, some portraying her as a young woman, but the one I picked was carved from a gnarled root.

"An excellent choice," said Foxy. "I think of her as a woman as old as the universe she created. You know, she gave birth to the moon, the sun, and the universe, then retired. Creation was enough. She let the moon and the sun take care of the day to day. An excellent reminder."

"Do you mind if I borrow her?" I asked. "I'll be careful, but I don't want to destroy an alter."

Foxy laughed. "If she was powerful enough to create the universe, don't you think she can handle a little travel? Take her and let her bless the show."

"Thanks Foxy. I hope Fantasia likes her."

"I hope she finds my image of Nana Buruku as well as my Maman Brigitte barely adequate. Then I will not have to worry about her deciding to add them to her collection."

"I'll keep my eye on her."

"I believe they will take care of themselves. With items like this, we are only temporary keepers, never owners."

At that point, Nacho called. "Get your lard butt over here. Dinner's ready to get hauled to the mansion and I need it outta here so I can get ready for tonight's shindig."

"On my way," I said.

I thanked Foxy and Suave again. "Will you be coming tonight?" I asked.

"No, dumpling," said Foxy. "You know we are not the social butterflies we once were. Tomorrow night will be more than enough entertainment for us."

"See you then," I said and headed to Nacho's. The Twinks helping Nacho loaded my car and off I went.

Tia called as I was leaving. "I hope you are on your way, BB. The natives are getting restless."

"I'll be there in a few minutes as long as I don't stop along the way to sample Nacho's cooking. It smells wonderful."

"If you stop or slow, I will know and I will punish you and not in a nice way. Then I will set Petunia on you."

"I'm driving. I'm driving."

Soon all was unloaded and the royal tables were set and filled with queens inhaling Nacho's wonderful cooking. These ladies might be glamorous on stage, but at the table, they were a match for any pack of ravenous beasts I could imagine. The food disappeared as fast as I could bring new batches around.

As I hurried hither and yon, filling glasses and bringing food, being one of many, a great feeling of joy bubbled up within me. Yes, the churchies were trying to fuck with us. Yes, intrigue was swirling and dangerous. Unknown assailants were hounding us. But as I looked around this room filled with some of the most stellar entertainers and underground royalty, unknown to most "regular" Americans, but famous and respected in our world, who had come together to help unknown younguns who were venturing into a new life, so that they would not feel alone or despised, I had to smile. This is what life comes down to. Can each one of us do something to help one single person? And if we can, will we? I cannot change the world, but I can reach out to a single person and I have come to believe that great movements make great copy, but the world changes one person at a time. Each one of us has that power. Each one of us has that duty.

And then Hildy von Tickle from Austin caught Savannah Flambeau from Georgia, trying to make a move on her protégé and threw a drink in her face and the potential for a full-fledged food fight loomed, until TiaRa jumped onto the table.

"Ladies, you *will* behave. You have all come for the most divine purpose and if we cannot get along and sparkle as we have never sparkled before, then who knows how many crushed spirits of gaybe babies forced into hiding will haunt our souls. You all know how to please a man and how to reduce him to tears. So, please, no fucking with other queens or another queen's princess." She pointed at the two queens who started the fracas. "I will not ask you to hug, but I will demand that you each bow before the other and kiss her ring. Now!"

TiaRa knew how to make people behave. She pointed at Savannah, she of the wandering hands who had started the mess. "Give her a towel," she commanded. I hurried to obey and Ms. Flambeau toweled off.

"Now, you have a hand to kiss," Tia commanded. The room was still. If Savannah Flambeau refused, the weekend was over right then. It would be a free-for-all and it would end in tears. Everyone knew that. The room held its breath.

Finally, Savannah sighed and nodded. "You are correct, TiaRa."

She turned to Hildy von Tickle's protégé. "I am sorry. I am so used to using underhanded tricks to throw off the competition, I forgot that we are not here to compete, but to work together for other queens to be. Please forgive me."

The protégé was a bit overwhelmed by all the attention and looked to Hildy for guidance. Hildy smiled and stroked the newbie's cheek. "That is a good apology. We accept."

Then Savannah reached out and took Hildy van Tickle's hand, bowed and kissed it. Hildy grabbed Savannah's hand and pulled her into a hug. "Great queens should not fight. We have too much out there to overcome."

A great wave of pride and solidarity flowed through the room. Having been to the precipice and survived, we were all more determined that this event would be fabulous and the ripples of it would carry on into the future, to bring strength and joy to unknown, but beloved seekers of their own truth.

Tia, still standing on the table, led the applause for the two queens. Then she declared, "Now go get dressed. Your carriages await and we will go to Hoosier Daddy and show whoever is trying to stop us that we are too strong to be stopped. But do remember, no drinks on the premises, so drink up before you arrive. We have also provided liquid refreshment in the carriages and there will be livery standing by, should you need a little drive during the evening."

With that, she leapt down. Not a mean feat in heels. But TiaRa del Fuego was not a mere mortal. She was, and always will be, a goddess.

Chapter 32 - Party at Hoosier Daddy

Hoosier Daddy was packed. Word had spread that the liquor license was in jeopardy and while gay bars are no longer the only place those of the less than straight laces could feel safe and comfortable, they are still a crucial part of the community. In Magawatta, Daddy's was it. Of course, there were gay bars and more in Indy, but going there involved a drive and navigating one of those sprawling Midwest cities that seem to be one shopping center after another, broken up by a mix of quasi-industrial and/or quasi-suburban areas. For those of us who had grown used to a city you could scoop up and put in your pocket, the expedition was intimidating. Neither was it an easy jaunt that could be handled on foot if the evening's "one and done" pledges were conveniently forgotten.

Daddy's was our homo away from home. It was our place where we met, told lies, and occasionally found recreational activities. Daddy's was many things to many people and they all were here, giving generously in buckets and baskets placed throughout the bar for donations to help the fight against those who would shut us down.

The owners had decided not to charge a cover, as people were leaving and returning on a regular basis, seeking out additional libations before returning to their sodas inside the bar. When the cars with the guest performers began to arrive, an impromptu show was arranged. The mix tape was stopped for a bit, an old PA system was dug out of the back room (as the decent equipment was at the mansion for the next night's Legendary Cotillion), and one queen after another graced the crowd with a world-class performance. The protégés also were pressed to strut their stuff and it was apparent that the new crop of performers promised over the top, horrifyingly wonderful extravaganzas well into the future. TiaRa ran the show with a practiced hand, even though the quality of talent and size of egos was significantly larger than those she usually had to corral.

The crush in the main room was a bit much for a man of my delicate sensibilities, so after a few numbers, I retreated to our usual table on Nacho Mama's Patio Café. I would be seeing the performers again the following night and after a day of running, I needed a seat more than a show. Roger was back in the kitchen, strategizing with Nacho while Nacho continued serving up food with a practiced hand. Aunt May was describing the boy who had provided her afternoon's exertion and Beau was hanging on to every word, with a mixture of lust and jealousy.

"If I didn't love you so much, May, I would hate you," he said. "You can't even share, because by the time you have finished with them, they are too pooped to pop."

"Beauregard, you have many sterling talents. Cherish those," said Aunt May. "I have always had a knack for seduction. It is not something I studied or strove for. Just like the color of my eyes, it simply is and always has been."

"It's not fading, either," said Beau.

Aunt May smiled. "I believe it was Ms. Midler who quoted Ms. Tucker saying that twenty goes into eighty more than eighty goes into twenty. As I said, I did not strive to acquire my talents. They are a natural gift, but practice, while it may not make perfect, certainly makes better, if I do say so myself

... and am joined in that assertion by several of my previous lovers, this afternoon's addition included."

"Well, you had me worried," grumped Beau. "I do wish you would call when you are going to be out of touch for a while. Don't forget we are targeted by unknown goons."

Aunt May lay a hand on his arm. "It is very chivalrous of you to worry Beauregard. However, I believe we have ascertained that the ne'er-do-wells are after the box of jewels, not this old lady. You know I do not wish to carry a phone with me and the opportunity to call did not arise."

Looking to me to create a diversion, Aunt May asked, "Is all well back at the mansion?"

I nodded. "Everyone has arrived and has been properly stowed. TiaRa already stopped a major altercation. Most of the performers have come here to Daddy's tonight and will have enough attention to keep them happy until the bar closes. Foxy has arranged for a flock of drivers to take them back at the end of the evening. I figure they'll be glad to go, since the bar at the mansion is well stocked and free, and the bar here is under lock and key. As long as no one goes prospecting for nookie, all should be fine. I'm officially off for the night and I intend to indulge in nachos and relaxation out here."

I looked around for a waiter to order a plate of nachos for the table. I didn't see one, but coming through the door, away from his usual stool at the bar, was Lester, the old queen. He had introduced himself that way so often, it seemed wrong just to call him Lester. Lester looked around the patio, spotted me, came over, and sat down.

"I've been hearing some things that don't make sense," he said, after I introduced him to May and Beau.

"I'm glad you sought BB out," said Beau. "He can help you feel comfortable with that. Most of what he hears and nearly all of what he says makes no sense at all."

I shot Beau an appropriately withering glance. Lester ignored the comment.

"I've heard that the bar was closed because of an underage drinker who got busted walking home."

"That's right," I said.

"No it's not," said Lester. "You know I watch everyone who comes in and goes out. I would have noticed someone young."

"Maybe they just looked older," suggested Beau.

Lester shook his head. "No way. I was glued to my chair for at least an hour before the police showed up. People were coming in, but no one older than you folks left and I'm sure you won't be insulted if I point out that anyone who looks like you, could not possibly be underage."

"Did you take a bathroom break?" I asked.

Lester shook his head again. "Never. I may be an old queen, but I have the bladder of a teen. Comes from years of practice. Besides, have you seen the bathrooms here? Daddy's has a lot of charm, but that does not extend to the bathrooms."

I had to agree. I think the owners kept them a bit on the gross side to discourage quickies. It worked. I have never been tempted.

"That wouldn't surprise me," I said. "Nacho and Roger are pretty sure something underhanded is going on with the bust. They are looking into it. I'll let them know you can back up their hunch."

"There's something else, more important," said Lester. "You know what I used to do here in town?"

"Roger said you taught geology."

"That's right. I also consulted with the Department of Natural Resources. I know the land around here. I know what it's made up of."

"OK," said Beau. "You know rocks. That's great, but not exactly important unless you know about the gems that we got from Opal's."

"I know a little about gems, but that's not what I want to tell you about. There is no gold vein in Brown County. I'm sure of it. I've studied it. There is no question in my mind."

"Do you know about Foxy's problems?" I asked.

Lester nodded. "Foxy and I go back. That's why I want you to tell him. Whoever is saying there is gold in Brown County is lying."

"But you can't prove it. I mean, how can you prove there isn't anything, especially when they can show veins of gold?"

"They what?"

"They showed Aristide a place with large gold nuggets right near the surface."

"Where was this?"

"On the land that used to be that old commune."

"High Hopes?" Lester asked.

"That's the one."

Lester shook his head. "Then they found ..." He stopped and stood. "Tell Foxy that he just needs to delay a bit. I'm sure there's no gold and I can prove it."

He bowed slightly to Aunt May and hurried out the door.

We stared after him.

"That is a very odd man," said Beau.

Aunt May began to gather her things. "The same could be

said of us all. A dear friend once told me 'we're all here because we aren't all there' and I have found few exceptions to that observation." She stood. "I was unable to take my usual afternoon nap, engaged as I was. In addition, the lack of strong drink here tonight further makes a case for my returning home to relax, with drink in hand, and prepare for an evening's repose. I do hope you will excuse me."

"I have a flask hidden in my pocket," I said.

Aunt May shook her head. "Very kind BB, but my days of surreptitious sips from a flask are behind me. There is rarely enough for one and never enough for two and I am well supplied at home."

"Shall I walk with you?" asked Beau.

"There is no need, Beauregard. The night is pleasant. The walk is short. Besides, I am much steadier on my feet than I usually am at this point of the evening. There are still performances aplenty and I sense an added feeling of frivolity in the air. Perhaps my afternoon's luck will rub off on you. Do give my regards to the others."

With that, Aunt May nodded to us both and went through the doors to the bar and out to street.

Beau turned to me. "Now, about that flask," he said and held out his hand.

I let him drain it, then went in to catch a bit more of the show. It had been a long, demanding day and after a few more songs, I said my farewells and headed home where my bed and my cat were calling. I figured that all would be taken care of and if anything went wonky, I had no doubt they would call.

Chapter 33 - Saturday Morning

The day of the show dawned ... well, I'm not sure how it dawned. I was happily asleep, thank you very much. I woke up about ten on my own, grateful that no phone calls heralding catastrophes major enough to require me to do something had disturbed my sleep. I was into my second cup of coffee when Roger called with an update.

"Foxy has his whales sorted out. He rented the entire Garden Inn, which is the best Magawatta has to offer, so if anyone needs to have an impromptu meeting, there will be plenty of meeting rooms available. He has cars picking them up and has meals taken care of.

"He will escort them all out to the mansion just before the show and will spend the day pumping them with facts and figures about the need for a youth center. Aristide will be working the crowd to spread questions about the reality of a gold find where so many before have failed."

"That reminds me," I said. "I had a very short, but interesting talk with Lester last night. He seemed absolutely certain of two things. The first was that there was no underage boy in Daddy's that night."

"I agree," said Roger. "My people and Nacho's Twinks have been trying to identify the boy. I'm sure he was a plant and whoever is behind this has hidden him away."

"The other bit of information was even more interesting," I said. "When I told him where Aristide found the nuggets of gold, I could tell that Lester knew something, but he wouldn't share. He just said he was certain there was no gold and then left."

"Very weird. Lester knows the geology of Brown County. I told you he's an old professor."

"It was more than that. It seemed like he knew something about that particular vein. He said to tell Foxy to delay, then before I could get any more out of him, he hurried out of there."

"You tell Foxy. I'll tell Nacho. Maybe Lester has shared something before or Nacho knows what's up. If not, we have too many things going on today to try to make sense of Lester. We'll look into it after this shindig is over.

"Nacho is sending a bunch of Twinks to the mansion tonight. They'll be masquerading as waiters, carrying the little nibbles Nacho has been making. But they'll mostly be there to help in case some outside elements decide that crashing the party would be fun."

"I hadn't even thought about that. My god, of course they might and then ..."

"BB, don't wet yourself. All is taken care of. We have been handling this end of the planning and everything is in place. There will be obvious *and* surreptitious protection. Nothing to worry your pretty little head over. You focus on keeping your own special part of the show happy. I hear she's a real peach."

I thought of Fantasia Gloriousity and shivered. This was not going to be a barrel of fun. However, it was only for another day. By tonight, it all would be over but the shouting. Of course, it was the shouting during the day that had me worried. I poured another cup. This was definitely a three-cup morning. Maybe I should add a little something to mellow the caffeine.

"Don't start drinking this early," said Roger, reading my mind. "You have a full day and you are going to have to be on your best behavior all day long. You might say something untoward if you are a bit on the oiled side."

I sighed. He was right. "I have another call coming in. We should check in around lunchtime to make sure all is still going according to plan."

Roger snorted. "You mean to find out what is spinning out of control."

"Ever the optimist."

"Answer your phone."

He hung up.

"BB! May! She's gone! Kidnapped! BB!" Beau was screaming into the phone. Strange warbles and sobs occasionally let a word slip out. This was Beau at full-on freak.

"Beau, take a breath. What do you mean? You can't be sure. Aunt May probably found a new quarry on the way home last night. You know she's not one to turn down an opportunity." Slow, calm speech while offering alternate realities usually worked to short circuit Beau's hysteria. Not this time. He began to hyperventilate.

"No. She's gone! Taken! She's been kidnapped. They left a note."

"What? Where? What did it say?"

"I found it stuck in the mail slot this morning. One piece of paper with words pasted on it, just like in the movies.

It says,

'We got her. Box and all money and jewels or else. Dry Lake Rec Center at 6 p.m. Come alone.'

"What am I going to do, BB?"

His wails turned to guttural groans with random gasps for air.

"I'll be right there," I said, hurrying out the door.

Aunt May and Beau lived a couple of blocks down the street, so it was quicker to walk. I stayed on the phone with Beau. He was not a sturdy rock in any kind of traumatic current and this was a major flood. I hurried down the street, continuing to make soothing comments that meant little and were based on no truth but a wish to provide solace. I got to his house, banged on the door, and let myself in.

He was standing in the middle of the living room, phone in one hand, note dangling from the other, snot and tears flowing freely down his face. When he saw me, he dropped both note and phone and I scooped him into my arms. Beau is larger than me and as he lolled against me, I was afraid I was going to collapse. I aimed us both toward the couch where we fell, still holding on to each other. His body shook with sobs and confusion. I continued to squeeze and pat him, providing an anchor to dry land.

When a truly awful shock hits us, the best a friend can provide is quiet steadiness, so that somewhere deep inside, we can believe that there is an island of hope in the sea of sorrow. Figuring out next steps would come soon, but for now, Beau needed to get his head above the waves of fear and worry.

After long minutes of weeping on his part, "there thereing" on my part, and equal parts of rocking back and forth, Beau struggled to the surface, able to finally form words.

"I came in late last night and assumed she had gone to sleep. I was a little tipsy, so I didn't notice anything. This morning, when I opened the door, the note was there."

I called Roger.

"Five minutes," he said, and hung up.

It was less than that when Roger and Petunia came through the door. Roger examined the note, then passed it to Petunia.

"Nothing special," said Petunia. "Words are from the *Student Daily*. Common enough words that they are probably from yesterday's issue. No leads there."

"I agree," said Roger pulling out his phone. He called Nacho and described what was going on. He looked at Petunia. "Merle around?"

Petunia nodded. "Where we going?"

Roger looked at his watch. "He should be at the main office now." He spoke into the phone. "Thirty minutes enough time?" He listened. "I think as many as possible. Best to show we aren't fucking around."

Roger nodded, hung up, then looked at Petunia. "U-Betcha Pawn on South Walnut. Thirty minutes. Tell her to bring something heavy, that doesn't shoot. We want a show of force, but not a battle. Freddy's smart enough to know the difference."

Petunia nodded and called.

Roger called Timmy and explained what had happened. "I need you and Cosmo to come over to Beau's right away. He can't be alone and we have to go somewhere." He listened. "Good. We're waiting, hurry."

"I can stay with Beau," I said, aware that the alternative meant going with Roger to what I guessed was not a peaceful walk in the woods.

"No you can't. You're needed."

"You're going to see Freddy Flash, aren't you? He's a gangster or at least as much a one as we have in Magawatta. The only thing I can do in any situation with him I can imagine, is get shot."

Roger pinched my chin. "Oh, BB. You are such a drama queen. You're coming with as a symbol, just like before."

"What do you mean?"

"You're like a cute little kitten or a baby. If we show up with you, Freddy will know that we aren't going to start a war, at least not right now. We wouldn't want you to get caught in the crossfire. We're there to talk. We'll have enough muscle to show he should talk to us, but we aren't there to do any more than talk right now."

"What if Freddy doesn't understand my role as a symbol?"

"Well, then it won't be a symbol role, it will be a cymbal crash, if you catch my meaning."

"I'm about to walk into a potentially deadly situation and you're making bad puns."

Roger shrugged. "If it makes you feel better, it's the best way to help Aunt May. That should be enough."

I had to admit it was. I sighed. "Let me call TiaRa and tell her. She can explain to Fantasia why I'm not there this morning."

I called. TiaRa did not freak. She was so used to trauma dancing around her, she could keep on dancing no matter what. She had probably been an entertainer during the Blitz in another life.

"We're working on the group number with all the children. They are a talented group and thankfully they haven't yet learned the finer arts of cutting each other down or upstaging to grab the attention of the audience. I will explain to Fantasia. Do you need anything else from me?"

I relayed the question to Roger who shook his head. "Just keep on going like nothing is wrong and everything will work out fine."

This brought a new fit of wailing from Beau. I leaned over and grabbed his hand. "Look at me, Beau," I commanded. "Everything *will* be fine. We will get May back and we will have a wonderful story to tell afterwards. But you must keep it together. For now, you should gather all the jewelry and put it in the box, OK?"

Beau looked up, tear-stained face trying hard to be brave. He reminded me of a little boy who had scraped his knee wanting to melt into tears, but was trying not to. He nodded and struggled to his feet and went looking for the box and any of the jewels he had pulled out to play with.

Roger said to Tia, "Nacho's Twinks will serve lunch. This is probably going to take all afternoon. Can you handle things there until early evening?"

"Certainly. But BB must be here by seven. That is when Fantasia will start getting ready. If he is not here to help, she will not go on and we might as well cancel the whole thing."

"Don't do that. If things have gone south by then, it will be best to have BB out of the way." He looked up to make sure Beau was out of earshot. "And we go on, no matter what. Aunt May would have wanted that. She would not want to be the reason we don't raise the money to start the center."

That stopped me. I knew this was a hiccup, but it had not occurred to me that Aunt May might not make it out of this safely. Now that it did, I started to shake. This was a bit much for me. Roger noticed. He said goodbye to TiaRa and disconnected. Then he walked over to me and punched me, none too gently, in the shoulder.

"OWWW!" I yelled. "What was that for?"

Roger leaned in and spoke low, but fiercely into my ear. "Do *not* freak out BB. This is not the moment for it. We have only a little time and each of us has a job to do and if we do it, all will be well. But if any one of us starts running around yelling, there's a good chance everything goes sideways. So, get it together—now. Do you need another punch to help you focus?"

I immediately wrapped my arms around my torso, trying to protect my shoulders. Fear of immediate pain completely drove away fear of future peril. I was not pleased that Roger knew me so well, but there it was. I shook my head. "I'm ready."

By this time, Timmy and Cosmo had arrived, so Petunia, Roger, and I headed out. Soon we were pulling into the parking lot of U-Betcha Pawn. For so early in the day, the parking lot was surprisingly full. Well, surprisingly until we got out of the car and I saw that all the cars were full of the butchest of Nacho's Twinks, the ones from town who were usually on hand when a bouncer was needed. I don't know where they went when not at work. I never saw them around town. Maybe they lived in gyms and workout rooms, oiling up each other and expanding their already enormous muscles. Whoever they were and wherever they were from, I was glad they were there.

Nacho got out of a car parked in the single disabled spot near the door. "You ready?" Nacho asked Roger.

Roger nodded.

Nacho looked out at the cars in the parking lot. All the windows were down and the Twinks were paying attention. Nacho's voice carried. "Everyone stay put. I'll be near the door. If you hear me yelling or see me backing out of the door, come in hard, heavy, and fast."

I saw heads nodding. I wanted to suggest that it would be best if I waited outside, too, but I knew I'd just be wasting my breath and in moments when one's last breath is potentially looming, wasting it seemed foolhardy.

Petunia, Nacho, Roger, and I entered the shop. It was dark and crowded with a varied assortment of stuff. Pawn shops fascinate some. They make me sad. Much of the merchandise represents the last, desperate attempt to stay afloat by someone. A failed attempt, because the items had not been redeemed. They are up for sale. Other pieces were emotional cast offs, never intended to be redeemed, just sold quickly for a fraction of their value.

Standing behind the counter was Freddy Flash. There was no one else visible in the store, but I was willing to bet that there were a few helpers in the back room. Great, big, unpleasant helpers. I imagined there was also some kind of weapon behind his counter within very easy reach, if not actually in Freddy's hands. I noticed a couple of monitors behind him with ever-changing shots of the parking lot. Freddy knew what was out there.

In his store, he had ditched his Uncle Murray sweater and persona. He looked the part of a gangster boss who could and would hurt anyone who got in his way.

Flashing an oily smile, Freddy nodded to us. "Welcome. Are you looking for something in particular or would you like to browse?"

"Aunt May," said Roger. "She's sweet. She's old. She doesn't have any part of this and you've stepped over a line."

Freddy shook his head. "I'm sorry. We're fresh out of little old ladies. We do have some lovely pendants in the display case."

Nacho stalked forward and slammed a piece of paper on the counter in front of Freddy. "This is a list, a partial list mind you, of aliases you have used, jobs you have either pulled

240

yourself or brokered, and laws you have broken. You've crossed a line and you are done in this town. We want the old lady back and we want her back now."

Freddy glanced down at the paper, then with growing alarm, picked it up and studied it. He looked up at Nacho. "How did you..."

Nacho cut him off. "We're still digging and we're still discovering. You've been a bad boy, Freddy. Now, your only chance is to get that sweet little old lady back."

Freddy's confidence was gone. Nacho had broken him quickly and completely. He was trying not to cry as he studied the list. "I ... I can't," he said, voice cracking. "I just brokered the deal. A guy contacted me on a special phone. Before you ask, I don't know who called. Only a few people know the number to that phone. It's used for one job and then burned. A week or so later, I get another phone. My connection sells the number to that phone. It's only used for one job.

"So, that phone rings. The guy on the phone has a password and tells me what he wants and that the only way to get it fast is to snatch the old lady. I called a team I knew."

"Who are they?" asked Roger.

Freddy shook his head. "Again, I don't know. I know how to contact them. I know they work fast and don't fail." He glanced down at the list. "I've used 'em for a couple of these jobs. In fact, I just used em for the old lady who died. And before you ask – no they didn't kill her. They were after the same box, but they pooched the alarm and split."

"How'd they know about the box," asked Nacho.

Freddy looked nervous. "I spread the word. Dumb kid who was boinking her told me about it. I don't do stolen jewels, but I make bank on setting up jobs. I let people know when I hear something is available. Someone got back to me and said they were interested."

"So some stranger called you and wanted the box," said Roger. "You called up your unknown gang, set it up, and figured you'd collect a commission. You get to stay clean in a very dirty business."

Freddy shrugged. "It's a living."

"Not no more," said Nacho. "Your sweet little deal is done. Call your crook friends. Call em right now."

Freddy shook his head. "Don't have a number. Same deal. Phone is used once, then it's burned. I'll get a new one in a few days."

"Then how do you get the box?" asked Roger.

"I don't. I never touch the stuff. I stay strictly out of it. I'll get a call at six from the buyer. They'll tell me where to have the guys deliver the merchandise. The guys call me at 6:15 when they have the box. I tell them where to deliver it. Then we all forget we ever heard of each other."

Nacho looked thoughtful. "How do you know that the call at six is legitimate?"

"I recognize the number. They have to call using the same phone they first called on so I know it's them."

Nacho smiled a dangerous, evil smile. I was very glad it was not pointed toward me. "Give me the number."

I could tell Freddy would usually have dickered. Bargaining was in his nature, but Freddy Flash was gone, leaving behind a very frightened Sheldon Flaxman holding a list of sins he could quite certainly be punished for. He recited the number.

Nacho whipped out a phone and dialed. "Cosmo, it's Nacho. I need everything you can get on a phone number and on a phone. Who bought it? Who's got it? I need it fast." Nacho recited the number and hung up.

Nacho growled at Freddy. "You have one more job to do. I know you ain't stupid enough to fuck it up. You probably won't have to do this. We intend to take care of things before, but if that phone rings at six, you get that address. You don't give any hint there's a problem. Then you call me. And if the shits who took May call you at 6:15, you tell them to deliver the goods to this address." Nacho handed Freddy a card. "Again, no hints that anything is up or else."

With that, Nacho turned and headed toward the door. We all followed. At the door, Nacho turned and looked back at Freddy.

"We'll be watching you until 6:15 to make sure you don't decide to slip slide away. Don't try it, because you know we'll stop you. After that, you're on your own. But by 7:00, I suggest you be gone, because that's when the cops are showing up with that list and anything else we can dig up. You crossed a line and you don't get to do that more than once."

With that, we left.

I followed Roger and Petunia out to the car. "What next?" I asked.

"We'll take you to the mansion," said Roger. "After that, we have some preparations for our friends."

"What about the money? May put it in the bank. How will we get it out?"

"We won't. They aren't getting the box."

"But how will you ..."

"Shut up BB. Let us take care of this."

"What about Beau?"

"Timmy will stay with him. I left a couple of presents to slip into his next drink, so he'll spend the day asleep."

"Do you think that ... "

"I need you to stop asking questions. Do you really think you
are going to come up with something that we haven't thought
of? You deal with the show. Let us deal with this."

I took a breath and considered. I know when I'm out of my
league. The best thing I could do was keep out of the way of
the adults. So, I went to face the demands of Queen Fantasia.

Chapter 34 - Preparations

I was worried. Fantasia was demanding. TiaRa was working with the protégés, putting the final polish on the closing number, which was a combination of dance and posing, allowing each one to strut their particular specialty, all to a recording of Queen's "Under Pressure," which I thought was quite appropriate for a competition to raise money for a questioning youth center. I had little time to enjoy the practice, as Fantasia had no end of needs.

I was foolish enough to attempt to iron one of her scarves. I figured, how hard could it be? A scarf is basically a single piece of cloth. We weren't talking seams, creases, or god forbid, pleats. I had the iron set low enough that I wasn't going to destroy it. However, Queen Fantasia nearly exploded when she saw my work. I still have no idea what I did wrong, but I was banished from having anything to do with her outfits. That was not, in my mind, a punishment.

I was assigned the role of gopher. A constant flow of demands for items had me running all over town. Foxy had several cars placed at our disposal, so I didn't have to worry about gas or wear and tear on my car, but on me—that was a different story. I procured. I returned things when what I had procured did not meet Fantasia's requirements. By the time I got back, a new item *had* to be fetched. At least it kept me busy and gave me less time to worry about Aunt May. I called Roger on a regular basis and he usually told me to fuck off and let him work. I called Timmy to see how Beau was doing. He stayed unconscious most of the day. About five, he came to, but there was still enough sedative floating around his bloodstream to keep him calm. I picked him up and brought him out to the mansion. We arrived in time for dinner. The show was scheduled to begin at nine. Guests would begin to arrive at seven, when they would be served drinks to loosen their grip on their wallets.

I was very aware that the scheduled time for the exchange of Aunt May for the ammo box was fast approaching. I desperately wanted to know what was going on, but I knew that my presence would do no good and could potentially screw things up. I also knew that calling anyone would just take their attention from what they needed to be focusing on. So, I kept busy running errands for Fantasia, keeping Beau in food and drinks, and helping out where I was needed.

At 6:15, I got a text from Roger. *"She's safe!"*

I sank down in a chair for a minute, finally allowing my worry and grief to wash over me. I think when we face a crisis, we can't allow ourselves to get lost in the emotion. There is too much to do. However, once the crisis passes, there is no holding back the terror that has been gnawing at us.

I still had too much to do to fully indulge myself. When this was over, I had earned a good cry and, dammit, I was going to have it, but for now ...

I ran down to where Beau was sitting. "She's fine," I said. "Roger has Aunt May and all is well."

We looked at each other, then grabbed into a hug and held on, tightly, tightly. The world had ripped at us, but we had come through one more time. We knew there was too much to do right now. We couldn't start to sob or it would all be over. But we could squeeze. Squeeze until it hurt. Self-inflicted pain to balance the pain some unknown had tossed our way.

After long minutes, we broke our embrace. We didn't say anything. With friends, you don't have to talk. Beau nodded. "Fantasia probably needs you."

"Almost certainly," I said.

"Get to it. I'm OK. But BB?"

"Yes?"

"Before you go, would you get me another drink?"

I smiled. "Sure. But from now on, you're off the injured list. You can get your own damn drink. Just flag down a waiter."

Beau smiled. "And they'll supply *whatever* I need?"

"Dream on. They're busy."

At this point, Fantasia texted, demanding my immediate presence, so I got Beau's drink and ran up to Her Majesty's dressing room.

She kept me running from then on, so I had no idea of the time. At one point Roger, Petunia, and Merle escorted Aunt May through the door. She had gone home and freshened up and she never looked so good. She was being swarmed and Fantasia's demands had risen to a fever pitch, so I could only give her a quick squeeze.

The whales began to arrive. Drinks were served. Foxy was the perfect host, greeting each person as they came through the door, directing them to drinks and delectables. Finally, a few minutes before nine, he called out, "Everyone, the show is about to begin! If you would step through to the theater, we will favor you with a show like no other that has ever graced any stage, anywhere in the world. It is for you and for our youth. For it is they who hold the future and it is we who can offer them safe harbor before they set sail into that glorious adventure."

I had hoped to follow the crowd in and watch at least some of the show. That was not to be. Fantasia sent a text summons, demanding drink for her and a food offering for her alter. I hurried to obey. I brought a tray up to her dressing room. She gazed over it with a critical eye.

"Is this the best they had to offer?"

"I tried to get a bit of everything. I don't know what your goddesses eat."

She shot me a look. "Are you attempting to mock me, BB Singer? Or to mock my worship?"

I knew better than to admit that. "No. I really mean it. I'm not being smart. I'm being ignorant. I really don't know."

She relented. "They like sweets. Go back down and collect a small selection of sweets. Pay close attention to the ones you choose. Form is important. Do not choose any that are damaged, even in the slightest. Then hurry back."

I went on my errand and came back with a second plate. She inspected it carefully and nodded. I wondered if she wanted me to go away so she could chow down on the treats, which I suspected was where they were going to end up. However, I didn't want to walk out. I had done that earlier and it had resulted in a severe scolding. An inspiration hit me and I began straightening up the room.

Fantasia cleared her throat. That was her, "Pay attention, you moron" signal. I looked up.

"BB Singer, what do you think you are doing?"

"Well, I'm your maid."

"Yes. And what does that mean to you?"

I wasn't sure where this was going, but I had a feeling it wasn't leading up to a pat on the back. "I thought maids should hang out and help when you need it."

"BB Singer. What I need as I prepare is solitude. I must channel my spirits to guide my talent so that I may be flawless. If you are here, how am I to be flawless? Your spirit," she looked me up and down with a tad too much disdain for my taste, "is rather work-a-day. I must ascend to the heavens. I cannot do that if my preparation is sullied by you."

"So what should I do? TiaRa said I'm supposed to be here to help you. Where should I go?"

Frankly, with all that was going on, I was about to tell this legend-in-her-own-mind where *she* could go or what body part she could climb into, since she was obviously so in love with herself that the smell of her farts would send her into ecstatic rapture. But I kept my mouth shut. Tia had made it clear that Fantasia was the bow on this particular birdcage and the success of the evening lay on this dilettante's very meaty, sequin and feather bedecked shoulders.

"Go away, BB Singer. Go outside of this room and let me center myself."

"Fine." I turned to go, glad to have an excuse to get away.

She called out after me, "But stay close enough so that when I need something, you can respond quickly."

I sighed. I thought of the youth center. Then I sat on the floor in the hallway outside her door and tried to think happy thoughts. I could hear the show going on downstairs. Fantasia Gloriousity was scheduled to be the final act, before the group number by all the protégés. It would all be over in less than an hour. I could suck it up and cope. Suddenly, a screech came from inside Fantasia's room.

"You out there! BB Singer. Come here at once!"

It sounded like Her Majesty had severed a body part. I rushed into the room. Fantasia was seated in front of the alter she had constructed. She had draped a small table with a purple cloth embroidered with mystical signs. Offerings of rice and crumbled sweets would be attracting various creepy crawlies for days. The four statues of the goddesses Suave and Foxy had loaned were carefully placed. Two candles and five sticks of incense burned, making the room very smoky. And standing before the table, now adorned in a towering dress, bedazzled all over with spangles and feathers and tiny bells, turning her into a spectacular (as derived from spectacle) creature of power and glory, was Fantasia Gloriousity, eyes blazing in anger, hell's own bitch demon unleashed, barely holding herself back from attack. She turned all that power and fury on *me*.

"Where is the Blessed Virgin Mary? You promised me all five of my goddesses."

The BVM! I could picture her on the table, where I had left her so that I wouldn't forget. But I had forgotten. The news about Aunt May had driven it from my mind. I had gone from May's to U-Betcha Pawn and then straight to the mansion. The BVM was still at my house.

I began to explain what had happened, but Fantasia stopped me. "I am Fantasia Gloriousity. I have performed for royalty across this world and I have never, and I mean never, performed without first blessing my act before my five goddesses. Five, BB Singer. Not four, five!"

I began to apologize, to explain, but again she stopped me. "You do not seem to understand, BB Singer. I am scheduled to go on in forty-five minutes. If the Virgin Mary is not here in forty minutes, I will not go on. I advise you to shut your mouth and drive as fast as you can and get what you promised here or prepare to explain why you have prevented me from performing this evening." Then she turned, went to her mirror, and began to touch up her makeup. I no longer existed. I weighed what I could do and the end result of each option was clear — I ran.

Foxy had rented a batch of cars for any needs that arose. I ran to the fastest looking one. I actually spun tires as I tore out of the lot and kept my foot on the accelerator all the way to my house. I unlocked the two locks that Petunia insisted I always locked. I grabbed the BVM from her spot on the table and shot back out the door, slamming it behind me. I dashed to the car and realized I had forgotten to double lock the door, but there was no going back. It had already taken twenty-two minutes. I had eighteen more and I better not hit any red lights, traffic, or officers of the law on the way back or I wasn't going to make it. I offered a quick prayer to St. Lance and sped away.

I made it back in sixteen minutes, dashed up the stairs, flung myself through Fantasia's door and handed her the lovely Blessed Virgin Mary, peacefully standing atop her mountain of shells. As she gazed upon the Virgin, Fantasia's anger slipped away and peace wrapped her magnificence. She placed the BVM on her alter. Lit another stick of incense. Muttered a short blessing. Then, she picked up her boa from the back of her chair and swept past me, down the stairs, and to the waiting crowd.

As I collapsed, panting, I heard the crowd below roar as the music to Aretha's "Respect" rang out. Fantasia Gloriousity did not lip sync. She was a singer and her gravelly voice grabbed you by the heart, pulled you up out of your seat, and kicked you behind the knees, so that joy overwhelmed you and you had no choice but to dance.

And dance they did. I danced down the steps and watched from the side of the stage. Fantasia had grabbed the audience and they had no ability or wish to get free. She finished the song and everyone exploded in applause. In complete control of every soul in the room, she quieted them with a wave and spoke into the microphone.

"Each one of us has come here tonight for a purpose. We are here for our youth. Each one of us has faced struggles and hate, but we have risen above that and we always will. The laws have become less evil, but many still feel they are free to debate our humanity ... our right to be who we are. We are here tonight to create a space for those who are coming up and coming out and coming into who they know they truly are. And for that, we give everything we can, to line the paths that we have struggled to create with diamonds and love."

A sparse bass line started and toes began to tap and smiles spread and Queen Gloriousity proved her royalty as she hissed and sizzled into "Fever." It is always a danger for a singer to take on a performance that is indelibly joined to another performer. However, had Ms. Peggy Lee been there, as Fantasia Gloriousity told us that we gave her fever when we touched her, she would have smiled as broadly as everyone in the audience did. We swayed through the stories of Romeo and Juliet and then Pocahontas and Cap'n Smith and we had to agree that Fantasia gave us a fever and it *was* a lovely way to burn.

The bass line sizzled off and the audience roared. *How could she top that?* All her demands and scolding that I had endured since she had arrived ... well, I didn't want to marry her, but I was happy to have carried her crown and would do it again.

And then ...

Bass. Then conga. Then piano. Jackie Wilson had made the world jump to it in 1967. The Divine Bette Midler brought it, special delivery, to the happy, hippy, homos six years later, making us scream and shake like crazy monkeys. In 1989, it made the Statue of Liberty step off her moorings, lift her skirts, and boogie down the streets of Manhattan. And that night it lifted our butts out of our seats and our hearts up to the moon. "Your Love Keeps Lifting Me Higher" takes a special kind of performer to blast that energy to the stratosphere and Fantasia had all rockets firing. She sang.

She danced. She shook. And every single person, from the oldest whale to the youngest Twink was moving, shaking, and grinning with not a single thought to how cool they looked, because the joy exploding inside them was immeasurable and could not be sullied by such insignificant concerns.

She brought the house down. I'm surprised she didn't make the mansion crumble with the sheer energy blasting out. And with a final shout, the music stopped, silence echoed for an instant, and then the screaming and clapping exploded.

"Thank you, my darlings," Fantasia panted into the mic. "And now, the Sorceress of Song, Miss TiaRa del Fuego and all our babies will end our entertainment, throwing ourselves and the future of all the youth of this area, upon your tender mercies."

With that, Fantasia strode off the stage. I was waiting, with her robe, her towel, and a drink, my eyes shining my appreciation and thanks. As TiaRa and the babies began their choreographed version of "Under Pressure," I followed Fantasia up to her dressing room.

"Queen Fantasia, I just want to say ..." I began, but Fantasia held up a hand for silence.

"BB Singer, I can see you enjoyed my performance. I am, however, extremely tired and need solitude. Please leave me. In ten minutes, bring me another drink. Knock once and wait until I allow you to enter. Then, without speaking, give me the drink and leave. I will require nothing more from you this evening, except silence and distance."

I nodded. She was a pain in the butt, but a very talented one, so who was I to quarrel? I did what she commanded and then went down to help wrap up the party. I was sure Foxy or Nacho could use help and if Fantasia changed her mind, as she had proven many times, she knew how to text.

The initial cleanup was done. Most of the performers had gone to Hoosier Daddy to continue the celebration. Although it was closed to the public, the entertainers, staff, and whales were all welcome. Alcohol was still verboten there, but enough had been soaked up during the evening to last well into the night. Nacho had opened the Patio Café, so those with the munchies could be satiated. Those of us who had been setting up since early had stayed behind to do the essential cleaning, tucking away everything of great value, and setting individual rooms right so returning divas would not find fault.

Aunt May stayed back at the mansion with us. She now sat at the mansion's largest table, safe and sound, with a drink before her and her friends all around. We all felt relief and gratitude that she had been rescued unscathed. Petunia and Merle were the uncomfortable heroines of the hour.

"Tell," demanded Beau. "How did you pull off getting Aunt May back unharmed without giving up the ammo box?"

Neither Petunia nor Merle were talkers, but Petunia also knew that Beau could outlast even her with his constant insistence for details. Finally, she broke.

"We used Little Neil to deliver the box. He looks enough like you to pass, but we knew he wasn't going to freak out like you almost certainly would have. The kidnappers had picked the parking lot at the Dry Lake Rec Center because there are three or four little league games going on every Saturday afternoon. The place is packed."

"Seems they'd want an isolated spot," I said.

"Some would," said Roger. "But this was a good choice. The advantage of a crowded place is that there are too many civilians around, so no big police action. Also, there were lots of ways in and out, so they had a good chance of escape. No way to cover all the exits."

"Why Little Neil?" asked Beau. "I know he's one of Nacho's Twinks, but I figured his strength was seduction. I didn't know he had any combat skills."

Roger grinned. "He doesn't, but he has no fear and can bargain with the devil and win. He was standing in the middle of the parking lot, holding the box. They pulled up and pointed a gun at him, but he stayed calm. He told them there was only one way he would give them the box. They had to drive over near the snack shack and let May out. Then he would put down the box and walk away. They could come and get the box and May would be safe. If they wanted to shoot him, they could, but they wouldn't get out of the parking lot. Worked like a charm."

"OK, that's how you got Aunt May. How did you get the box back?" I asked.

"They never got it," said Roger. "We had Merle dressed as an umpire. Looked like she was walking from her car to the game. But once May got out of the van, Merle stopped, turned, and threw her baseball through the side window and beaned the driver. You know she has a thing for baseballs. Knocked him right out. He was lucky. His foot slipped off the brake and the van started forward, but his partner pulled the emergency brake before the van ran into a car."

I looked at Merle. "You threw a baseball across the parking lot, through the safety glass of a van, and it still had enough zip to knock the driver out?"

She smiled, embarrassed. "Side windows ain't that strong if you hit toward the edge with enough force. Plus, I'm pretty good with a baseball. I actually held back a bit. I didn't want to kill the guy. Too many questions." She shot me a significant look. "I hate questions."

I may not be all that bright, but I could take a hint like that—I shut up.

Roger continued the story. "I drove up and collected Merle, Neil, the box, and Aunt May. Petunia hopped in the kidnapper's van and had a brief Q & A session with them. It didn't take long. They were hired by Freddy Flash and with Petunia persuading them, they were very talkative. Petunia has that effect on people. Just like Freddy said, they didn't know who wanted the box. Petunia suggested they drive to the hospital to have their injuries looked at and then leave town. I'm pretty sure they will follow her advice. We'll check later."

"And what about Freddy?" asked Beau.

"Freddy seems to have taken a vacation," said Roger. "He waited until 6:15, left the pawn shop, and went out to his girlfriend's place. He must have had an escape route through some of the connecting condos, because we didn't see him leave, but he's gone. Nacho's network is looking for him. They'll find him eventually and tie up that loose end, but for now the important thing is that the jewels were recovered, the most precious one being our Aunt May." He raised his glass. "To Aunt May."

Aunt May smiled, raised her glass, and quickly emptied it. "They were most gentle with me, so I was lucky. But I am luckier still that I have such talented friends to rely upon.

Merle, Petunia, I know that being the center of attention is not to your liking, so I will not wax as lyrical as I feel toward you. I will simply tell you that I am exceedingly grateful and am in your debt and those are words not to be taken lightly. Thank you."

I poured another round from the bottle on the table and we all drank to Petunia and Merle, who gritted their teeth and didn't run away from all the attention.

I looked toward the door and saw Cosmo hurrying toward our table. It didn't surprise me that he had missed the event. Timmy loved an occasion and Cosmo loved isolation. While they loved each other, they had realized that an essential part of living together was allowing each other to indulge in their personal joy without foisting it on the other. Cosmo didn't try to explain his fascination with his latest digital adventure and Timmy didn't force him to endure loud crowds.

Cosmo was so excited, he only gave Timmy a quick kiss and squeeze, instead of their usual extended greeting ritual which lingered somewhere between endearing and gack. Then he turned to Roger.

"I found it," he said, putting a printout on the table in front of Roger.

"Found what?" asked Beau.

Cosmo began to explain the various databases and search terms he had used. I lost track of any meaning within the first sentence. Roger was following the narrative, but everyone else's eyes were glazing over. Timmy gave Cosmo a little squeeze.

"Honey, you've gone tech on us. Why don't you tell the what, not the how?"

Cosmo nodded with a bit of regret showing. He was much more interested in how he had untangled the problem than what the final answer was and didn't understand why that wasn't the universal opinion. However, he relied on Timmy to translate human interactions and guide him in norms of behavior.

"I found where the phone came from," he said.

"What phone?" I asked.

Roger rolled his eyes. "BB, your attention and retention are sorely lacking. I don't know how we're going to tell when you go senile. Already you are apparently impaired. Remember how the plan worked? Freddy got a call on a burner phone. He wrote down that number. At six, Freddy got a call from the same number telling the kidnappers where to deliver the goods. The kidnappers called Freddy when they had the box and he told them where to deliver it. The phone number that called Freddy is the way we can find out who made the call. The identity of who threatened Aunt May. That is the number that Cosmo has traced."

Cosmo had our full attention.

"The phone was one of a box of prepaid phones all purchased at the same time. I tracked down the purchase order. They were bought by an oil and gas industry support group."

"That means lobbyist," I explained to Beau, who was looking completely befuddled.

Cosmo continued. "And that particular phone with that particular number was activated about ten days ago."

"I don't suppose whoever activated it was stupid enough to use a personal credit card," said Roger.

"As a matter of fact," said Cosmo, "the card was a business card and it was issued to Peter Ponce."

Roger actually giggled. "Got him. I love it when bastards are stupid bastards. Peter and Matt are in this together and won't be able to say otherwise. Matt said he was going to get that box, no matter what. So, he did all this for some fake jewels, money we never put in the box, and his pride. Now he and his brother are busted."

"But why?" I asked. "Why take such a risk? Sure it's a pile of money and they thought the jewels were worth more, but they've both got plenty."

"No," said Roger. "Their mother has money. And while I am sure she would be happy to help them fund their school, I doubt they want to tell her about their shady land purchases in Brown County. She's too smart and would smell a scheme. My guess is that they are up to their asses in short term loans from shady sources and are desperate for some fast cash to get a little breathing room. I've go to tell Nacho about this."

He pulled out his phone and called Nacho, relaying the information.

"We meet tomorrow morning at Nacho's," he announced after disconnecting. "Aunt May and Beau, you've been through enough. You two just relax. We'll take care of this."

I was going to suggest that my absence might also be more useful. Unfortunately, before I could make my argument, the attention of the table was diverted. Arriving were Foxy, TiaRa, and Dr. Tarkington, who had been Foxy's guest, not because of his wealth, but his position with the state educational establishment. Aristide had been spreading questions about the gold find in Brown County among the guests. He also had occasionally slipped in the requirement for regular inspections by the state board of education, hinting that the cover story of an educational campus would not hold water. Dr. Tarkington was there to back him up. Aristide did not make a clear declaration that the plan couldn't work, but introduced doubt and doubt encouraged delay and delay was all we hoped we needed. Foxy and Tia had been counting up the evening's proceeds. Their less than ecstatic faces telegraphed the news.

Tia, ever the optimist, said, "We did well. Very, very well. We did not make enough to match the churchies offer, but perhaps Mr. Dick will accept a lower offer from the better group."

"Or give us some more time to raise the money," Beau said.

Foxy shook his head. "We raised nearly one million dollars, but Mr. Dick wants $1.5 million and the churchies have held up $1.75 million and may well go as high as two million. I could easily make up the difference if my company wasn't under attack, but ..." He trailed off.

Dr. Tarkington was carrying two bottles of champagne that obviously had come from Foxy's cellar. Lack of celebration or not, there was no way I was going to pass up such a treat. I ran to get fresh glasses, opened the bottles, filled the glasses and passed them around. I wasn't sure what to toast. We were all tired. The opposition seemed to be fracturing, but time was not on our side. Once the block was sold, we had lost and they had won. They already had the connections. They would have enough time to raise the money to start the school, force Daddy's out, and lay waste to Brown County. No one seemed to have any inspiration for a toast, so we just drank. The champagne was good, a delight to the senses. But it didn't fill us with joy. There was too much pressing down on us to be lifted by the small bubbles.

I looked at my BVM, which I had retrieved from Fantasia's alter as soon as she left for Daddy's. Mary sat on the table, so calm and hopeful. I'm not a religious man, but Fantasia had just blessed her and Virgin Mary had certainly helped her deliver a show beyond all expectations. Desperate times call for desperate measures.

I placed the BVM statue in the middle of the table.

"Everyone," I commanded, "fill your glass again. Then make a little request. A little prayer, if you will. Ask Mary for help.

Why else is she here? Then pour a little at her feet so it runs down the river."

Roger opened his mouth to make a snide remark. I held up my hand. "Chicken soup, Roger. Chicken soup. It can't hurt. It might help and right now—we are fucked. This is at least worth a try."

Roger closed his mouth, picked up the bottle, and filled his glass. He poured a little at the feet of my BVM, then poured the rest down his throat. He passed the bottle to Beau, who turned Mary to face him and repeated Roger's actions. He was about to pass the bottle to Aunt May when Dr. Tarkington shouted, "That's who it is!"

We all looked at him. When Beau had turned the BVM to face him, the back of the statue had faced Dr. Tarkington. I remembered that he had evidenced quite a little interest in the inscription "and when I deviate, punish me" and the signature, Eppie J.

"It just hit me," Dr. Tarkington was very excited. "I have been searching for the name and it just hit me. You recall the Ponce brothers who are involved with the online charter school project, I am sure. Well, their mother came from a wealthy, religious, and powerful family. She is the one who has always controlled the purse strings as well as her husband before his death and her sons since their birth. Her father's name was Ephraim Ward. Her husband's name was also Ephraim, but he had neither the fortune nor the stature of her father. She insisted he be called by a diminutive name—Eppie J, for Ephraim Junior. That is how he signed this statue. Obviously, it is a gift to his lover and dominatrix. What you have here is proof that the father was unfaithful to the mother with Opal Milbank.

"I believe all you would need to do is send the mother a picture of the declaration and signature. Not only does it show that her husband was unfaithful, but is also defiling the

Virgin Mary. She will be furious. She has sworn she would take the entire fortune and donate it to a convent, leaving his darling boys with nothing, if he was ever unfaithful and this is proof. She will act immediately. You may not have the money to meet Mr. Dick's offer, but the money the Ponce's were planning to use to purchase the block and start the school, will no longer be available. They will have to wait for some other source of funds. So, Mother Mary has at the very least granted a delay and very possibly has provided a path to your success."

We all turned the BVM around and looked at the inscription. It was clear that if Dr. Tarkington's research was correct, we had been privy to a miracle.

"Then, I believe a round of drinks to toast our good fortune is called for," said Foxy. "Tomorrow I shall take it upon myself to visit Madam Ponce and show her the evidence. BB, you had better go home right now and take her with you. Keep our lady safe."

"Hold on there bucko," said Roger. "Excuse me if I don't trust our fate to BB's strong, manly hands. If you don't mind, I'll ask Petunia and Merle to keep watch tonight, just in case any unwanted visitors come a-knocking." He looked at the two for confirmation.

"I think it would be a better plan to locate across the street," said Petunia. "I'd rather catch someone when they are in the middle of trying something than just scare them off. It gives me more latitude with how I handle them. We'll station ourselves there right after we escort Foxy home with the proceeds from tonight. Don't you worry, BB. We'll be seconds away. If anyone tries to break in, we'll be there before your first scream leaves your throat."

All the planning scared me. I had no desire to be the weak link in a chain. "But what if you miss someone? What if they somehow slip by?"

TiaRa reached into her purse and pulled out a tiny silver whistle on a string. "This is small, but very loud. It has rescued me in a few situations. Take it. Put it around your neck. If anything or anyone is crafty enough to avoid Petunia and Merle, which I supremely doubt, then blow it. It will be heard down the block."

I took the tiny thing and hung it around my neck. "Thank you, TiaRa."

Foxy spoke up, "Dr. Tarkington, we owe you a great debt. You have once again proven to be most entertaining and helpful. I hope we will see you more often, both at Casa KitTan and at Hoosier Daddy."

We all raised our glasses once more to the man. This finished the sparkling contents of the bottles and the end of the libations, as always, was a signal among our group that it was time to go home. Foxy's crews would finish the cleanup of the Ontario Mansion over the next few days. We were well on our way to owning the block. We had stuck at least a finger in the eye of the Ponce brothers. Now we only had to raise the remaining money and save the Pie Hole. Two impossible tasks to go. Everyone was feeling pretty positive as we set off for our respective abodes.

Chapter 36 - Homecoming

They were already inside waiting for me when I got home. I hit the light switch as I walked in, but nothing happened. Well, no light came on. What happened was I felt cold metal against my neck. Funny. I've never had anything to do with guns and yet there was no question in my mind as to what was poking me. I recognized Matt Ponce's voice.

"OK faggot. Hands up. Mouth shut."

More than anything, I wanted to obey. However, I was holding the BVM and while the concept of Mary was ethereal, the statue was not. She was a two-hander clutched to my stomach, not a one-hander held above my head. I'm sure someone who had not avoided working out as diligently as I had could have done it. For me, not so much. This presented a problem. If I tried to set the statue down, it might be taken as an evasive maneuver. I could explain, but I had been told to keep my mouth shut. It had been a long day and there had been several glasses of champagne. I was confused and unsure what to do. My mental gymnastics were taking too long. Matt wasn't privy to my thoughts and didn't like the delay. He delivered a sharp punch to my kidney.

"I said hands up."

The punch solved my problem. The sudden pain rocked me and I dropped the BVM. She fell to the floor with a crash. Of course, I knew what the sound was, but Matt didn't. He was behind me and wrapped a thick arm around my neck and squeezed.

"What the fuck was that?"

He had told me to keep my mouth shut. In addition, with his arm choking off my air, I couldn't do anything more than gurgle. I thought about Tia's whistle. Even if I could reach it, I wouldn't be able to blow it.

"Peter, turn on a lamp," Matt commanded.

A light came on. Matt was still behind me, but in front of me stood Peter Ponce, his plastic face actually registering an emotion. He obviously wasn't used to having or expressing emotions, so it wasn't all that clear, but from where I stood, gasping for air, he looked worried. He was holding a gun pointed generally in my direction, but I could see that he had no idea how to use it. Of course, that didn't make it any less lethal.

"Matt, are you sure?" he started to say.

"Shut up Peter. You're a pussy. You've always been a pussy. You tried to take care of this your way and it didn't work. Now we don't have time to fuck around."

"But what if he reports us? What if he goes to the police?"

Matt tightened his grip on my throat. I didn't see stars. I saw black spots. Hmmm, even my strangulation was more boring than I had imagined. "He's not going to report us, is he? Not to the cops. Not to his friends. Not to anyone."

He gave another squeeze. I tried to nod my head.

"He knows if he talks, then me or one of my friends will come back and finish the job, doesn't he?"

I couldn't talk or else I would have assured him I would not tattle. I might also explain that he should have said "I or one of my friends" instead of "me or one of my friends". However,

I was more concerned with not dying than correcting his grammar.

Peter looked at me with actual tears in his eyes. "We really don't want to do this to you, even though you're a sodomite. But God wants me to help those children and I can't stay my course without my inheritance. You are standing in the way of God's plan."

"Oh shut up, Peter," said Matt. "Find the goddamn statue and let's get out of here."

Peter clapped his hands over his ears. "Matt, you shouldn't take the Lord's name in vain."

"Bite me. Pull your head out of your ass and find the statue."

Peter pointed to the BVM at my feet where it had fallen. "It's right there. He must have been carrying it. That's why we couldn't find it."

Matt threw me aside. I collapsed onto the sofa, gasping. We both looked at the BVM. She had broken into several pieces when she hit the floor. Seashells had scattered. Her calm face, head broken from body, smiled up at me. Matt picked up a couple of the bigger pieces, then glared at me triumphantly. "Betcha didn't know how valuable this little lady was."

Now that I was not being choked, a bit of anger managed to surface. "I know it's going to cost you and your little brother your fortune. I know it's going to stop you from fucking up a bunch of kids with that hate school and fucking up Brown County when you try to dig it up."

"We're saving those children," cried Peter. "We're going to show them that they don't have to live in sin. They can embrace the Lord."

"Shut up Peter. I've got work to do." Matt grinned at me and picked up something from the table. It looked heavy. I had a nasty feeling that my grand outburst was going to hurt me more than it hurt him. He held out the something to show me. It was a very old, very well-made, cast iron frying pan. New cast iron is lighter, both in color and heft. This was strong and heavy. He must have brought it from one of the booths at his antique mall. To bang home the point, as it were, he brought it down on a cute cut-glass dog I had recently acquired and proudly displayed on the living room table. The dog shattered. When I looked where the dog had been, there was nothing but a small pile of shards.

Matt grinned again and lifted the frying pan high over his head, holding it with both hands, the better to pulverize me, I thought. I couldn't look away from that looming black metal implement of death. They say time slows down when we're facing death. It was not going nearly slow enough for me.

It swung down, Matt putting his considerable muscles into the swing and *WHAM*, slammed it into the BVM. Relief that I was not the target assuaged my heartbreak at the loss of my statue. Dear Mary, once again she had suffered for and from the sinner.

The first hit shattered the statue beyond repair. Poor Mary, she would never stand atop her mountain of shells again. Then Matt, crazy, raw anger pouring forth, brought the frying pan down again and again on the shattered remains, reducing the statue to pieces of shells and plaster. He laughed wildly as he swung again and again.

He stopped and looked at me. "Can't prove anything now. Your evidence is nothing but dust. Maybe I should take care of you, too. That way you won't ever be tempted to talk."

I could see he was weighing the idea and having enjoyed the destruction of Virgin Mary, was leaning toward continuing the fun.

"Matt! Please!" yelled Peter. "Let's get out of here. I can't get caught like this. Think of my public. I won't be able to complete my mission."

Matt turned to Peter. I could see what he was considering, although I couldn't tell if Peter realized the danger he was in. Holy Cain and Abel.

Suddenly, the door burst open and two whirlwinds of punching, kicking, throwing, and every kind of mayhem imaginable spun into the room. Petunia and Merle were large women. I always thought of massive stone idols when I saw them. But they were demonstrating how fast they could move. I had never doubted they could be destructive and they did not disappoint. It seemed that between one breath and another the tableau changed from my imminent destruction to both Ponce boys barely conscious, face down, with their hands tightly handcuffed behind their backs.

Petunia turned to me; concern writ large across her face. "Are you OK, BB?"

Realizing that I was not going to die, the part of my mind that wanted to run around in circles shrieking stepped forward. I managed to stay on the sofa, mostly because my throat hurt and my back hurt, plus I was shaking uncontrollably.

Gentle as a mountain gorilla cradling her baby, Merle scooped me into her arms and held me and let me shake, rocking slowly and making soothing sounds. After a bit, I managed to straighten up and dry my eyes.

"Thanks," I whispered.

Merle stroked my face and smiled.

Petunia had jerked Matt to his feet. He was spitting mad. Actually, spitting and calling the ladies every evil word he could think of. Peter, on the other hand, was sobbing. As Petunia pulled him up, he quieted. His hair, which I had always suspected was coated with shellac, was actually mussed. A bit of the lobbyist-politician flickered in his eyes.

"Young lady," he said, addressing Petunia. "Perhaps we can come to an understanding. As you can see, your friend is not hurt. I have many very powerful and wealthy friends who would be very grateful if this could be resolved without resorting to the police. Perhaps we could ..."

At this point, Petunia pulled back her arm and slapped him hard across the face. I was surprised it didn't knock him over. A bright red hand print blossomed on the white skin. It was a pleasure to see.

"Don't give a shit about your friends, your power, or your money," said Petunia. "We're going to the station now." She turned to me. "Roger's on his way. I don't want to wait. Can you hang until he gets here?"

I nodded.

Merle stood and grabbed Peter's shoulder, pushing him toward the door. Petunia grabbed Matt's handcuffed hands and lifted until his arms threatened to dislocate. He groaned, bending away from the pain and stumbled forward. At the door, Petunia turned. "How's about you remember to lock the door this time?" she said. Then they were gone.

I looked around at the wreck of my living room. Spot came out of the bedroom, where he had been hiding, to see if there was some food. I sighed. Cat duty. Back to my real purpose in life.

In the kitchen, I grabbed the dustpan and broom. I was a bit too shaken to deal with the glass shards. I didn't want to end up with a glass splinter to end a perfect experience. However, the Virgin of the Seashells deserved a proper disposal. At the very least I didn't want plaster powder tracked all over the house. I bent down and began to sweep up the remains. Matt had done a fine job. There was next to nothing recognizable left. There was no evidence of Eppie J's confession of adultery. I sighed as I swept the pieces into the dust pan.

But, as I swept, I noticed a small object that had escaped Matt's pounding. It must have been secreted inside the BVM. I poked through the powder and pulled it out. A key. A small key. No markings. No indication what it opened, but if Opal had decided it needed Mary's protection, it must be important. I tucked it into my pocket.

I was considering possibilities when Roger unlocked my front door and rushed in. He grabbed me and looked me over carefully. "Come on," he said.

"Where?" I asked.

"Doctor," he replied. "Petunia said you were shaken, but didn't seem hurt. I think this is more than a delicate flower like you can handle. I want you examined and then drugged. You'll stay at Beau's tonight."

For me it had been a bit much of a day. I didn't have the energy to argue. Besides, being taken care of sounded very good right then. I let him lead me out. As we left, he locked the door, with both locks.

Chapter 37 – Sunday Night at Nacho Mama's Patio Café

Sunday dawn dawned without my notice.

I had a few bruises, but the doctor had declared I was basically unharmed. Whatever she gave me had me nodding before Roger got me to Beau's house. Aunt May took over at the door and got me into bed. I woke up actually feeling pretty good.

Unfortunately, all too early I was summoned to the mansion. Performers were leaving and had to be packed up and squired into cars, buses, or ferried individually to the airport. Even TiaRa was present helping. I couldn't recall a time she was up and glowing so early in the day. Tia at her core, is a creature of the night, where subdued lighting and garish makeup artfully applied allows magical transformation. However, the previous evening had been sublime and there was royalty to be thanked and helped.

I took Fantasia Gloriousity to the airport. She was too grand a queen to be packed with the others on the bus, no matter how luxurious it was. She insisted on stopping three times during the forty-five-minute drive. The first was to get coffee when she noticed a roadside café that was a large enough chain for her to feel safe with their quality, but not so large that it seemed, to her, common. The second was to get a different cup of coffee, as the first cup did not meet her standards. The third was at a roadside hotel where, for a tip to the front desk clerk, she was allowed to primp, because she didn't want to appear in public bedraggled from the drive. All the while, she kept up a running commentary on the benefits available in a so-called real city and the difficulties she had endured coming to such a backwater. I concentrated on remembering her stellar performance from the night before and all that it had contributed to the project and to all who attended. I nodded at appropriate times and kept my mouth shut. This continued all the way into the airport, where she strode ahead, leaving me to trail behind pulling a cart stacked high with suitcases. I helped her check in and turned her luggage over to the ticket agent, of course paying the excess baggage fees. At the entrance to the security gate, she stopped, turned, and placed a hand on my forehead, as if giving me a blessing.

"BB Singer," she said. "You did well. You have my thanks."

As annoying and demanding and wonderful as she had been, I felt a pulse of grace flow from her hands and all through me. I nearly fell back a step. She smiled and touched a finger to my lips. Then she turned and went through security, never looking back. I watched until she made it past the guards and down the hallway, out of sight. Then I headed home, to my sofa, my cat, and an afternoon nap that had my name written all over it.

Early Sunday evening, we were gathered around our table in Nacho Mama's Patio Café. The liquor license for Hoosier Daddy was still suspended, but Nacho's legal team had assured us all that once the state offices opened on Monday, all would be made right. The arrest record for the alleged violator had been uncovered. He turned out to be the son of an Indiana State Trooper who sometimes did security work for Peter Ponce events. The boy had not been served at Daddy's, had not had any alcohol in his system, and had not actually been charged. The record had been deleted, but some very clever computer hacker, who shall remain nameless, had discovered and retrieved it. Nacho's lawyer visited the boy's father and, after explaining numerous potential lawsuits and penalties and the associated cost, convinced the man to admit he had recruited his son at the behest of Ponce.

TiaRa had announced a special show for that evening. It would be a little shorter than usual, but some of the divas had stayed around and would be performing, so the show would be a monument to talent. All of us were there, feeling pretty good about ourselves. Roger was in boy-hunting mode. Foxy and Suave had deigned to attend, bringing Aristide to enjoy the show. Foxy had smuggled in an imported luxury soda in a large, beautiful, cut-glass bottle and an Italian amaretto. He gave me a small taste. It tasted of nuts and money. I could learn to love it, but decided I had better not, unless I planned to turn to a life of crime. Cosmo and Timmy were engaged in staring into each other's eyes. A little gooey for my taste, but their usual behavior. That left Aunt May, Beau, and me to carry the conversation, if there was to be one. However, it was mostly a night to lie back on our laurels and feel a bit smug, which is what we were doing.

The coming week held challenges. We still didn't have enough money to make an offer. We didn't know if the plan to take over the Pie Hole was going to be successful.

"At least Matt and Peter Ponce are in deep shit," said Beau. "I'll be surprised if they can cover up or wiggle out of a kidnapping charge. Peter will probably claim the phone and card were stolen, but it's going to open him up to some very careful examination. Then there's the visit to BB's. Breaking and entering, he can wiggle out of. The gun, well, his followers will actually love him all the more for that. But inside a homo's house at night, even though the homo was BB, is not going to look good in the papers."

"What do you mean, even though it was me?"

"Face it, when most politicians get caught with a guy, the guy is at least cute. But you ..." Beau looked me up and down.

I shot him a dirty look. "I have been traumatized and barely escaped with my life and instead of offering me comfort, you resort to insults. Typical."

"Oh, you poor, poor, delicate flower," said Beau. "You were never in any danger. Petunia and Merle knew better than to leave you to your own devices. They were just a bit delayed. Where would you be without the protection of the women in your life?"

Aunt May laid a hand on his arm. "Beauregard, I suggest you limit your name calling and consider how much you also rely on the strength, kindness, and protection of others."

To avoid considering Aunt May's obvious truth, Beau summoned Jackie and ordered another round.

"Matt is probably going away for a while," said Roger. "But a couple of years in jail will just teach him new skills and introduce him to new friends. Of course, there's always the possibility he'll turn on his little brother and cut a deal, but I doubt it. Peter's the one you have to watch," said Roger. "Someone that plastic on the outside tends to be able to wipe off all kinds of dirt. He uses that clean but stupid front to cover for what he's actually doing. Matt is just a crook. Peter thinks he has been chosen by God himself and in his mind, that excuses any fucking thing he wants to do."

"While I agree with your assessment," said Foxy, "tonight is not for such concerns. Our worries will wait for us to deal with them tomorrow. This evening is to celebrate how far we have come! Look, even TiaRa has come out to bless us with her presence before the show begins."

He was correct. Tia had come out from backstage to join us for a few minutes to bask in the glow of a truly legendary

274

show. After the success of last night and now another show packed to the tits with professionals, TiaRa del Fuego seemed to be pulsating. She had grown used to a life in a small Indiana college town, but this weekend had brought forth the memories of a thousand exotic revels in spots of mystery and intrigue.

"Aunt May, I have brought back your broach," she said, pressing the large silver piece into Aunt May's hand. The green glass blob, that was the body of the spider, glowed under the patio lights and the little stones around it sparkled. "It was the perfect piece for last night. However, I am sorry to say it does not go with this evening's ensemble. Many thanks. It certainly brought its blessing to our efforts last night."

Beau and Aunt May had come pre-lubricated and I had a pretty good idea that May's purse held a flask. She took the broach from Tia with a smile. "I am pleased it helped. While it is not of the highest quality, I find it charming. In addition, it does seem to carry a certain gift of luck, particularly for new beginnings. At least that is what Opal always said."

She began to tuck it away in her purse, but Suave stopped her. "Aunt May, don't banish your little spider. Put it on. See what magic it brings to you."

We all agreed that Aunt May should wear it, to celebrate her escape from danger. Beau pinned it to her dress and while the broach was really too flashy for the plain lines that Aunt May always wore, it was pleasing to see a bit of flash on our dear friend's bosom.

It was a perfect Sunday evening, as the stars began to twinkle beyond the strings of bedraggled Christmas lights that lit up the patio. Far enough into spring, the night was still warm, but summer had not been let out of the cupboard, so humidity's steamy, wet blanket did not intrude. Nacho rolled up to the table and slammed down a plate of perfection.

Nacho had, as usual, somehow appeared without anyone seeing the approach. "One plate for free," Nacho grumbled. "You done good last night. Besides, I figure that if you ain't drinking, you'll need something to fill your faces. I expect more orders over the evening and don't even dream that you won't be payin' for them."

We dove in. Looking up from a loop of cheese trying to escape its inevitable consumption, I saw Lester walk through the door that led to the bar, escorting an older lady who I had never seen before. She had an understated elegance I have only seen in people who came from wealth. Not money, wealth. She didn't display any unease at being in a rather seedy gay bar. I've only seen that combination with the few trust fund hippies I've met. Her clothes said middle class. The cut said money. The frizzy hair and rainbow scarf at her neck said undercover hippy. Very interesting combination. They came up to the table and sat.

"Foxy," said Lester. "Your conspirators are still in town, aren't they?"

"Regrettably," answered Foxy. "They have insisted on a meeting tomorrow and are going to force a vote. Aristide and I had hoped to delay some more so I could have more time to work on specific individuals, but that is what they fear. We are not optimistic about the outcome."

Lester smiled. "That's fine, just fine. Everyone, I would like to introduce my friend, Cathy Canada. Actually, you know her as Mary Jane Ontario."

"As in the Ontario Mansion?" I asked.

"Yes indeed," answered Lester.

Nacho came out from the kitchen holding a plate. The old pirate set the plate in front of the lady. "I heard you might be coming by. I remember you liked these."

The lady beamed at Nacho. "A stuffed sopapilla! You

276

remembered." She lay a hand on the meaty arm, then reached up and tweaked Nacho's nose.

I repeat. She tweaked Nacho's nose.

No one would dare lay a hand on Nacho, except TiaRa and that was an occasional pat on the arm. I could not imagine someone taking such liberties.

"So, you two know each other?" I asked before I thought better than to pry. The glare Nacho shot my direction quickly reminded me of boundaries and the danger of over-stepping them. Hastily I looked away.

Ms. Canada took a bite of the pastry in front of her, a pastry I had never known Nacho to make. Her eyes closed and a smile flickered around her mouth. I wasn't surprised that a special concoction de Nacho was good. I wanted to try it, but knew better than to ask. So, as Nacho settled into a chair across from her, I decided to feed my hunger from a less dangerous source. I turned to Lester.

"You knew where Ms. Canada was all these years, didn't you?"

Lester nodded. "Mary Jane and I have been good friends for a while. I used to pal around with the Canada boys. All the radicals knew each other. But a few went off to California and joined up with the SLA and got involved in bank robberies and kidnapping to take the system down. Didn't work out too well for them and the backlash made it all the way back to Magawatta. I was safe. I just went back to the geology lab. Mary Jane went out to High Hopes, but they were watching her and she needed to get away."

By this time, Mary Jane had finished Nacho's treat, pushed away the plate with a happy sigh and looked around the table. "I knew I had to disappear, but I had gone through most of my money. I had a plan. I thought it was a pretty good one. Of course, I was young ... and stoned."

We were all captivated. A juicy story that we didn't know. "Do tell," urged Beau.

Mary Jane smiled as she considered the past. "I had spent a lot of my inheritance on gold. We thought the system would fall apart, so I had gold jewelry and even few gold bars. I decided to scam some of the straights who were running the town and the state. It was my little act of revolution."

"What did you do?" I asked.

"Lester helped. We made fake nuggets and rocks peppered with gold. I had enough gold to make them look real and Lester had the knowledge of how to model the rocks. Then we planted them around the edges of High Hopes. The plan was to take some investors out, get them to find the gold nuggets and think they had discovered a new vein worth millions, let them keep their discovery *hidden* from me so they thought they were ripping off the little hippy girl, sell them the land and let them discover that they had a few thousand dollars of gold covered pieces of art. Well, several thousand dollars' worth of gold. We wanted it to look like a really big vein, but of course it would be worth much, much less than they had paid for the land. One final way to stick it to the man."

"Why didn't you just take the gold and go?" asked Beau. "That would have been easier."

"I needed cash. If I'd tried to sell gold, I would have had to provide ID so they'd know I didn't steal it, but if I disappeared with a pile of cash ... no worries. The squares I had lined up were more than happy to do the deal with money, because they thought they were ripping me off. They didn't want something that could trace back to them. Banking laws weren't so tight then."

Foxy smiled. "I am sensing parallels with a current situation. How is it that your plan did not come to fruition?"

"Friends," she said. "Lester and Opal. Lester didn't want me to go out with a cloud on my name. He talked to Opal. She knew most of the people in the area who were rich, powerful, and not strict believers in honesty. She convinced me that once these people found out I had ripped them off, they would not let it go. They'd be after me forever. Plus, she offered me an alternative."

"And what was that?" asked Foxy.

"Opal bought High Hopes for cash. She had plenty tucked away. We didn't register the deed, but had it notarized. She had one of her lawyer friends write up a document that gave ownership to whoever held the deed. She said she'd hide it where no one would find it, but she'd make sure the taxes on the property were paid. That way, any old hippies who found their way back there would have a safe place to land."

I laughed. "MoonStar is still out there."

Mary Jane smiled. "He was a very pretty boy, long ago. Bit of a narcissist and well on his way to being a full-time stoner, but I'm glad he stayed and didn't get lost in a city of needles. That would have killed him."

"But how did you vanish?" asked Beau.

Mary Jane shot a significant look at Nacho. "Friends. I have been blessed with loyal friends who were able to keep a secret."

Nacho blew smoke in our direction, "As opposed to a few here that I could name—BB and Beau."

"So what prompted the reappearance?" asked Roger. "Seems you went to a lot of effort to leave Magawatta behind."

"Lester called and told me about Foxy's dilemma. I think I can straighten things out. Plus, it will help my current situation."

"How?" asked Beau.

"What happened to that seashell virgin?" asked Cathy. "You know, the BVM statue on top of a mountain of sea shells."

"I got it," I said. "But last night, it got smashed. You see ..."

Nacho interrupted. "We've heard the story and if she needs to hear it, I'll tell it. It will take half the time. Why do you need the BVM?"

"There's a key hidden inside her. I need that."

"I found it," I said. "I put it on my key ring. I thought it might be lucky or something." Fetching it I handed it to her.

"How about the ammo box Opal kept in her room? Where is that now?"

"It's here. Back in the vault," said Nacho. "We figured that if it was worth kidnapping Aunt May, there was something we was missing. Go get it Roger. The key for it is still in the lock."

Roger was back in a minute with the box. He passed it over to Mary Jane. She turned the key in the lid, opened the box, and turned it over, spilling the few costume jewels that had not sold at the auction the night before out on the table. Then she picked up the key I had given her.

"I noticed there was another lock in the bottom," said Aunt May. "But I didn't know where the key was. I could hear something inside when I shook it. Is it ..."

Cathy nodded, unlocked the lower lock, opened the false bottom and pulled out a sheaf of papers. "The deed to High Hopes." She looked at Foxy. "I believe if you invite me to your little conspirator meeting, I can accomplish three things. I can reveal that there is no gold, so the gold mining scheme will collapse. All those who wanted to ravage both you and the countryside will find they now are the proud owners of land that they cannot exploit, except for its beauty. Second, I can prove that I own the final piece of property, the only one that has gold on it that happens to sit right in the center of their proposed walled-in sanctuary and I'm not going to sell, so they will never be able to even fall back on their hopes of having a little rural retreat to pray the gay out of their kids. They'll have to try other forms of child abuse. I would guess they will sell at a loss, as they probably overextended themselves to pull off their dirty little game." She sat back with a smile.

"You said three things," said Beau. "I counted two."

"Ah," said Mary Jane. "Well, living in obscurity, I have run through most of the money Opal gave me. Since I now possess the deed and so the land, I also possess the gold that we used to set up the scam. There is actually quite a bit of gold in them thar hills, if you know where it is and I know, because I put it there. And now, I plan on going prospecting."

Aunt May looked uncomfortable, which was unusual. She was shifting in her chair. She picked her glass up. She put her glass down. She opened her mouth, then closed it. Patted her lips with her lace hanky. Then opened her mouth and closed it.

I was fascinated with the ballet of emotions that danced over her perpetually serene face. I was not the only one to notice. Beau glanced over at her and became hypnotized. Mary Jane looked over and, while she was not used to Aunt May's usual taciturn demeanor, she could tell something was amiss. She began to stare as Aunt May continued to, well—squirm. Foxy noticed and began to watch. Finally, Roger glanced away from the boy he was perusing and saw what was going on.

"Aunt May, are you having an attack of some kind?" he asked. "You look like you are in the middle of a stroke."

This seemed to break the spell and Aunt May spoke. "I'm not sure ... it's that I don't quite know where I ... Ms. Ontario, we do not know each other well, but ..."

Mary Jane reached over and patted Aunt May's hand. "What

is troubling you? I'm sure we can work it out."

"It is not for myself, you see, but for the boys and for the youth. You see we have been raising money for ..."

Mary Jane broke in. "Lester has told me all about that. It seems that the challenge has been delayed and with my news, the chance of the others buying the block is nil. Isn't that right?"

"Well, yes and no. You see, Mr. Dick has offered the block to us at a special price, but if we cannot meet that price, he will sell it on the open market. The church was attempting to purchase the block first, but we still have been unable to raise the full amount to purchase it ourselves."

"Do you want a donation?"

"Well, that is what is troubling me and why I find myself pulled in two directions. You see, Opal left me the box. However, I also know that at one time the land and the gold belonged to you. In addition, you have shared your knowledge of both the deed and the location of the gold, so I am uncomfortable asking for the substantial amount required to complete the purchase of the block, but I also cannot in good conscience allow the block to go onto the open market when the opportunity to complete the purchase lies right here." Aunt May looked at her, the turmoil between gentility and commitment to her adopted family clear in her face.

Mary Jane smiled, but looked a bit confused. "Are you asking me to give you some of the money from the gold?"

Aunt May was embarrassed. She was raised that a lady might hint, but never outright ask. "Not for myself, you understand."

"But why do you need any? Opal left you the emerald."

"What emerald?"

"You are wearing it."

Aunt May shook her head and touched the spider broach. "This is glass. It is pretty glass, but it is certainly just glass."

Foxy held out his hand. "May I examine that broach, Aunt May?"

Aunt May shrugged, unpinned the broach, and handed it to Foxy. "Opal gave it to me because I thought it was pretty and she liked it. For her it had personal history and she knew I would cherish that. It was one of the first pieces one of her gentlemen friends gave her."

Foxy was looking closely at the large glass piece that made up the body of the spider and the spray of green, purple, and blue stones that traced the outline of the silver web. He pulled a small jeweler's loupe from an inside pocket. He would, of course, carry one. Foxy took time to examine the piece. Then he pulled a large kerchief from a pocket and wrapped the broach in it. He set the kerchief wrapped broach on the table, picked up the ornate soda bottle, and brought it down once. He then carefully unwrapped the broach. The glass had broken into pieces and Foxy brushed the pieces away, showing us what was revealed.

Where an interesting green blue glob of glass had been, a brilliant green stone caught the light.

Foxy looked from the stunning piece to Cathy. "Could it be? The Taylor?"

Cathy nodded.

Foxy looked around at us. "The story goes that Richard Burton bought it for Elizabeth Taylor during the filming of *Cleopatra*. When they split, she had the piece deconstructed and sold the individual stones at auction for many millions out of spite."

Cathy took up the story. "One of Opal's admirers talked a bit too much about a deal that could have sent him to jail if discovered, yet made him and his estate enormously wealthy because of her silence. He purchased the stone and surrounded it with emeralds, musgravite, and benitoite, the most expensive gem stones in the world. Opal had the broach reworked so it looked like it was a plain and simple thing, because it gave her pleasure to be the only one in the room who knew what she was wearing, while all the other ladies sneered at the glass and silver. However, Aunt May, if you need money, well, I'm not sure how many millions that is worth, but it is certainly enough to meet your needs."

Aristide, who had been sitting quietly, sipping a glass of Foxy's soda from a beautiful blue glass stem, spoke up. "What a wonderful story. I would love to add it to my collection. While I am certain you could get more for the piece at auction, as time is important to you, I would be grateful if I could offer $5.5 million for the piece when the banks open tomorrow. That would allow you to both close the deal and begin the process of setting up your youth center."

We all looked around and agreed that this would be a wonderful outcome. Aunt May was pleased not to have to worry about an extremely valuable piece and had only one requirement. "I would like the center to be named after Opal. I think that would be a lovely way to keep her name alive and I'm sure she would support the idea behind the place."

We all agreed it should be the Opal Milbank Questioning Youth Center and raised our glasses to toast the decision.

"Great story," said Nacho grunting upward. "I still got a place to run and I figure you oughtta be sending back some orders to celebrate. If you weren't absolute cheapskates, I would think you should buy everyone in the joint a special plate of nachos. It would make all the time I've spent on this hoopla worthwhile."

Foxy raised his glass. "As ever, my dear Nacho, you are correct. Make it so. Give me the bill and add a substantial surcharge for your continued help."

"You got it, Foxy," said Nacho, clumping away toward the kitchen, where the best nachos in the world waited to be waved into existence by those magical hands.

Foxy turned to Mary Jane. "Would you like to stay in your old mansion for a few days? I still have access while the cleanup and restoration from our celebration takes place."

Mary Jane shook her head. "No. That's a past I have no desire to relive. I have a new life. I'll stay with Lester for a couple of days. Tomorrow I'll go out to High Hopes and go prospecting. That will take a couple of days. Then, I have a life that I'm very happy with to get back to."

She shot me a look. "You should come out there before I go. I went by earlier today and saw MoonStar. He remembered you. You stirred something in him. You might want to stir back. Not as a long term anything, but he does clean up nicely and, as I remember, was quite flexible and pleasing to look at, in various positions."

I considered. "Let me think about it."

She nodded. "Perhaps you can offer me a ride one of these days. It would be a kindness." She kind of cackled at me and winked.

At this point, Jackie brought out plates of nachos for us and the other tables on the patio, so we busied ourselves with what we do best—eating, drinking, and talking about the amusing little things that make up this life full of friendship, spiced with a bit of drama, and a touch of tawdry, to end another Sunday night at Nacho Mama's Patio Café.

Chapter 38 - And In The End

"Come over. Now," said Beau.

"What's up?"

"Come over," repeated Beau. Then he disconnected.

It was a short walk and a pleasant day.

I gave a quick knock and opened the door. Beau and Aunt May were sitting in the living room, each with a drink in hand, contemplating the ice cubes as they swirled through amber liquid. Beau shifted his eyes to me and pointed with his chin to a card that lay open on the table.

"Just came this morning. You know how they've been trying to kill the post office? Well, this went to Indy, god knows where else, and then back here. About two weeks to accomplish a fifteen-minute drive. We should have got it a week ago, right after she died."

The picture on the front of the card was a derelict building at the edge of a field, peeling paint over rotting boards. An opening framed by a sill showed where a window had once been. Below the window, planted long ago, a patch of red and orange day lilies showed that someone had once lived in this house, had looked out this window, had smiled at these lilies, perhaps had brought some in to brighten their table. Perched in the gap that had been a window, looking off into the distance, a dove sat, content to enjoy what was there.

I picked up the card and read.

My Dearest May,

We both know that life is most enjoyable when grabbed with both hands and celebrated with no regard for the wrinkled noses of those who wish they would allow themselves to have as much fun as you, yet choose scorn over joy again and again.

We also know that every party has an end and to try to squeeze any more out of it once it is over, reaps nothing more than flat seltzer and spilled wine.

I have fully and joyously lived my hour upon the stage, savored every experience, and now my party is ending. I am taking my wrap and leaving, rather than waiting to be shown the door. I am sure you understand.

A lawyer will contact you. He is less than honest, but will behave. You will discover why. You will be given a few hours alone in my house. I know you have no interest in things, but there are a few loose ends I ask you to tie up for me.

In my bedroom, in the wardrobe, is a metal box. Please take that. Take also the small statue of the Virgin Mary surrounded by sea shells. Downstairs in the library, you will find a small room behind the bookcase with a rug in front of it. I'm sure you will be able to figure out how to open it. Inside, on the desk is a letter for you, which will explain what I wish you to do. In that envelope is a key to the box from my bedroom. Inside the statue, you will find another key. That opens the door in the bottom of the box.

If Beau wants anything from the costume room, of course he is welcome.

Thank you May. You have been my last true friend and life, as wondrous as it always seems to be, has saved the best for last.

Yours,

Opal Hungerford Milbank

I put the card back on the table. I went to the kitchen and poured a drink and came back and sat down. We looked at each other. Then raised our glasses.

"To Opal."

"To a magnificent life," added Aunt May. "Could anyone wish for anything more?"

And we drank.

The End

About Steve Schatz

Steve Schatz has been a clown, theatrical lighting designer, tour guide, college professor, television producer, organizational consultant, conference lecturer, focus group supervisor, and comedy traffic safety instructor. He holds degrees in Government, Instructional Design and a PhD in Education. He lives in the college town of Bloomington, Indiana with his very patient husband of many years.

We hope you have enjoyed **Seashell Virgin**.

Check out our other books
- Any Summer Sunday at Nacho Mama's Patio Café
- Who Plugged the Dyke

Middle Grade Ghost Story
- Ghost Girl

YA Fantasy Adventure (From Absolute Love Press)
- Adima Rising
- Adima Returning

Please!

Let others know. Leave reviews on book sites.

Order audio, epub, or print of this and other books. www.AnySummerSunday.com

Write to us, we'll write back. Really we will.
Nacho@anySummerSunday.com
520 S Walnut #3306; Bloomington, IN 47402